DiMAGGIO

For my sons—
Joe Jr., Peter, Christopher, and David
—And the proud memory
of their mother, Elsie Durso

Joe DiMaggio is the last American knight.

— Bob Considine

CONTENTS

PREFACE

THIS STARTED OUT as an autobiography. But Joe DiMaggio decided that he would rather have his privacy than two million dollars.

The signal came in a telephone call one morning in March 1989, when I was in Florida covering spring training for *The New York Times*. It was a few days after Joe had driven north from Miami with his friend Joe Camilleri to spend an afternoon with me in Port St. Lucie at a game between the New York Mets and Boston Red Sox. We got to talking about cosmic things like Mikhail Gorbachev and Ronald Reagan and never did see any of the game. But we must have done something right because a couple of days later his lawyer, Morris Engelberg, drove up from Hollywood to see a game, too.

Joe and I had been talking about writing his memoirs for a long time, kind of vaguely because Joe used to say that thirty-three books had been written *about* him and he didn't like *any* of them. But how could he not like his own book about himself? Especially since he was almost seventy-five years old and this seemed like a good time to reflect on a career and a life spent in the spotlight and in the shadows.

The telephone call that March morning came from Morris Engelberg, and it meant that the vow of silence was about to be broken. He said that Joe had "selected" me to write his memoirs, he had confidence in my writing style and in my discretion, he was authorizing me to bring in the best publisher, and he didn't even want to haggle about money, *but* the "best publisher" should know in advance that the money we weren't going to haggle about was two million dollars.

The first publisher I contacted didn't have any problem with that; but he did have a problem, or at least a healthy curiosity, about how much talking and remembering Joe would do for the two million. And when we all gathered in Engelberg's office in Hollywood a few weeks later — Joe and Morris and myself, flanked by my designated publisher and editor — the question came up pretty early in the conversation: How far into his personal life would Joe be willing to go? And without missing a beat, Joe replied: "You mean about Marilyn?"

They meant about Marilyn, all right, but they didn't make a fail-safe issue of it. They sort of took it on faith that she would somehow find her proper place in the life story of her onetime husband and longtime protector. But in the months that followed, even with book contracts drawn, presented, amended in dozens of places by Edward Bennett Williams and his legal battalions — even then, DiMaggio was wrestling with the memories and was losing the fight to release them from the safe depths of his mind.

There was something touching about this. Morris Engelberg even kept saying: Give Joe time, you know that he does things only in his own time and in his own way. And Joe said that he wondered if he had enough free time to go through with it, and I guess he really meant that he wondered if he had enough free will to go through with it.

The overriding fact was that he cherished, preserved, and

sheltered the memories of Marilyn Monroe, and he didn't know if he could unfurl them even in a shallow way without a sense of betrayal. Not even for two million dollars.

The months of hesitation stretched into years, and it seemed almost impolite to badger a man with such strict feelings, especially an old friend with such strict feelings. Besides, you couldn't very well "do" DiMaggio without DiMaggio.

Or, we asked, *could* you? In fact, maybe the *only* way to "do" DiMaggio, with all of the closed vaults of his memory, was *without* DiMaggio. That is, without his holding the reins on his own remembrance of things past.

So, here we are, five years after he asked me to help gather his memoirs. He is eighty years old now, and it is half a century and more since he reported to the New York Yankees in spring training and walked for the first time onto the national stage.

Nobody can pinch-hit for Joe DiMaggio. But let's say that I am here to pinch-run for him, to complete the journey that we once embarked upon, to record his story, his career, his life and times — and, for better or worse, to measure his impact on American life in the twentieth century.

Joseph Durso

DiMAGGIO

1

WHERE HAVE YOU GONE, JOE DiMAGGIO?

On a clear and cold morning in February 1972, a man named Robert Pierson strode through the front door of the classical and stylish building at 110 East Forty-second Street in Manhattan, diagonally across from Grand Central Station, and entered the world and the architectural splendor of the Bowery Savings Bank of New York. It had vaulted ceilings, marble walls, a main banking floor the size of the Grand Canyon, and one boardroom that dazzled even bankers because it was two stories tall and stocked with the trappings of success and wealth. And somewhere down there in all that magnificence, it had $3.5 billion in deposits.

But, Robert Pierson reflected as he walked into the world of The Bowery, it did not have a voice or a face.

It didn't matter too much to Robert Pierson whether The Bowery spelled its name with a capital "T," as if to suggest a kind of institutional permanence and a title for the ages. You know, something like The City for London's financial center. Or The Rock for Alcatraz Island.

But it mattered that The Bowery had a voice or a face, and to him it mattered urgently, because he had been hired from the think tanks of Madison Avenue for precisely that reason: to breathe personality into The Bank the way Frankenstein breathed life into The Monster, to transform it from an immovable organization renowned for escrow accounts and fiduciary funds into something more personable — like a place where people wanted to put their money. And to do that, he reasoned, to endow the institution with a capital tone to go with its capital "T" and whatever it implied, he needed to find a "spokesman" for all the values and virtues that this bank implied in its never-ending relations with the public.

This wasn't entirely Pierson's private target. It was also the brainchild of the top guns at the bank, Morris D. (Rusty) Crawford, the chairman of the board, and John W. Larsen, the president, who began to get the feeling as the 1970s unfurled before them that nothing lasts forever. After all, in the allied field of commercial banking in New York, the First National City Bank had overtaken Chase Manhattan as the front-runner; and in the insurance field, Prudential had caught Metropolitan Life, which for generations had not seemed likely to be caught by anybody.

And to bring the issue home, to get to the trend that mattered most, even The Bowery was hearing footsteps in the dark: Some of its biggest competitors were now narrowing its margin of leadership in the savings-bank world that Robert Pierson was striding into on that cold February morning.

It wasn't that The Bowery was getting paranoid and was hiring wise men to figure out ways to keep the demons from juggling the league standings. Actually, it was getting smart. Times were changing, and commercial banks were snatching more of the action that historically had belonged to savings banks. In 1945, at the end of World War II, savings banks had 29 percent of the nation's savings; by 1965, they had just under 18 percent. They had been created to protect the interests of "little people" who wanted to stash their savings in rigidly regulated ventures, safe and sheltered from speculation. Now they were fighting for their fading fraction.

At the peak of its power with the public, the bank simply made things work. It could even play a paternal role in people's lives, as it did when William Levitt started building "developments" after the war and stocked them with schools, churches, shopping centers, and police and fire departments. To furnish the financing for one of the textbook developments, Levittown on Long Island, the bank made a total of 7,736 home loans, and did not take a bath.

By 1951, only twenty-nine of the loans were in arrears, and most of them came with explanations that would be hard to reject: seventeen were caused by sickness, five by economic conditions, four by absence for military duty in the Korean War, two by marital difficulties, and the twenty-ninth and last case of arrears probably had the best explanation of all — the death of both the husband and wife in a Pennsylvania Rail Road wreck.

But this kind of sterling record of rapport with the public was eroding a few years later, so the call of distress was aimed at Madison Avenue, where it was heard by Robert Pierson, an economics graduate of Lehigh University, later an alumnus of Klemtner Advertising and Johnson & Johnson, and now a headhunter hunting for the perfect link between The Bowery and its public.

Banks had not been exactly famous for the wit or ingenuity of their messages or their pitches, but at least The Bowery had done some dabbling in the arts of reaching out. In the early 1930s, it set up the first public relations department in a mutual savings bank. Later, it installed an advertising department, and anointed it with an aggressive attitude, as far as any bank could have an aggressive advertising attitude. It even sold itself on the radio for years, but did it with the properly tame jingle: "It pays to save at The Bowery."

That, plus a couple of TV spots. And now, Robert Pierson: tall, athletic, good-looking, a man with an engaging manner and a low golf score. And a mission.

"From the start," he remembered, "we determined that the soft-sell and the shotgun approach were gone forever, and that from now on we had to begin zeroing in on more specific targets through public relations, promotion, and market research as well as advertising. This made the choice of *spokesman* crucial.

"We wanted a spokesman who conveyed something of the good old-fashioned values and who, by his very presence and bearing, would be convincing. If he had a clear-cut identity with New York, so much the better."

Strictly speaking, Pierson wasn't alone in thinking The Bowery needed a voice, a face, and a personality, and it didn't require a giant leap of faith or genius to come to the same conclusion. But on the scale of advertising values, banks rarely ventured past "tame." They tried to exude confidence and durability, the Rock of Gibraltar in your otherwise fragile life, the immovable object that looks on tempests and is not shaken.

But once the tempest of television struck the world of communicating, entertaining, and advertising, a great many things got shaken. Television could walk, talk, smile, frown, cry, laugh, sigh, roar. And could do it all in color. Right now, here in your living room, whether you liked it or not. Subconscious and subliminal, and set to music.

So, it pays to save at The Bowery, eh? Well, you'd better turn that one up a notch or lose the public's passion and purse. And where do you go from here, you headhunters headed through the revolving door en route to that two-story boardroom with its vaulted ceiling and its crisis mentality?

"I already had set aside some money in the budget," Pierson said, "to make an impact on New York. And I had an agenda. Day One: meet Ogilvy & Mather. Day Two: keep Ogilvy & Mather but fire the old agency."

At the time, Robert Pierson was one officer in a regiment of officers working to plant some soul into the corporate body of The Bowery. There were 18 vice presidents, 17 assistant vice presidents, 19 assistant treasurers, 9 mortgage officers, and a herd of department heads, including Pierson in marketing.

Twenty-one years later, he sat comfortably in his wood-paneled, leather-lined office as president of the Montclair Savings Bank in New Jersey and peered back across the years like a pioneer who had blazed a trail. He remembered blazing this particular trail with a pair of creative prodigies from Ogilvy & Mather. They were Robert Spero, vice president and copy group head, and Seymour Waldman, the art supervisor, and they in turn flanked J. Robert Watts, the account supervisor, and all three joined Pierson in recasting the image of The Bowery.

"The first thing we had to do," Pierson said, "was to figure out the product. Do we have dancing bears, or prancing ponies? How do we get The Bowery across as trustworthy in a memorable fashion? That was it: How do we get The Bowery across in a memorable fashion?

"The guys at Ogilvy came up with the key suggestion: Why don't we do it with a spokesman?"

A spokesman. Strong, silent, sure, solid, honest, loyal, trustworthy. Something like an Eagle Scout. The kind of person who made you proud to be an American. Or, closer to the point, proud to be a depositor at The Bowery. Recognizable, credible, believable, honorable, maybe even lovable. Thrifty, not shifty, prudent, comfortable, respectable. How about avuncular? Honest, direct, neighborly, healthy, wealthy, and wise.

How about John Wayne? Not bad. He was all of that, and a superstar, besides. First and foremost: Duke. The whole thing was about television and the revolution it was bringing into your living room, capturing your mind and getting your attention with pictorial firepower, carrying "the message" into new dimensions of color and character created by "the medium." That's what the whole issue was about: not a newspaper ad announcing the highest savings-bank interest rate (7.90 percent) in New York State, but a friend, ally, hero if possible, spokesman at all costs, standing there telling you for God's sake to save at The Bowery

and not play Russian roulette with your kids' future. Take it from
Duke.

Hold it, boys. Somebody beat you to the punch: John Wayne
was already being earnest in TV commercials for somebody else's
bank on the West Coast, the Great Western. Scratch John Wayne.

When you scratch John Wayne from the "short list," the list
becomes a lot shorter, especially when the next name is Robert F.
Wagner Jr., former mayor of New York, alumnus of Yale, prac-
ticing lawyer, and son of a distinguished United States senator.
Honest, sincere, well-known, committed to New York. Also:
somewhat ponderous, very political, not what you would call
dashing. How about dull? And hundreds of thousands of New
Yorkers, and maybe hundreds of thousands of people who banked
at The Bowery, had voted *against* him at one time or another.

Scratch Bob Wagner. The list was getting shorter now, and
they were sitting around trying to rocket their way through
what Pierson remembered as "a brainstorming session" when
the name was dropped onto the table.

"One of the agency people dropped it on us when we were
straining to come up with exactly the right person, the spokesman: *Joe DiMaggio.*"

They glanced at each other across the conference table and
tested it. *Joe DiMaggio.*

"We kicked it around," Pierson said. "Nobody had ever met
him. Bob Spero of the agency was there, and Cy Waldman and
myself, and Bob Watts, the account executive, and others would
come floating in and out.

"We drew up a list of the pros and cons. And, believe me,
there were plenty of both.

"*Against* using DiMaggio: He's fifty-seven years old and he
retired from baseball twenty-one years ago. Since then, he's
faded from public view. He's done a couple of radio commercials and even some TV. But nobody remembered seeing him in a
spot since he did those Blue Brylcream commercials in the early
1960s. You know, there was Joe telling you, 'It works for me.'

"He also kept coming close to a job with the Yankees, but it never quite happened. Nobody thought he wanted to be a manager, and he didn't seem like the type to do anything serious in the front office. Five years before we started auditioning his name that first time, back in 1967, he went to work for Charley Finley, the guy who owned the Oakland Athletics and before them the Kansas City Athletics. He made Joe an executive vice president for community relations, and he doubled as a coach for the manager of the team, Bob Kennedy. He looked strange in those yellow-and-green uniforms Finley put on his team.

"Anyway, the point of all this was: Would young people relate to him?"

Pierson paused, and added: "Would they even *know* him?"

Strike one, the umpire said. And that's not all, the guys from the agency said. Another potential point *against* using DiMaggio: The Bowery had one of the largest blocs of Jewish depositors in the banking business, and Joe DiMaggio was obviously and unrelentingly Italian. How would the ethnic "thing" work, especially if you were creating a spokesman to reach out and relate to people like some solid, solitary, strong, silent, suave, and sure-handed uncle?

And if that wasn't strike two, how about this one: He lived in San Francisco now, so how could he symbolize New York? How could he even suggest New York, unless you were going to dress him up in pinstripes and a Yankee windbreaker? Remember, he hadn't gone to bat in New York in twenty-one years, and Spero and Waldman and the rest of the think-tank heavy hitters from the agency were big on the "identity" factor.

"Besides," said Pierson, sniping away with the best of them, "how about the basics of broadcasting? What was his voice like? Porky Pig? And did he have any acting ability? Could he read lines and project trust and take cues and make rehearsals and make you want to believe that The Bowery 'works for me' the way good old Blue Brylcream worked for *him* more than a decade before?"

They were throwing so many strikes by now that you had to start wondering why DiMaggio didn't just strike out with the search committee without even taking a cut at the ball. Then somebody sitting around the "search table" reached back and fired this one at their candidate: Since 52 percent of the depositors in the bank were women, maybe the shrewdest move would be to sign up a coed team as the "spokesman," a man and a woman touching all the gender bases and encircling the audience, too.

Against the *againsts,* so to speak, there were a lot of things *pro* the old pro, too. Tall, dark, and handsome, for one thing; maybe one big thing. The very model of the model New York Yankee, for another. The class act in Yankee Stadium, the guy who ran down the ball in center field, the king of the hill and the toast of the town, the cleanup hitter, the boyfriend, the man acclaimed only three years earlier as "the greatest living ballplayer." The Yankee Clipper, for God's sake.

"Even at his stiffest," Bob Pierson conceded, bestowing the ultimate accolade, "he projected humility, dignity, integrity."

He stepped back to appraise his candidate, something like Henry Higgins appraising Eliza Doolittle, and said:

"DiMaggio met all these requirements, and more. He was a true popular hero, even if most of his contemporaries were middle-aged. Even though he hadn't lived for years in New York, no celebrity was more clearly identified with New York, not if you turned back the clock and let your memory coast. And he seemed to convey the quiet virtue of someone like Gary Cooper."

So, they did what any red-blooded American pitchman would do: They kicked it around. Then they remembered that none of them had ever met DiMaggio, and none of them had the slightest idea whether he could be sold on the grand design or even whether he had the slightest interest in joining it. So, naturally, they invited him to breakfast at the Stage Deli on Seventh Avenue to find out.

"He always ate there," Pierson said, sounding like a man with the guilts for picking such a déclassé place to transact such soaring business. "Bob Spero and I got in touch with him through somebody on the creative side of the agency who got him on the phone through the Yankees. And so we three met at the Stage Delicatessen on Seventh Avenue. As I say, he always ate there. The owners liked him to come in, naturally, and he went there for years. They kept the wackos away from him, and he could hide out, in a manner of speaking, right there in midtown Manhattan.

"Joe always went straight to a table where he could sit privately, and he did the same when Spero and I took him to breakfast. We broached the idea that morning, but didn't clinch it. And we got his attention. You know, he seemed to like the idea of being the spokesman for a bank, nothing sleazy or seamy. When we left the Stage Deli, we figured we were on first base."

Rusty Crawford, the chairman of the board at The Bowery, thought it was a good idea and promptly wrote a letter to DiMaggio inviting him to play golf at the Greenwich Country Club in Connecticut. John Larsen, the bank president, had been a little crustier about the whole thing at first. But he became a quick convert as soon as they made the initial approach to DiMaggio and then poured out his approval.

"He's my hero," Larsen announced. "I've loved him all my life."

And to clinch *that*, sounding more and more like the chairman of his board, he said: "He plays golf. I'll bring him over to New Jersey to play with me at the Ridgewood Country Club."

"It all clicked," Pierson said. "If it hadn't clicked, I would have been left holding the bag."

But the old hero of the Yankees still wasn't off the hook with the new heroes of the think tank who had been analyzing and rationalizing and institutionalizing him, matching the *pros* against the *cons* and slicing him six ways before unleashing him on their public as the voice, the face, and the soul of The Bowery. They may have been taking it all pretty seriously, almost as if the banking system itself was at stake, but they had been hired to take it seriously, and they accepted the mission with all the grim purpose of men who had also taken it seriously when they were selling the public on a bar of soap, a package of cigarettes, or a bottle of beer.

But just as they were approaching the crucial point in their deliberations, the market researchers fired one salvo after another, and got everybody off the hook.

"We found," Pierson said, "that he had an OK voice. We were assured the Jews liked him as much as the Italians. The kids had heard about him from their parents. New Yorkers thought of him as a New Yorker. And the women didn't particularly know him as a ballplayer, but they all remembered that Joe put roses every day or two at the grave of Marilyn Monroe."

In other words, all those reasons for voting *against* DiMaggio, or at least putting him to a list of litmus tests on age, sex, ethnic appeal, and even national geography — all those possible downers in electing him The Spokesman had been answered. The market researchers, pitching for the wise men of Ogilvy & Mather and the Bowery Savings Bank, had thrown every curveball in the advertising book at DiMaggio. And, you might say, giving it the tone and the spin of Madison Avenue, he rose to the occasion and hit a home run with the bases loaded.

Kids liked him, women liked him, Jews liked him, and New Yorkers liked him as one of their own. It was contract time, gentlemen.

"We signed him for two years plus a two-year extension," Robert Pierson remembered. "The extension would be at the bank's discretion. It also had a morality clause. Contracts often had things like that in those days. A lot of people resented them, and still do. But he liked the idea of the morality clause, whether it was in there as a formality or not. Don't forget: He was being signed to become the spokesman for a savings bank. You know, to convey the virtues of someone like Gary Cooper."

But virtue didn't pay outrageously in those days. The contract said DiMaggio would film three spots each year and would be paid $60,000 the first year and $65,000 the second. He agreed to make two public appearances, but he would have to approve them.

"He didn't want to be paraded out like a circus horse," Pierson said. "He also understood that he had to play golf once a year with Crawford and Larsen. You know, fly into New York and all that. Limo going and coming, first-class hotel, things like that were all spelled out. And the contract became a little more complex after nailing down those things. We went into some ten-second outtakes of the thirty-second spots on TV.

"But basically, that was it. We had exclusivity for money institutions nationally and for all products within twenty-two counties in the New York City area. They called it prime-time access.

"After the spots started to be shown on the tube, we did a lot of research again and found that they were a smash. People identified him with The Bowery, and that was the whole ball game. They saw him on the screen, and knew he was talking about putting your money in the bank.

"A couple of years later, he agreed to do some TV spots for Mr. Coffee. He did it as a favor for his friend, Vince Merada, who owned the company. We couldn't keep him off the Mr. Coffee thing. It was a national product, and the commercial came into a big part of our market. We were pissed off, but we couldn't stop him from doing it.

"I guess we got some satisfaction out of it, anyway. People would see Joe having a cup of coffee on the screen and think he was appearing for The Bowery. How's that for identity? It worked so well that I began to think: Why not do a commercial for the bank with Joe having a cup of coffee?"

The huckster's mind never sleeps. But Pierson and his think-tank colleagues didn't have too much to worry about. Their "spokesman" brought it off handsomely, and he exuded the grace and style that fairly shouted the virtues of saving your money you-know-where. He also turned down offers to become the spokesman for Grecian Formula hair preparation and Polident denture cream on the perfectly proper ground that he neither colored his hair nor came equipped with false teeth.

But everybody put their money in the bank, or wished they did. A thrift hero was born.

It didn't take much shrewdness to pick the venue for the first commercial. It was shot at Yankee Stadium with DiMaggio hitting a few flies to get the investors in the audience in the mood. Somebody had to pitch to him, naturally, and for a while the brothers of the brain trust entertained the illusion that they might carry their advertising coup into another dimension by casting themselves as the batting-practice pitchers for Joe D. himself.

"Spero had pitched in college, at Northwestern," Pierson said, "and he had visions of making a fool of himself. Actually, he was torn between two visions: He also could imagine that he was reaching back and firing his heater past a helpless DiMaggio.

"Joe was fifty-seven at the time, and he was unbelievable. He knocked line drives all over the place with fabulous grace. Later, I saw him in the locker room and I wished that I had his muscle tone.

"Anyway, in the first commercial that we shot, there was Joe talking about how when you get older, you have to take care of yourself, you have to take care of your money. And he said 'your money' as though the words were in italics or boldface. We also surrounded him with a bunch of singing kids, a rainbow of kids. We had white kids and black kids and Chinese kids."

Pierson let himself grin with a touch of guilt, and explained: "We had a branch at 130 Bowery."

Nobody had to tell the think-tank team that the kids must stay, the old hero and the young singers from the neighborhood, no choirboys, just singing boys. And they got along so well with DiMaggio backstage that it was a natural to keep the act together.

DiMaggio also didn't hide the fact that he rather liked the idea of appearing on TV for a bank. He told Pierson one day: "I don't want to be remembered for liquors." He even said that he always had regretted posing with a cigarette in his mouth for that blockbuster billboard in Times Square. The part was growing on him.

He and the singing kids then were staged all over town in the most visible and recognizable settings in the most recognizable skyline in the country. They were caught on the decks of a Circle Line boat as it circled the city. They were arrayed on the carousel in Central Park (you know, Joe DiMaggio and a bunch of kids always took a ride and rode the hobbyhorses and talked or sang about the greatest idea on earth, saving at The Bowery). They were filmed back at Yankee Stadium, where he was seen chatting with some other baseball old-timers who, he reported, "sing worse than the kids."

In another scene, Joe was standing in the stadium telling you in all earnestness: "The Bowery pays you six percent while commercial banks simply do not." In a later scene, he appeared solo without the support of the boys' chorus and, making the pitch calmly and sincerely from an armchair, reminded you, "The Bowery pays a lot." And in yet another scene, he and the kids were reunited playing stickball on the street, no doubt in one of the many neighborhoods graced by a savings bank.

"He was fifty-seven years old," Pierson said, counting his blessings as only a marketing director can do. "He was the exact age of The Bowery's average customer.

"When we started with Joe in 1972, about a month later the Dime Savings Bank came along with cartoon bunnies and squirrels saving their money. It was a very effective campaign. But we had no idea Joe would turn out to be the phenomenal success he did turn out to be.

"On the set, he took coaching. He did his homework. We warned the TV director not to chew the fat with him. Forget saying you remember seeing him play ball. And above all, keep your mouth shut about Marilyn Monroe.

"Joe handled all the acting and coaching without grousing or stumbling. He was getting paid, but it wasn't all the money in the world. And there were a few perks."

Pierson laughed, and said: "Joe is — shall we say — thrifty. Under his contract with us, he was allowed to keep any clothes that he wore in the commercials. He wound up with lots of windbreakers."

The Bowery wound up with lots of new deposits, but it would take a brave or reckless marketing director to credit his own campaign for an upturn in company business. Still, they had set out to build an advertising campaign that would focus attention on the bank in the most trusty way at a time when the bank was being ambushed in the financial jungle.

As a result of *something,* deposits in the bank's eleven offices in 1972 reached a record level of $205 million. No other savings bank in the country could make that statement, no matter what it was doing with its TV time. When The Bowery opened an office at Third Avenue and Sixtieth Street in Manhattan, more dollars poured into its savings accounts than *any* savings bank had ever counted. And the research demons came up with this one, too: In terms of "unaided recall," the bank's name outscored every other savings bank in the New York area in recognition as the one that "pays the most."

But even if Joe DiMaggio played no telling role in the business revival, he was playing a new role in his own life that clearly was leading to a personal revival.

It was ten years since Marilyn Monroe had died, apparently of an overdose of barbiturates, leaving him with the emotional trauma of their brief but tumultuous marriage of nine and a half months and their longer but troubled alliance of eight more years. But worse, also leaving him with the torch that he carried for the rest of his time. It left him grieving but coping, not quite a hermit, yet not quite a man about town anymore.

The other love of his life, the Yankees, abandoned him to his years on the other side of the spotlight. He had always wanted, or at least expected, some role in the empire that he had helped to flourish. He didn't really enjoy the prospect of becoming a manager and directing the details of nine men playing nine innings with all the nuances and decisions involved. But he vaguely cherished the notion that the star of the empire days would reign in some comparable way as a star of the post-empire days. The only difficulty was that nobody could figure out what that role would be.

In March of 1961, he had joined the Yankees in spring training for the first time since he had retired ten years earlier. He reported to the team's base at St. Petersburg in Florida as a special but unpaid "assistant" to the manager, Ralph Houk, the onetime third-string catcher who rose to become general manager.

He looked good, still athletic and handsome, and he shepherded Marilyn to the camp with the kind of noble protectiveness that he showed in her company, especially now that she was mentally and physically declining and desperately needed his protection. But his duties with the ball club were not very urgent, not even very clear, and his hope of returning to the Yankees in some triumphant measure was never fulfilled.

By 1972, when he was blooming into the voice of The Bowery, the Yankees were owned by the Columbia Broadcasting System and were being orchestrated by the stylish and even gallant Michael Burke, who might have made a pretty good spokesman for the bank himself. But Burke ruffled DiMaggio by acknowledging in the newspapers that "he wants to come back with us" and by inflaming the situation even more by adding: "We'd like to have him if we can work something out."

To DiMaggio, language like that spelled hesitation, and hesitation about rolling out the red carpet spelled condescension. Burke frequently announced that he would rather be a lamppost in New York than mayor of Chicago. DiMaggio didn't particularly want to be either, but he wanted to be *asked,* in any event. He might not accept, but he still wanted to be asked.

So it was a little ironic that he should be flushed from his cover by something so glitzy and glamorous as television. But his very craving for privacy magnified his appeal on the least private of mediums. And the late-life popularity that it bestowed gave him the attention and the significance that he craved.

In 1974, he was honored by the New York baseball writers as the first recipient of an honor that came with the title of the Casey Stengel-You-Could-Look-It-Up Award. What you could look up was the fifty-six-game hitting streak that he fashioned in 1941, a feat that won the American League pennant for the Yankees and the American League Most Valuable Player Award for him. And now, he was receiving — and accepting — the newest award named for the grand old man and grand old manager of the team who arrived in 1949 just as DiMaggio was winding down his own career. They weren't close; in fact, they were apart in most personal relationships. But here was Joe, more than two decades after he retired, flying to New York one winter's day to take the salute.

In 1975, he went back to Japan for the first time in nearly twenty years, worked for a few days as a guest batting coach with the Lotte Orions, and said tactfully that an international World Series might be five years away.

Two years later, he made a list of twenty-one Americans selected by President Gerald R. Ford for the Medal of Freedom. He accepted with Lady Bird Johnson and Nelson Rockefeller, and he glowed quietly at the distinction. And in 1979, he was lionized by the New York Board of Trade for his contributions to New York City, and he heard Senator Jacob Javits proclaim that Joe DiMaggio was "synonymous with what's great about New York."

It wasn't exactly that the commercials for The Bowery had created a media monster and thrust him back onto the national stage after years in seclusion. But there wasn't any doubt that he had been in the right place at the right time when Robert Pierson and his creative colleagues showed up looking for a spokesman for the savings bank, and the relatively new force of television showed up with them looking for stars and multiplying their brilliance.

"In 1977," Pierson said, "Joe and my wife, Virginia, and I were on the West Coast having lunch at the Fairmont Hotel. We had Joe on the screen talking about the bank's one-year certificates. 'The Bowery pays six percent.' And he'd hold up six fingers to clinch the point.

"After lunch, we left the Fairmont and took the cable car down California Street, and as we were getting off to switch to the Powell Street car, some guy shouted, 'Hey, Joe,' and held up six fingers. We thought Joe had hired the guy as a trick on the bank. But Joe laughed and said no way, people did it all the time to him: six fingers. The Bowery pays six percent. I'll tell you, it was great identity."

Now it was Pierson who laughed. "We had a problem," he said, "when our interest went up to seven and a half percent."

"The TV spots were shown only in the New York area," he said. "We had twenty-five branches there. But the commercials revived his image and made him a national folk hero."

DiMaggio stayed on as The Bowery's spokesman on TV for ten years. Then he got into print ads in newspapers and magazines, later into radio spots. The bank meanwhile went through some transformations. Richard Ravitch headed a group of investors who took it over in 1983, then sold it in 1986 to the Home Savings Bank of America, and they later changed the name of The Bowery, too. So DiMaggio stayed on as the spokesman for most of twenty years on TV and radio both, as well as in the newspapers. He actually lasted longer than The Bowery.

His relationship with Mr. Coffee wasn't quite that smooth, and his role wasn't quite that durable, although he apparently got people to drink coffee brewed by *Mr.* Coffee machines just as he got other people to put their money in The Bowery.

Paul Schneider, who worked closely with DiMaggio in all his business dealings and endorsements in later years, after Joe had shifted his base of operations to the Hollywood area in Florida, remembered it this way:

"He represented himself on the Mr. Coffee deal. He was

friends with the guy who owned the company. The guy asked him to do a commercial, so Joe did it as a favor to him. And Joe was so believable drinking the coffee on the screen that people thought *he* owned the company.

"But years later, he was reading the contract — Joe read all his contracts — and he noticed a change in it that hadn't been called to his attention. He trusted everything his friends said. But this time, he got so angry that he tore up the contract and ended the deal. And the friendship.

"That's the way Joe always was. He needed an entourage of friends and he trusted them. But he was sensitive and proud, and easy to offend."

He also was a natural when it came to setting the stage and the mood, and it was a marriage of true minds when he set the mood for the savings bank and the coffeemaker that nudged him out of obscurity in the seventies and projected him onto the TV screens of a country that had been wondering: Where have you gone, Joe DiMaggio?

Wherever he had gone, he was back. He was back as the voice of reason, reinforcing the obvious value of saving money, reminding an audience of mature men and women that 2 and 2 still made 4 and that you got more for your money at the good old Bowery.

He did the same for Mr. Coffee, sharing with you the warm confidence that this was the nicest way to start the day. He didn't look or sound like a man making a pitch, or a celebrity reading lines. He came across as a guy who made the coffee and drank it, and wanted to tell you about it. He may have looked and sounded like an aging Eagle Scout, but to Robert Pierson and the rest of the market men he looked and sounded like the noblest Roman of them all.

He also had grown into a runaway horse, and nobody was certain how to handle, treat, feed, or pay him.

"By the time he had worked his way through the two-year contract and two-year extension," Pierson said, "he was making seventy-five to eighty thousand a year for the bank commercials. And we had to renegotiate the contract.

"Every year, one of my jobs was to brief the board of directors on our marketing campaigns, operations, and plans. We had an all-star board, too. People like Eugene Black, the head of the World Bank, and the chief guy at Goldman Sachs. A wide variety of very good and very big people.

"So, I'd give them the report and they'd listen and approve and maybe ask questions. But once, in the third year of Joe's deal with us, I got the question I'd been dreading: How much are we paying Joe DiMaggio?

"I took the Fifth on that one. I don't remember how I ducked it, but I hemmed and hawed around, and finally Rusty Crawford said to me privately: 'But you've got to answer the question.' He figured it was legitimate enough, and he couldn't have his marketing guy withholding stuff like that from the board of directors.

"So, I said: Seventy thousand. They all kind of gasped, and I wanted to crawl under the table before they sacked me for squandering the bank's assets. They were aghast, and said so. They thought it was too *little.*

"At that rate, they all said, we'll lose him to somebody else. In fact, *anybody* else would pay him more, he's so effective now. And they made me pay him $100,000, which surprised Joe as much as it surprised me."

The key to the relationship was that DiMaggio felt comfortable and secure with the bank, just as the bank felt with him. Pierson and DiMaggio became close friends, they talked business and politics and presidential visits. Joe had been invited to the White House for one social or ceremonial reason by every president since Franklin Roosevelt, and the thought caressed him.

There was nothing frivolous about him, nothing free and easy or glib, nothing to betray his sense of privacy. Once when he was shooting a commercial, he seemed unusually tight in his delivery and his bearing, and the director went to Pierson on the sidelines and asked for help. Pierson pried a little that time, and DiMaggio unbent that time. He explained that he'd been having some growing-up trouble with his son Joe Jr. and talked it through with Pierson in a rare moment of sharing family ties.

Pierson always believed that DiMaggio had a tangible effect on the bank's business, too. It would be hard to prove that "the spokesman" created prosperity, but deposits grew during his television tenure, the mortgage side of the business boomed, and The Bowery recovered its grip and seemed to keep money from leaking to other banks.

"It was a whole lot of chemistry," Pierson said. "It happened. We had our voice and our face and our spokesman, and it worked. We won a Cleo, we won all the top awards, every award in the book.

"We'd go to lunch at La Scala or some other fancy place, and some guy would come up and say, 'Joe, *paisan.*' And before he could say anything else, Joe would cut him off. The commercials revived him as a public hero. But he was still a private person. Remember, the average American had never seen Joe in color or in person or on TV. And believe me, TV did it."

It was twenty years after Robert Pierson had walked through the revolving door at 110 East Forty-second Street in Manhattan, twenty years after he had launched "the search" and found "the spokesman." He basked in the memory of his courtship and friendship with Joe DiMaggio, and the hours they had spent chipping away at the wall that Joe had built to hold back the invaders. But he also winced at the memory of the wall that had not been breached.

"One topic I never discussed with him," Robert Pierson said, "was Marilyn Monroe."

2

SAN FRANCISCO

IT WAS thirteen minutes past five o'clock on the morning of April 18, 1906, when the earth trembled in San Francisco.

The tremors ripped across the city in surges, splitting open the ground, caving in the streets, collapsing one block of buildings after another. The force of the earthquake measured 8.3 on the Richter scale, and it seemed all of that as it struck the filled-in marshland to the south of Market Street, toppled the Valencia Hotel, rocked the Opera House, near Third and Mission, where Enrico Caruso had sung the night before, and devastated mansions on Nob Hill, where the new Fairmont Hotel was poised and polished and primed to open its doors in splendor.

The mighty quake also fractured the water mains beneath the surface, and that was the coup de grâce. When massive fires began to spread through San Francisco, the shining city by the Bay was defenseless.

Ellsworth Quinlan remembered that he was five years old and sleeping with his grandmother when the house started trembling. His grandmother swept him up in her arms and tried to run outside, but the hammering of the earthquake knocked her down a flight of steps. Ellsworth held on to her and went tumbling down the stairs in her arms. Somehow, they weren't hurt.

He had no trouble reliving those moments when another earthquake rocked San Francisco eighty-three years later. He was living on Beach Street in the Marina district then, just down the way from the house that Joe DiMaggio had bought for his mother and father and where he still was living with his older sister Marie. This time, Ellsworth Quinlan was eighty-eight years old, and he had the distinct feeling that his second major earthquake was stronger than the first.

"By God," he said, crawling out of the debris of his house, "you couldn't get your balance."

Elizabeth McKenna was twelve years old and was living in the Mission district in 1906, and she lived through the second big one in 1989, too, but she figured it wasn't quite as powerful as the earlier one.

"It was heavier, it lasted longer," she said, sorting out the earthquakes the way people in other cities might compare snowstorms. "The whole city was on fire."

Some of the newspapers in town, joining forces to record the moment under the combined flag that read *The Call-Chronicle-Examiner,* agreed that doomsday was dawning. Across the top of the front page in two tall and screaming lines of block-letter headlines, it told starkly what everybody already knew:

EARTHQUAKE AND FIRE:

SAN FRANCISCO IN RUINS

Below the fold of the page, another headline reported: WHOLE CITY IS ABLAZE. Then, with an almost provincial touch of local grieving, the headline to the right said: ST. IGNATIUS CHURCH IS DESTROYED. And, putting the catastrophe back into broader focus, the headline to the left of the page advised: NO HOPE LEFT FOR SAFETY OF ANY BUILDINGS.

Caruso got the idea immediately. He rushed out of the ornate and elegant Palace Hotel and tried his luck in the relative safety of Market Street. He was draped with a towel around his neck, ostensibly to protect his vocal chords, and he was clutching a signed photograph of President Theodore Roosevelt.

A. P. Giannini had the same desperate thought of trying to save *his* chief valuables, too. He was the owner of the Bank of Italy, later to become the colossus known as the Bank of America, and he rescued the cash in his vault by loading it onto a vegetable cart and hauling it to his home on the Peninsula.

John Barrymore was in town, too, and he was sleeping off a late-night case of drinking too much at a party. Sleeping it off, in fact, on the couch in his hotel room. When the earthquake struck, he also fled to the street, found it heavily patrolled by soldiers, and promptly offered to pitch in. His cousin and fellow-actor John Drew later told Ethel Barrymore: "It took an act of God to get the fellow out of bed and the United States Army to get him to work."

Nobody knows if Drew actually put it that way, but it seemed characteristic of the high-living Barrymore family, and it was absolutely characteristic of the bustling and beautiful city of San Francisco, a city that had always lionized heroes, swashbucklers, and oddballs and that had never lost its Gold Rush frenzy and zest for life.

Only sixty years before, it was a scenic little town of about 450 people. Then gold was discovered at Sutter's Mills in the foothills of the Sierras.

At first, everybody headed for the hills. But by the end of 1849, the stampede for gold was reaching high tide and the population had multiplied to 25,000. People came flooding in from the East by covered wagon, coach, and anything else on wheels. And the harbor was getting thronged by ships abandoned by their crews, who jumped ashore and joined the rush for gold themselves.

When California became a state on September 9, 1850, wild celebrations were touched off. By then, six major fires had also been touched off in San Francisco, and each time the city was rebuilt and redeemed. Fire fighting even grew to be a socially prominent pastime, with firehouses achieving the status of private clubs that on certain occasions served champagne to the busy volunteers.

The population was soaring past 40,000 when the Wells Fargo Company was founded in 1852 at 114 Montgomery Street as an express and banking company that carried passengers and gold (sixteen days by Concord coach to St. Joseph, Missouri) and that came to symbolize the city's growing passion for commotion. And if more commotion was needed, it was guaranteed when the city's Big Four of business and power — Charles Crocker, Collis Potter Huntington, Leland Stanford, and Mark Hopkins — connected their Central Pacific Railroad with the Union Pacific in Utah and opened the gates even wider.

They were a bold bunch; or, at least, proud to the point of being bold. When the railroad link was joined, one headline shouted: SAN FRANCISCO ANNEXES THE UNITED STATES. And when the Palace Hotel was opened a few years later, in 1875, chic and stylish and dazzling with its carpeted hallways and glass-ceilinged dining room, one report noted: "There are also 457 bath tubs, which is an important consideration."

Even after the earthquake and fire scorched the city a generation later, causing five hundred deaths and wide ruin, the spirit was still bold. Billboards sprang up around town saying: "Don't talk earthquake — talk business."

And they did. Within three years, San Francisco was rebuilt. The city spent $150 million to restore it, the fire-insurance companies spent $225 million more. The Civic Center rose from the ashes with fountains of water and Renaissance buildings and auditoriums. The public library was constructed. The M. H. de Young Museum, a gift of the publisher Michael de Young, was opened in Golden Gate Park.

It was an ethnic, energized jewel of a city with 345,000 people, a violent past, and an epic future.

North of the city, in the town of Martinez on the eastern shore of the Bay, it didn't take long for a fisherman named Giuseppe

Paolo DiMaggio to decide that something momentous was happening on the day the earthquake struck.

It certainly wasn't going to be a day when he could board the skiff that he had built with his own hands and spend the daylight hours fishing. Besides, his wife, Rosalie, was expecting their fourth child two months later, and Giuseppe was in no mind to get reckless when the Pacific Coast seemed to be churning.

It had been eight years since Giuseppe DiMaggio left his home in Isola Della Femmine, a small island northwest of Palermo in the Golfo di Carini in Sicily. That was where he was born in 1874, and that was where Rosalie Mercurio was born five years later. And that was where they met and married and started looking for a better life.

There were only about nineteen hundred people in the town, and most of them were poor and all of them worked hard. Like generations of the DiMaggios before him, Giuseppe worked at one trade: He was a fisherman. And he didn't begin to look for wider horizons until after he had served in the Italian Army in its inglorious and losing expedition to Abyssinia in 1896.

When he came home, he wasn't nearly so willing to bury himself in the old grinding routines. So he made one of those decisions that can change the lives of generations. Rosalie was expecting their first child and stayed home to anchor the family while he sailed off to establish their beachhead on richer shores. In 1898, Giuseppe joined the tide of migration and headed for the New World and its opportunities and fantasies and, he hoped, its green pastures.

He took a somewhat unconventional route to the green pastures, though, skipping New York and its torrent of voyagers from Europe and continuing across the country to California, where a colony of his old neighbors from Palermo had already settled. They included Rosalie's father, who was living in a small town north of San Francisco, the island town of Collinsville, and he sent back word to his son-in-law to join the waves of their countrymen chasing rainbows across the Atlantic.

The streets of Collinsville were paved with good intentions but not with gold, and Giuseppe even had trouble finding steady work at his old trade on the fishing boats that crossed the Bay. For a time, he signed on as a laborer and section hand on the Union Pacific Railroad, where they paid about ten cents an hour. But small boats, not railroad cars, carried his hopes.

"He was born and raised a fisherman," his son Vince remembered. "There was nothing he could do over there. He wanted to be a fisherman. There were friends and family here from Italy that used to write and tell him how good the fishing was. So he decided to come over and try it by himself."

Somehow, Giuseppe put aside enough money to set the grand design into motion. In 1902, he sent the signal to Italy for Rosalie, and she headed west along his route with their daughter, Nellie, who had been born in Sicily on September 1, 1898, not long after he had left for America.

By the time they were reunited, he had moved south along the Bay to the town of Martinez, where he got back to commercial fishing with no further side jobs or distractions, and the family began to bloom.

A second daughter, Mamie, was born a year later, on September 25, 1903. Their first son, Thomas Paul, arrived on January 12, 1905. A third daughter, Marie, on June 17, 1906. Two years later, to the day, a second son, Michael Paul. Two years after that, on July 13, 1910, Frances was born; and two years after that, on September 6, 1912, a third son, Vincent Paul. And two years and two months later, on November 25, 1914, the fourth son and eighth child arrived at the house in Martinez: Joseph Paul DiMaggio.

The following year, Giuseppe moved the whole herd across the Bay into the city to the North Beach section of San Francisco, where a small but energized colony of Italian immigrants already lived and where many of the men went to sea every day, as they had done back home in Sicily. And that was where the ninth child, and fifth son, was born on February 12, 1917. He was named Dominic Paul, and he gave Giuseppe Paolo a clean sweep for his namesake and favorite saint: All five of his sons carried the middle name Paul.

In their new home, where they lived for the next twenty years or so, the eleven DiMaggios made a life in the bottom flat of the three-story building at 2047 Taylor Street. The rent was twenty-five dollars a month, and it was only a quarter of a mile to Giuseppe's fishing boat, which he properly named the *Rosalie.*

They went to school in the neighborhood, and they went to church at St. Peter and St. Paul, the landmark standing at Filbert and Powell Streets. They all played games at the North Beach playground, nothing very violent, and no particular omens for careers not yet shaped or even imagined.

Dominic, the baby of the family, was a kind of whiz at the sedentary sport of checkers. Vince even confessed to some feeling for music, especially opera. Joe showed a certain flair for tennis.

But sandlots and ball fields were just over the next hill. And for those who see signs of destiny in common things, the older sister Frances sometimes pitched tennis balls or rubber balls or unidentified flying objects to Joe in the alley behind the house.

The family ties were bound together by a mixture of respect, discipline, old-world commitment, and hard work. The parents spoke Italian to each other; the children spoke Italian to their parents but English to one another. After all, eight of the nine children had been born in America; only Nellie came from the old country, and she was four years old when she and her mother quite literally got off the boat and joined Giuseppe in what history portrayed as "the melting pot." And it didn't violate the lifestyles of the time for Rosalie to wait until 1944 to become a naturalized citizen and for Giuseppe, one year later.

"He was a good father," Joe said later. "We had some rough times, but there was always enough bread in the house, even though our clothes were hand-me-downs and we never had any extras. I can remember my father coming home from work, drinking a glass of wine, then playing with us. And his hours were long. He used to have to get up at four o'clock almost every morning. My mother always worked hard, too. I can't recall a time when she wasn't working."

"We were poor," Vince said, "but we were never without food or clothing. We were like all big families: When the older ones grew out of their clothes, they passed them down to the ones who were next in line.

"Nobody put any great pressure on us to finish school. We were more or less expected to go into fishing. That was Dad's view: We were going to be fishermen."

Tom DiMaggio, the number one son, went straight into fishing with his father. He was a good sandlot baseball player but strained his arm and never looked back. Then when Mike became old enough, he joined the crew. So Giuseppe bought another boat and suddenly had a fleet: He and Mike manned one of the boats, Tom handled the other one by himself. They went out every day, cast their nets into the Bay or the ocean, and came home with herring, bass, and salmon. Tom became a crab fisherman, and eventually even became vice president of the Crab Fisherman's Protective Association and, in the family councils, the business adviser and consultant to the three younger brothers who pursued their fortunes on land rather than on sea.

San Francisco was a good place to pursue fortunes, even half a century and more after the forty-niners pursued theirs in the gold fields. More than 350 fishing boats put out to sea every day and came home with 300 million pounds of fish every year.

There was no crisis within the family over who should chase fish and who should chase fly balls. The two older brothers, Tom and Mike, followed their father to the boats almost instinctively. The three younger brothers just as naturally gravitated to the ball yards. And if San Francisco was a fisherman's paradise crammed in every direction with boatyards, it was also a baseball paradise crammed with ball yards and embellished by a perfectly professional and highly successful hometown team that played in the

Pacific Coast League at the peak of the triple-A minor leagues: the San Francisco Seals.

Joe didn't like to put the knock on the number one family business at the time, but he conceded later that it wasn't exactly for him.

"I'd get seasick when the water was rough," he said. "And I couldn't stand the smell of the fish and the crabs."

So while Giuseppe walked from the house to the wharf with Tom and Mike every dawn, his three younger sons embarked on a dramatically different course that carried them on separate tracks and at varying levels toward the same destination. They all peddled the *Chronicle* together at the corner of First and Howard. But Joe had a more lasting memory: waiting outside the Lido café at Columbus and Lombard for the great Lefty O'Doul to come out, perchance with baseball in hand, but in any event with the bearing and stride of a batting champion and hometown hero. It was totally unthinkable at the time, but O'Doul was to be cast one day as Joe's coach, manager, and friend for life.

They went to Hancock Grammar School, then to Francisco Junior High School, and finally to Galileo High. But Joe dropped out of high school, took a job in a plant that bottled orange juice, decided it was "a lousy way to make a living," and dropped out of that, too.

He began to spend more time playing baseball on the dairy-wagon parking lot near the wharf. But he didn't have a very exalted opinion of himself.

"When I first started playing on the lot," he said, "I couldn't throw at all. I tried the infield, but I was a real scatter-arm. Even later on when I was trying to play shortstop for the San Francisco Seals, I made lots of errors, all on throws. The people sitting back of first base used to get up and run.

"I also couldn't run much myself. I used to wear braces on both knees when I was a kid; I had some kind of problem, the way they were lined up. But after a while, my arm got better and my legs came around, too."

"After that," he remembered with towering understatement, "I was all right."

Almost everybody who saw him play agreed that he was "all right," especially after he began to play for organized teams with committed coaches. His first team was the Silesian Boys' Club. Then an olive-oil dealer in the North Beach neighborhood, John Rossi, organized a sandlot team to play semipro ball and Joe played third base and shortstop. He was a tall, wiry kid with horsey, aquiline features and no expression, and he was a natural.

Off the field, he wasn't so natural. It was 1931, he was sixteen years old, and his family was feeling the strain of the Great Depression, which was one of the main reasons he quit Galileo High. That was when he went to work in the orange-juice plant and hated it. He also worked for a while as a laborer on the docks, he got another job in a cannery, he delivered groceries, he loaded trucks. His brother Vince, who was eighteen, had quit school to work in a fruit market. But he also played ball on Sundays, and he came home with two dollars a game. You would have to say the handwriting was on the wall.

In fact, it was on the wall in screaming letters. Joe also didn't have any other direction to travel, and he didn't seem to have any other interest to develop. Frank Venezia, one of his cronies from the old neighborhood, who went on to become a teamster, once told the writer Maury Allen that this was an unadorned teenager.

"Joe was really shy," he remembered. "Every once in a while, we'd have dances over at the boys' club. You couldn't get Joe to go. I'll tell you the truth, I don't think he knew how to dance."

But he knew how to hit. And although baseball ranked somewhat below dancing as a social skill in the eyes of old-line parents in the neighborhood, it was clearly the escape route to take *out* of the neighborhood and out of the Depression. When Vince was signed by the Seals the following year for $150 a month, the economic issues were unarguable.

Joe looked back on this later with total recall, especially the primitive way he started to follow Vince up the ladder. When he first began playing ball on the Horse Lot, the parking lot for the dairy wagons, he said: "We used rocks for bases, and most of us played bare-handed because we couldn't afford gloves."

But after John Rossi organized his sandlot team, things started looking up. He entered the team in a league, bought good equipment for his players, and gave them some notions about fundamentals and tactics to go with their teenaged skills. In the game that decided the championship, Joe hit two home runs and was rewarded with two "gold" baseballs and merchandise worth maybe sixteen dollars. It was the first time he was paid for playing baseball, but not the last.

He did even better after he raised his game a notch by playing for the Sunset Produce Team. He batted .632 in eighteen games, and he went home that time with a pair of baseball shoes as the prize. More rewarding than that, he was now seventeen years old, a six-footer with long legs and good upper-body strength, and he was living and playing in a city that had two high minor-league teams, the Seals and the Missions, competing for the local talent. And in a short time he received offers from both teams and promptly followed Vince into professional baseball.

The first offer came from the Missions. It was triggered by the team's manager, Fred Hofmann, who had played in the major leagues as a reserve catcher for the New York Yankees between 1919 and 1925, just when the storied Babe Ruth was powering them to great success, and for the Boston Red Sox in 1927 and 1928. He spotted DiMaggio playing on the sandlots, invited him to a tryout with the Missions, and promised him $150 a month if he made the team, about twenty-five more than the regular rate.

Joe liked the idea right away, but took the proper family route straight to his oldest brother, Tom, who had grown into something resembling the senior American in the family, too. Besides,

Tom had already led the brothers' way into baseball, even though he had been thwarted by a sore arm, and he was a practical and solid man with a sense of business strategy.

Joe also went to Vince for advice, knowing that Vince had meanwhile signed with the Missions' rivals, the Seals, and was hitting .347 that season for the Seals' highest affiliate, the Tucson club in Arizona. When Vince was called up to the Seals late in the season, Joe went over to the Seals' ballpark one day to consult with his brother. He already knew that Vince wanted him to take a shot at joining him on the Seals, but Joe did have the offer from the Missions, and for the moment it was the only offer on the table.

What happened next isn't entirely clear, not even in Joe's memory. But it is clear enough that Joe was taken to the owner of the team by a sandlot coach and local scout with the penny-novel name of Edward (Spike) Hennessy, who had watched him play around town. The exact route they took to the front office, though, may have been the earliest legend of Joe DiMaggio. One version portrays the kid ballplayer squinting through a knothole on the outfield fence trying to sight his big brother inside until the scout comes along and says: "Never stand on the outside looking in, unless it's jail."

Another version reports that Spike Hennessy vigorously escorted the young player into the office of the owner, Charlie Graham, and predicted: "This kid is going to make the big leagues." And yet another version suggests that Hennessy and Graham had already talked about DiMaggio around the office since he was building a reputation on the sandlots and was also the brother of Vince, who was established in the lineup. In any event, Vince later struck a blow for the whole and unvarnished truth, saying: "No, Spike Hennessy did not discover Joe at the knothole." And Joe later took away some of the intrigue when he admitted: "I was already aiming for the Seals."

The Seals were in last place in 1932, so it was fine with them. Graham invited him to join the team, more or less as an unpaid apprentice since it was already late in the season, and turned him over to his first manager, Ike Caveney.

But nothing much happened as the season wound down and the seventeen-year-old rookie from Taylor Street sat and watched. Then the curtain parted and Joe DiMaggio walked onstage. It happened with three games to go before the season closed; Augie Galan, the regular shortstop who later became a star in the big leagues, went to the manager and asked if he could leave early. He didn't have the most compelling reason in the world: He just wanted to travel to Honolulu with "Prince" Henry Oana, an outfielder and pitcher with the club, who was going home. Considering the state of the Seals, Caveney had no problem with that, even though he still had to find somebody to play shortstop for three days. And Joe remembered how that problem was solved: "Vince spoke right up and said, 'My kid brother can play shortstop.' "

Vince's assessment wasn't literally true, but there wasn't much doubt that his kid brother could handle the bat. The first time he went to the plate in professional ball, he hit a triple. For the three games, he hit only .222, but he did it with grace, and the Seals were interested.

"Everybody wants to get the credit for bringing Joe into pro ball," Vince said. "But I brought him in. I made the contact for him. After Ike let Augie Galan leave, Joe played the three games, threw a couple up in the stands, made a couple of good catches, got a couple of good hits, and they liked him.

"They liked him so well that they wanted to sign him right then and there. But Tom was the boss, so it had to be under Tom's jurisdiction. Joe was still underage, so Tom took over. In all Joe's dealings as far as San Francisco was concerned, Tom was Joe's manager."

So Tom DiMaggio became the senior eminence of the business life of the brothers, the crab fisherman setting the party line for his three younger brothers as they tilted the family's involvement and fortunes toward baseball. But the family legends go too far when they create crises between the fishing father and his sandlot sons as they arrived at the point of professional no return. Giuseppe was skeptical because he had always worked hard and long for his livelihood, and the idea of playing baseball for a living seemed frivolous. But he wasn't driven to the warpath to change the course of the boys' careers. At least, not after Vince went to him in December 1931, after his first season with the Seals and their Tucson farm club.

"Don't forget," he said later, "this was the big Depression. And I had to show my folks that there was more money in baseball than in fishing. So I took the money and the bonuses the club owed me, something like fifteen hundred dollars, and went home and put it on the kitchen table. Cash. It was a lot of money. And the first thing Dad wanted to know was where I stole it.

"I said I earned it, and right away took him with me the next day to meet Mr. Graham, the owner. They got along good, even though Dad was speaking in broken English and every now and then I'd have to get into the conversation and kind of explain what he was saying.

"He and Mr. Graham got to be pretty good friends. And later I said, 'Dad, you ought to go out and watch a ball game.' And he did, and he turned to me one day and said: 'I guess there is money in that.'

"Believe me, I really broke the ice for Joe and Dominic, as far as baseball was concerned. When Joe started talking to the Seals the next year, he didn't have any opposition from our father. I had already set the pattern for the family."

With Vince's pattern and Tom's smarts and Giuseppe's blessing, Joe signed with the Seals for the 1933 season. He was eighteen years old, and he was suddenly making $225 a month, which was twice as much as the average rookie was paid in the Pacific Coast League. And, like the average rookie, he sat on the bench for the first two weeks of the season with Vince, who was suffering from a sore arm.

Then one afternoon the Seals were trailing by a score of 6–1 and Ike Caveney shouted down the bench for the younger DiMaggio to grab a bat and pinch-hit for Ed Stewart, the rookie right fielder, who was playing but not hitting.

"I went up to the plate in a trance," Joe remembered. "And I drew a walk, which was just as well because I doubt that I could have swung the bat with any force."

He stayed in the game and went out to right field, which was terra incognita to him because he was billed as an infielder who could play shortstop or third base. But the next day he started the game in right field, got two hits, and launched a career.

They played long seasons in the Pacific Coast League because they had long stretches of sunshine, and DiMaggio not only made the most of his first moments in the sunshine but also stepped into a spotlight that followed him from home plate to right field and back again. Everything he did seemed to defy the truth that he was a teenaged rookie making his debut one rung below the big leagues and making it with Olympian numbers.

He played in 187 games that summer, batted .340 with 45 doubles, 13 triples, and 28 home runs, led the league by knocking in 169 runs, and made 17 errors but also led the league by throwing out 32 runners from right field. And during one thundering streak of two months, he hit safely in 61 games in a row, breaking the league record set 18 years before.

Did somebody say *streak?* That's right. He was 18 years old, and he hit in 61 games in a row.

By now, he was the toast of a town that was caught in the Depression and that urgently needed to lift its sights and spirits. The Italians in North Beach cheered and strutted. Giuseppe beamed. Mayor Angelo Rossi presented a wristwatch as a token of civic pride. And, more to the point, all sixteen teams in the big leagues sent scouts to see for themselves.

Nobody was more impressed by all this than Tom DiMaggio, the business shark of the family, who quickly sensed that his kid brother's instant success had created a value of its own. He went straight to the one man in town who could take a bravura performance like this and run with it: Charlie Graham, the owner of the Seals, who also was caught in the Depression. It took no time to figure out that Charlie Graham could do several things with Joe DiMaggio's contract: renew it, extend it, cancel it, improve it — or sell it.

It was probably a little cheeky for those days, since all baseball contracts were ruled by the "reserve clause," which reserved the player's rights to the owner automatically from year to year, but Tom did it, anyway. He leaned on Graham to cut the family in when he sold Joe's contract to a major-league club, and he put a value on that, too.

The value of the contract, he suggested, should be something like $75,000. The family, he also suggested, should come in for $6,500 as the price of Joe's success. There was nothing wrong with either calculation, except that Tom was a little ahead of his time. Everybody was being stifled by the Depression, and nobody was biting. At least, not yet.

For the skeptics who might like to see him do it again, Joe obliged. The following year, he played in only 101 games because of an injury — 86 fewer games than in 1933 — but he still batted .341 with 18 doubles, 6 triples, and 12 home runs, and he drove in 69 runs.

However, the most memorable thing he did that year, the rest of the baseball world suspected, was to tear up his left knee. He did it in the same sort of down-home way that he did most things then: He played in a Sunday doubleheader early in the season, hustled from the ballpark to have dinner with his married sister, then jumped onto a crowded jitney bus to his family's apartment on Taylor Street. He sat cramped in the crowd, hopped off when he got home, and, he remembered, his left knee "popped like a pistol shot."

The shot was heard loud and clear round the baseball world, and front offices in big-league stadiums lost interest overnight. It was one thing to pay hard dollars for a phenom from California, but it was unthinkable to pay hard dollars for anybody with a torn knee. And after the knee was blocked into a cast the next day and he limped through seventy games on the bench, his statistics and his price plunged on parallel tracks.

"Once you had a bad leg," the celebrated umpire Jocko Conlon observed, "it was nearly impossible to get a major-league club to take a chance on you. The only one I can remember back then who did get a chance was Joe DiMaggio."

DiMaggio got the chance because he was still a teenager with time to outgrow an injury, and because his performances suggested that he might become dynamite if another team signed him in spite of the knee. But there also was no doubt that when his knee buckled, his price buckled, too. Dan Daniel, who wrote endlessly about DiMaggio and the Yankees in his baseball columns, guessed that the injury lowered his value "in the open market by something like $100,000." He also reported that it "scared fifteen big-league clubs away from him." But that wasn't entirely true: Money was tight in those days for every club, but Joe Cronin said later that, as both the general manager and manager of the Boston Red Sox then, he was ready to pursue DiMaggio if the Yankees had not got there first.

It wasn't just that the Yankees were wiser than everybody else. Richer, maybe. Probably luckier. But they also were still basking in the powerhouse success of their 1932 championship and in the depth of a cast led by the nonpareils Babe Ruth and Lou Gehrig, and they also had just hired a shrewd and aggressive farm director named George Weiss, who had come aboard in 1932 and promptly started beating the bushes for the talent the Yankees would need when their marquee stars left the Broadway stage in the next few years.

Weiss was the son of a "fancy-grocer" in New Haven and got his first job in baseball as the student manager of the baseball team at New Haven High School. Five years later, while still studying at Yale, he became manager and master-of-all-trades for the New Haven Colonials, a semipro team that soon made life competitive for the professional team in town, which played in the Eastern League — but never on Sunday, because of the blue laws that spared the Sabbath the clamor of organized sports.

Weiss immediately filled the Sunday silence with imported shows that added some spice to the life of the Colonials: an All-Chinese team, a Bloomer Girls team, and a team led by the renowned Ty Cobb, who used to insist on a $350 guarantee to make a side-trip to New Haven from either Boston or New York, where his Detroit Tigers were being kept idle by the laws every Sunday. When Weiss forked over $800, Cobb was impressed and came back often for encores, with no written guarantee.

The Colonials became studded with famous athletes like Charlie Brickley and Eddie Mahan, the Harvard football heroes, and Wally Pipp, Walter Johnson, and Cobb from the big leagues. Once, in a moment of booking genius, Weiss even imported the Boston Red Sox and their star pitcher, Babe Ruth.

Ruth played first base for the Red Sox that day, but the Colonials still defeated them, 4–3. Nobody knows how hard the Red Sox were trying, but Weiss still advertised the game as "the greatest baseball attraction ever offered New Haven fans."

That was in 1916, the year Boston won the World Series, and in another exhibition game staged by Weiss, Ruth pitched for the Red Sox while Cobb played for the Colonials and knicked Ruth for a single and double. The score that time was 3–3, and you might say the Red Sox bombed in New Haven again.

After that, evidently to forestall the spectacle of a semipro team team defeating the best in the major leagues, the National Commission of baseball ruled that only three members of a championship team could take part in postseason exhibitions.

George Weiss turned into such an enduring part of New Haven life that Damon Runyon, contemplating the memorable features of covering a football game at Yale, once wrote:

New Haven — what fond memories the name conjures:
Elms.
The Campus.
More elms.
George Weiss.

"In 1919," Weiss said later, "the New Haven club apparently decided to stop fighting me. They came to me and said: 'You want to buy the club for $5,000?' I had to borrow the $5,000, but I did it."

Ten years later, he moved up to the International League as general manager at Baltimore, succeeding Jack Dunn, who had died after falling from a horse. Weiss arrived in Baltimore with the Depression, and cash was already tight, but he still sold eight players to the major leagues in the next three years. Then in 1932, the telephone rang and Colonel Jacob Ruppert invited him to join the Yankees.

One year later, he was arguing the merits of signing Joe Di-Maggio and his torn knee. Ed Barrow, the general manager of the Yankees, put it bluntly: "We just don't have any more cash to go after minor league players. We'll have to build from our own farm system." But Weiss found a pair of allies in a pair of scouts: Joe Devine, who had been watching DiMaggio play for the Seals, and Bill Essick, who even lived for a time across the street from DiMaggio's house.

Barrow later wrote in his memoirs that "I made the decision to gamble on DiMaggio." But he actually needed some prompting, and he got it when Weiss drove with Essick and Devine to visit Colonel Ruppert at French Lick, Indiana, and made the case in person. And when Ruppert agreed, in the words of his general manager, "to gamble," they pitched the proposition to Charlie Graham and the Seals.

"That I got to the Yankees at all," Joe said later, "or even stayed in baseball, was due to the persistence of Bill Essick."

Since he had missed eighty-six games that season, it was also

due to the persistence of Charlie Graham, who had to bargain
strenuously to get the Yankees "to gamble" for a reasonable
price. After all, Essick had advised Barrow: "Buy DiMaggio. I
think you can get him cheap." And Barrow, after ordering a series of medical tests on the celebrated knee, tried to get him
very cheap.

Graham still was aiming for the $75,000 in cash that he and
Tom DiMaggio cherished as the ransom price. But when the deal
was finally struck, they settled for one-third of the target price,
$25,000, plus something else the Seals needed almost as much as
the money: five players. They were players from the Yankees'
farm system, and they were intended to help the Seals fill the
one mammoth vacancy that would be created when DiMaggio
left. But they were mostly journeymen: Ted Norbert, an outfielder; Les Powers, a first baseman; Ed Farrell, an infielder; and
Jim Densimore and Floyd Newkirk, both pitchers.

Three of them played in the big leagues, but they weren't
men of distinction. Powers made it to the New York Giants in
1938 and got into three games, then made it to the Philadelphia
Phillies the next year and got into nineteen games. He got eighteen hits in those nineteen games, but the fling subsided there.
Newkirk made the Yankees' roster in 1934, but pitched only one
inning and was probably best remembered for his middle name:
Elmo. And Farrell, who was known as Doc, played for the Giants, Boston Braves, St. Louis Cardinals, Chicago Cubs, and Yankees, and later for the Red Sox. But he didn't play for the Seals.
In fact, he refused to report, apparently not willing to go back to
the minor leagues, so the Yankees paid an extra $5,000 to
Graham to compensate for his nominal loss.

Graham had an ace up his sleeve as he haggled into November with the Yankees: Since he was receiving only one-third of
the money he wanted, he could use DiMaggio "to help the gate,"
so why not leave him in San Francisco for one more season,
anyway? The Yankees mulled that one over, calculated that he
had a point about the money, further calculated that the famous

left knee could use the extra time at home, and agreed. DiMaggio would play for the Seals in 1935 and report to New York in time for spring training in 1936.

But if DiMaggio was distracted by either the knee or the Yankees, he didn't show it. He played in 1935 for the new manager of the Seals, one of his original hometown heroes, Lefty O'Doul, who had just finished eleven years in the big leagues with a career batting average of .349. So he knew something about hitting, and DiMaggio listened.

He also got the chance to play against some senior pitchers "on the way down" from the big leagues, and he even took some swings against touring black pitchers who had the talent but not the complexion for the "lily white" big leagues, including the top gun in both the black and white baseball worlds, the legendary Satchel Paige. And all of the elements in Joe's two previous summers in professional baseball came together and exploded.

In his booming last hurrah to San Francisco, he got into 172 games, batted .398 with 49 doubles, 18 triples, and 34 home runs, stole 24 bases in 25 attempts, lost the batting title by less than one percentage point, and was voted the Most Valuable Player in the Pacific Coast League. And the Seals won the pennant.

A few months later, in February of 1936, he said goodbye to his mother and father, his four sisters and four brothers, and headed east.

He was actually chaperoned by two of the Yankees who lived in San Francisco, the shortstop Frank Crosetti and the second baseman Tony Lazzeri. The Yankees brought them together by urging the two veterans to shepherd the rookie to spring training, so they set out with Lazzeri at the wheel of the new Ford sedan he had just bought for the trip. Each of them ponied up fifteen dollars for expenses, although Crosetti remembered that they each had to throw in another five dollars to make it.

"Anyway," he said, "we got by on fifty bucks or so, three guys eating, sleeping, gas, everything."

They also were supposed to share the driving as well as the tab. They weren't long on the road before they learned that the rookie couldn't drive. But there was no doubt that he could play.

They drove into St. Petersburg on the Gulf Coast of Florida late in the day on March 1, chiefly to shield their rookie prodigy from the newspaper writers. The next morning, he put on his Yankee uniform for the first time, and Dan Daniel wrote in the *New York World-Telegram:* "Here is the replacement for Babe Ruth."

3

THE BATTLE
OF BROADWAY

THE "REPLACEMENT" for Babe Ruth probably never lived, and he certainly didn't drive into the Yankees' training camp as a twenty-one-year-old rookie in the spring of 1936 after a cross-country drive from San Francisco. But the *heir* to Babe Ruth did arrive in St. Petersburg on that March morning, the heir to the tradition that began with Ruth in 1920 and that stretched for nearly half a century through the Yankee career of Mickey Mantle. And for the middle years of that Yankee era, Joe DiMaggio became the centerpiece.

But it was historical truth that the booming bat and the booming personality of Babe Ruth were absent from the Yankee scene. Lou Gehrig was there, but he was fated to be there for just three years more before his physical power was destroyed by the exotic, unknown, and fatal attack of amyotrophic lateral sclerosis.

During the time that he shaped and dramatized the Yankee Age in sports, Babe Ruth hit 714 home runs, knocked in 2,211 runs, batted .342, and rescued baseball from the ruins of the Black Sox scandal of 1919. Even before he crashed into the public's mind and mood with his bat and his roundhouse swing, he had already reached star standing as a pitcher for the Boston Red Sox. An accomplished left-hander, he won 94 games, delivered 107 complete games, and twice won more than 20 in a season. But the image he cast was the image of a cheerfully roguish man hitting a baseball past the fences and enchanting people who were hungering for life and style and heroes in the days after Johnny came marching home from the war fields of Europe.

To the public, the passion of war switched to the passion of peace, or maybe just the passion for passion wherever you could find it. There was no doubt about that from the moment the Seventy-seventh Division came home to New York and marched up Fifth Avenue from Washington Square to 110th Street in the parade to end all parades after the war to end all wars.

Mail was being flown by air for the first time, and New York was forming an air police squadron of 150 wartime pilots headed by the vice chairman of the Mayor's Traffic Committee. Nobody, including the mayor, knew exactly what it would do, and nobody cared what it would do.

Brigadier General Douglas MacArthur was named commandant at West Point. Baseball, which was played never on Sunday, began to be played on Sunday, and 35,000 persons turned out at the Polo Grounds in Manhattan and 25,000 at Ebbets Field in Brooklyn on the *same* Sunday to "celebrate the death of a blue law." The *Ladies' Home Journal,* reveling in the end of federal restrictions on paper, announced that it was immediately going to 184 pages with color pictures of the war and articles like "How I Wrote 'The Battle Hymn of the Republic,' by Julia Ward Howe."

That is, the United States was spiraling happily into the decade of wonderful nonsense. It was a time of suffragettes, heavyweights, and hoopla; of Suzanne Lenglen in flowing white dress socking a backhand on the courts at Cannes; of Mary Garden taking up her new duties as "directrix" of the Chicago Opera

Company; of the great red racehorse Man O' War winning twenty times and losing just once and becoming one of the symbols of an age that reveled in winning twenty times and losing just once.

John Barrymore, having survived the earthquake and fire in San Francisco as well as numerous other more personal adventures, was appearing at the Empire Theatre in New York with his sister Ethel in Michael Strange's new play, *Clair de Lune.* And the great tide of Prohibition was causing Barrymore little inconvenience, and was causing the public inconvenience only in the new "rum courts," which were doing a landslide business in bootleg cases.

In its gentler moments, as the decade barreled on, American society might applaud "Madame Curie's genius," as the newspapers put it; or attend Sunday-afternoon tea dances at roadside spots like the Pelham Heath Inn; or follow the high life reflected in rotogravure pictures of Billie Burke as Mrs. Florenz Ziegfeld walking with her daughter Patricia at Palm Beach. Or, in its frenzied moments, which seemed more frequent, it might rail at the Bolshevik threat in Russia; issue ultimatums on occupying the Ruhr Valley; or rush to get some cash down on the Dempsey-Carpentier fight.

It was a time of idols, and sometimes of idols stacked on other idols. Douglas Fairbanks posed with Jack Dempsey perched comfortably on his right shoulder, and insisted cordially that it was "just as easy as holding up the Woolworth Building." And Dempsey just as cordially announced that he was studying French to understand what Georges Carpentier might say in the ring. He didn't say much, and the fight ended in four.

It was a time properly portrayed then and now as the Roaring Twenties, and they roared.

"The vandals sacking Rome," observed Gene Fowler, "were ten times as kindly as the spendthrift hordes on Broadway. The Wall Street delirium was reaching the pink-elephant stage. Chambermaids and counter-hoppers had the J. P. Morgan complex. America had the swelled head, and the brand of tourists that went to Europe became ambassadors of ill-will. The World War killed nearly everything that was old Broadway. Prohibition, the mock-turtle soup of purists, provided the *coup de grâce.*"

So, all things considered, there was no grander stage for his gargantuan talents than Broadway and its environs when Babe Ruth was traded to the Yankees by the self-destructive owner of the Boston Red Sox, the debt-ridden Harry Frazee, who was as unlucky in love as in business.

But when Ruth arrived on the grand stage of New York life in 1920, it was already occupied — and, in sports, dominated — by the many-splendored manager of the Giants, the master of the Polo Grounds by day and the downtown clubs and theaters by night, John McGraw. He was known affectionately as *Mr. McGraw.*

It was eighteen years since McGraw had landed in New York himself with a solid reputation, and a solid notoriety, as an original member of the old Baltimore Orioles, the cheap-shot artists who ruled baseball in the decade known as the Gay Nineties. His philosophy was terse, and unmistakable: "The main idea is to win." And the Giants did win after he was hired as the shortstop and manager during the 1902 season, when they were a last-place team in the National League.

One year later, they finished in second place, and for the next two years they won the pennant and in 1905 also won the World Series in five games over Connie Mack and his Philadelphia Athletics. All the games were shutouts, and three of them were pitched by McGraw's ace of aces, Christy Mathewson. They won again in 1912 and 1913, again in 1917, and they ran second in six other seasons.

Then, at the pinnacle of McGraw's power and popularity, Babe Ruth arrived from Boston with his bat, cast an instant shadow over McGraw's empire, and rang up the curtain on the classic confrontation of the Roaring Twenties, the battle of Broadway. And it was waged for the first three years in John

McGraw's own ball yard, the Polo Grounds, which the Giants were sharing with the Yankees while the Yankees' own stadium in the Bronx was being built.

Ruth wasted no time in firing the first salvos. He hit 54 home runs in 1920, the first season he wore the uniform of the Yankees, and then made it 59 the next year. McGraw's first baseman, Long George Kelly, unwittingly helped to dramatize the Ruth revolution when he led the National League by hitting a mere 23. But the public got the point instantly: the year before they acquired Ruth, the Yankees played before 619,162 customers; the year he arrived, attendance rocketed to 1,289,422 as he began driving home runs over the fences in John McGraw's stadium.

"The Yankees," he raged to Charles Stoneham, the owner of the Giants, "will have to build a park in Queens or some other out-of-the-way place. Let them go away and wither on the vine."

The Yankees, however, had no intention of withering on the vines of Queens or any other place. On February 5, 1921, they announced that they had bought ten acres of land in the Bronx between 157th and 161st Streets, from River Avenue to Doughty Avenue. They bought it from the estate of William Waldorf Astor and noted that "the running time from Forty-second Street by subway will be about sixteen minutes."

Moreover, the stadium planned for the site would be an oval like the Yale Bowl, and would be made "impenetrable to all human eyes, save those of aviators, by towering embattlements."

To McGraw, the worst architectural feature was the geography: The new Yankee Stadium was going to rise just across the Harlem River from his Polo Grounds, where it would not exactly be impenetrable to all human eyes. It was as though Ziegfeld had opened a new theater next door to Belasco, and had promptly hired the Barnum & Bailey Circus for an indefinite run.

There was more at stake than baseball, too. McGraw, as the master of the only game in town, also reigned as one of the stars of the sporting and stage life downtown, along Broadway, the center of his world of actors, athletes, touts, Tammany tigers, con men, chorus girls, boxers, and bootleggers. It was a world bathed in a hippodrome atmosphere, and it was bustling with people like Louis Mann, the actor, who once tangled for laughs with Gentleman Jim Corbett in a dressing room at the Palace. They mauled each other for ten minutes before Mann, now getting whacked, implored the massive former heavyweight champion: "For God's sake, Jim, let's quit before we kill each other."

The inner circle also included the celebrated, and often ine-briated, criminal lawyer William Fallon, who defended McGraw in a number of cases involving left hooks to the jaw, and who did it with the same zest that he displayed on behalf of his other clients, notably the tycoon gambler Arnold Rothstein and the trick-shot artist Danny Arnstein. It took some extra brilliance to defend Arnstein when he was accused of arranging a five-million-dollar heist of stock certificates. But Fallon performed with such tactical genius that Arnstein's wife, the actress Fanny Brice, named her son for the great mouthpiece.

Fallon and McGraw were regulars at The Lambs, where the lawyer sometimes would recite movingly from Tennyson and By-ron. But he gave his best performances in court. Once, during a tedious case, he bet a colleague that he could remember the names and occupations of all sixty prospective jurors. He won the bet, and later the case. On another occasion, the judge re-coiled when he detected liquor on Fallon's breath during a huddle before the bench and asked the lawyer if he had been drinking.

The judge was a noted teetotaler, but Fallon charmed him by replying: "If Your Honor's sense of justice is as good as his sense of smell, my client need have no worry in this court."

But there wasn't much that Fallon could do to shield McGraw from his confrontations with Ruth. And when the 1921 season ended, McGraw stood on top of the National League, where he would be standing on closing day for four straight years. And

Ruth and the Yankees stood on top of the American League, where they would be standing for three straight years. The irresistible force of Babe Ruth had somehow met the immovable object of John McGraw.

The World Series opened on October 5, and proved just as improbable as the stars of the cast. It was the first played under the jurisdiction and the bushy brows of Kenesaw Mountain Landis, the federal judge named for a Civil War battle, who had been anointed as the commissioner of baseball to clean away the debris of the debacle of 1919. It was also the third and last Series played to the best of nine games. It was the first for the Yankees on any basis, and it was the first played entirely in the Polo Grounds, where tenant and landlord were approaching the end of their strained occupancy.

The Yankees jumped off to a rousing start the first time they went to bat when Ruth singled and drove across the first run. It was enough, as Carl Mays pitched shutout ball and protected the lead that his former Boston teammate had provided. In ninety-eight minutes: 3–0, Yankees.

The next day, McGraw changed his catchers but not his luck. The Yankees found a new way to torture him when Bob Meusel stole home while the catcher, Earl Smith, watched and McGraw stewed. Smith had a clubhouse reputation as a talker, but his reputation must have preceded him: He delivered an inflammatory talk at home plate after Meusel crossed, and was promptly relieved of two hundred dollars by Judge Landis. The Giants, meanwhile, managed only two hits off Waite Hoyt and for the second straight day lost by the score of 3–0.

No team in the twenty-year history of the World Series had spotted a rival two games and survived, and the Giants hadn't even scored a run yet. Then the Yankees scored four runs in the third inning of the next game, and now the Giants were two games and four runs down and still hadn't scored a run of their own.

But the Giants finally revived, scored four runs in the home half of the third, then eight more in the seventh inning for a World Series record, and stormed along to win, 13-5.

McGraw felt better now, and he felt even better than that when the Giants won the fourth game, 4-2, and tied the Series at two games apiece. But Ruth unfurled his first home run in a World Series, the first of fifteen during the next dozen years, and an omen of sorts was delivered to the combative master of the Giants.

The next day, the Yankees went back in front by winning, 3-1, and Ruth made even bigger news: He beat out a bunt. But he also developed an abscess on his left elbow and, except for one appearance as a pinch-hitter, his Series was finished. So, for all practical purposes, were the Yankees. Without their champion, they did not win another game while the Giants tied the Series, 8-5; took the lead, 2-1; and won it all, 1-0.

McGraw, who had lost four Series in a row since 1905, treated himself to one of those rare moments of unmixed delight in the last inning of the last game. First, his nemesis Ruth pinch-hit for Wally Pipp and grounded out. Then Aaron Ward walked and Frank Baker lined a pitch toward right field. But Johnny Rawlings, the boy second baseman whom McGraw had bought from Philadelphia four months earlier, lunged for the ball, knocked it down on the rim of the outfield grass, and, still on his knees, threw out Baker at first base. Ward had rounded second and was en route to third, but he was thrown out from first to third, George Kelly to Frank Frisch, and McGraw's cup runneth over.

It ran over far into the night, in fact, in a roaring celebration in the Giants' suite at the Waldorf. They had won the World Series over the Yankees, and were headed for four straight seasons of unmatched prosperity. But for McGraw, there was only one victory that mattered.

"I signaled every pitch to Ruth," he said, savoring every memory of his first encounter with the new colossus in town. "In fact, I gave the sign for practically every ball our pitchers threw.

It was no secret. We pitched only nine curves and three fastballs to Ruth during the entire Series. All the rest were slowballs, and of the twelve of those, eleven set him on his ear."

He must have been doing something right: Ruth struck out eight times in the five games he got to play. But Ruth showed that his very strength was a rollicking attitude that never looked back to dwell on the past. And as soon as the Series was over, he embarked on a baseball barnstorming tour. Judge Landis ordered him not to do it, but Ruth didn't even wait to collect his loser's share of $3,510 from the Series pool, which Landis impounded, anyway.

He also was suspended for thirty-nine days at the start of the next season, and did not play until May 20. To complete the tumble, he then suffered through his worst slump as a player.

Yet he stalked the enemy like a lion. And there he was the following October at the Polo Grounds, flexing his muscles for another World Series between the Yankees and the Giants and for Round Two of his war with John McGraw. It was October 4, 1922, and the return match between the titans of baseball was waged with a torrent of public passion.

"Truly," wrote *The New York Times,* frankly impressed, "baseball is the national game. From east and west, from north and south, the fans are gathering to see two New York teams battle in the blue-ribbon event of the diamond, the World Series."

The fans, in fact, were gathering outside the bleacher gate at the Polo Grounds twenty-four hours before the first pitch. It was a queue that stretched for blocks, and it made social news when the waves of newspaper writers pursuing the flavor of the scene on the eve of battle discovered that the fifth person on line was a woman, Mrs. Carrie Lentz of West 141st Street, and, the press duly reported, "she will root for the Yankees."

In addition to Mrs. Carrie Lentz of 141st Street, two governors, four former governors, two mayors, and swarms of deputies were spotted and listed in page after page of minute detail carried in the newspapers. They even disclosed that

"J. P. Morgan is a boxholder, as are also Harry F. Sinclair, Harry Payne Whitney, Finley J. Shepard and Charles H. Sabin."

In a box near the dugout, Mary Roberts Rinehart entertained a group of friends. George M. Cohan, Louis Mann, and Jack Dempsey took bows, and when General John J. Pershing made an unexpected appearance, the crowd rose and cheered for the hero of the American Expeditionary Force, as it did for Al Smith and the old brown derby.

Christy Mathewson, the recent pitching sensation of the Giants, who was no longer a combatant, made the headlines just for attending. So did Babe Ruth, the new sensation of the Yankees, just for striking out twice. It was even noted with something approaching civic pride that Lord Louis Mountbatten, Grand Admiral of the Fleet, illustrious cousin of the Prince of Wales and uncle to an empire, had planned to attend the opening game with his bride, one of the reigning beauties of Europe, but at the last moment decided instead to view the polo matches at Meadowbrook, worse luck for *them.*

Casey Stengel, already ancient at thirty-two but still an irregular in McGraw's outfield corps, stood behind the cage during batting practice and thought he detected a Yankee "spy" watching. "Yankee secret service," he told Earl Smith, the Giants' catcher, who was batting at the time with no thought that it was possible to hide anything from anybody on the clamorous stage.

And there was the revolution of *radio,* spreading the noise and the action beyond the ball yard.

"Hear the crowd roar at the World Series games with Radiola," the public was exhorted in newspaper advertisements. "Grantland Rice, famous sports editor of the *New York Tribune,* will describe every game personally, play by play, direct from the Polo Grounds. His story, word by word, as each exciting play is made by the Yankees or Giants, will be *broadcasted* from famous Radio Corporation–Westinghouse Station WJZ."

Grantland Rice was manning the oval microphone when the Yankees fired the opening shots, as they had done the year before. Whitey Witt led off the sixth inning with a three-bagger but was thrown out trying to score on an infield grounder by Joe Dugan. However, before he surrendered, Witt hopped back and forth along the line between third base and home and did it long enough for Dugan to reach second. Dugan then scored from second when Ruth followed with a single to right field.

It was the second straight year that Ruth had struck first. But for the second straight year, McGraw was destined to have the last hurrah. It was the only run produced by Ruth in the entire Series.

The Yankees made it 2–0 in the seventh, and Bullet Joe Bush was stifling the Giants all the way. But in the eighth, the Giants crashed through for three runs and the game.

To the crowd of 36,514 persons inside the Giants' park, this was the Battle of Broadway at its theatrical best. But to a far greater audience huddled before loudspeakers in other parts of the city and for miles along the eastern seaboard, this was the new life of leisure and action at its unimaginable best.

"Radio, for the first time," reported *The Times,* "carried the opening game of the World Series, play by play, direct from the Polo Grounds to great crowds throughout the eastern section of the country. Through the broadcasting station WJZ at Newark, New Jersey, Grantland Rice related his story of the game direct to an invisible audience, estimated to be five million, while WGY at Schenectady and WBZ at Springfield, Massachusetts, relayed every play of the contest.

"In place of the scoreboards and megaphones of the past, amplifiers connected to radio instruments gave all the details and sidelights to thousands of enthusiasts unable to get into the Polo Grounds. Not only could the voice of the official radio observer be heard, but the voice of the umpire on the field announcing the batteries for the day mingled with the voice of a boy selling ice cream cones.

"The clamor of the 40,000 fans inside the Polo Grounds made radio listeners feel as if they were in the grandstand. The cheers which greeted Babe Ruth when he stepped to the plate could be heard throughout the land. And as he struck at the ball, the shouts that followed indicated whether the Babe had fanned or got a hit even before the radio announcer could tell what had happened."

Even Lord Louis Mountbatten was impressed with all that, and he duly abandoned his polo pursuits the next day and was seated in a box behind first base when the teams lunged at each other in Game Two. In the first inning, Heinie Groh and Frank Frisch singled for McGraw and Irish Meusel hit one into the left-field bleachers. But the Yankees got one run back in the bottom of the first, then another in the fourth, and then Ruth and Bob Meusel doubled to tie the score in the eighth.

While all this was going on, the press was keeping a box score on Lord Louis Mountbatten, noting that he ate six ice cream cones and two bags of peanuts, drank four bottles of soda pop, and rooted for Babe Ruth until he was hoarse. Lady Mount-batten, resplendent in brown, watched through a tortoiseshell lorgnette. When the mighty Ruth appeared alongside the Yan-kee dugout, she leaned over and shouted: "Atta boy, Babe."

When the umpire called a strike on Wally Pipp, Her Ladyship was heard to grumble, "Rotten." His Lordship said it was the greatest game he had ever seen.

It was the greatest game a lot of people had ever seen, and when it was unexpectedly ended with the score still tied at 3–3 in the tenth inning, it turned into the greatest mob scene a lot of people had ever seen.

It was 4:40 in the afternoon, and the sun was still shining as the Yankees went down in order in the bottom of the tenth, when the home-plate umpire George Hildebrand wheeled around, swept his face mask through a wide circle with his hand, and announced: "Game called on account of darkness."

Judge Landis, erect, dignified, crusty, had just been intro-duced to Mountbatten and his bride in the box of Colonel Rup-pert, the owner of the Yankees. For a moment, the crowd didn't quite grasp what was happening. But then the players began running from the field, and suddenly thousands stood and raged and poured from the stands, many of them heading straight for Landis. The old judge stood upright in his box, his white hair shaking like a mane, buried under boos, catcalls, and shouts of "crook" and "robber."

A police escort finally was marshaled to escort Landis and his wife through the howling mob. Lord Mountbatten, startled but also enraptured by the violent ending of "the greatest game ever," turned to the beleaguered commissioner and observed, in splendid understatement: "My goodness, Judge, but they are giving you the bird."

"I may not be the smartest person in the United States," the judge said later, "but at least I can tell day from night." Whereupon, to get the mob off his back, he announced that all the money from the game would be donated to a charity for disabled soldiers.

The Series was resumed the next day, and everybody forgot about Landis — except the club owners, who grumbled about his beau geste with *their* money, and except for dozens of organized charities who promptly deluged him with requests for a piece of the $120,554 giveaway.

As things turned out, that tie game was as close as the Yankees were to come to staging a palace revolt in 1922 on Mc-Graw's home grounds. The Giants swept the next three games, swept the Series, and for the second year in a row McGraw defended his empire against the upstart Yankees and their champion.

They did come face to face, though, and McGraw prevailed that time, too.

It happened after the second game, in the Giants' locker room. Ruth had been nicked by a pitched ball, and he retaliated by barreling into the stumpy Heinie Groh, and then spent the rest of the afternoon trading insults with the Giants' bench. Spoiling for a fight, he finally stormed into the Giants' clubhouse after the game with his burly teammate, Bob Meusel.

Just as the players on both sides were taking off coats and rolling up sleeves, John McGraw came into the clubhouse with his old Baltimore Oriole crony and coach, Hughey Jennings, and ordered Ruth and Meusel to "get out and stay out." And they did.

When the Giants completed their sweep, McGraw stood at the pinnacle. *The New York Times* put it this way:

"Every fan within hailing distance wanted a chance to slap the Little Napoleon on the back, to shake his hand or at least to yell his admiration at close quarters. McGraw, for the time being, was the hero of heroes. Men climbed on each other's shoulders trying to get near enough to tell him what a wonderful manager he was. They leaped and danced and yelled themselves blue in the face.

"His record stands alone and unchallenged. He is the outstanding figure among all the managers in the history of the game."

But the shadow and the specter of Babe Ruth not only hung over McGraw's empire but relentlessly threatened to darken its luster, especially after the Yankees at last opened their new stadium on April 18, 1923, just six months after the Giants had beaten them for the second straight time in the World Series. For two seasons, the Giants had withstood the challenge to their ranking as the best baseball team in the business. But now they found Babe Ruth regally installed in the newest and biggest ballpark in the country, Yankee Stadium, built to his personal specifications as a left-handed hitter with artillery power. It sat gleaming across the river from the Polo Grounds, setting the stage for the changing of the guard.

Even before the Yankees took the field for the first time there, the new ball yard captured the public imagination by its size and scope, one of the wonders of the skyline. Also, one of the wonders of concrete construction. Not exactly the Pyramids, of course, but close.

Before anybody could do anything else, they had to truck in 45,000 cubic yards of earth just to rough-grade the property.

Then 950,000 board feet of Pacific Coast fir had to be shipped in via the Panama Canal to erect the bleachers. For the stadium proper, 3 million board feet of temporary form work was required, as were 20,000 cubic yards of concrete and 800 tons of reinforcing steel; 2,200 tons of structural steel then had to be fabricated and erected. The playing field needed more than 13,000 cubic yards of topsoil, and finally was covered with 116,000 square feet of sod.

The seats for the grandstand were manufactured at the site and required 135,000 individual steel castings and 400,000 pieces of maple lumber, which was secured to the castings with more than a million brass screws. The seats were expansion-bolted to the decks and necessitated the drilling of 90,000 holes in the concrete.

The White Construction Company, which did all this, got a little carried away when it recorded the deed in the corporate archives in proud language that might have portrayed the epics of the Suez Canal or the Great Wall of China.

"This is the story — briefly told — about the construction of the largest baseball stadium in America," it reported, grandly but not too briefly.

The official language may have been soaring, but nothing was soaring more than the mood of the city over its landmark. On the afternoon when the gates opened and the multitudes swarmed inside, the Seventh Regiment Band paraded back and forth across the field, Governor Alfred E. Smith made his way cheerfully to Judge Landis's box, the great and the small crammed the three tiers of seats, and, at three o'clock sharp, the Yankees appeared in their white home uniforms and the Boston Red Sox in their gray, with red sweaters, red caps, and red-striped stockings.

The band headed across the infield to the Yankee dugout on the third-base side, where John Philip Sousa took baton in hand and stepped to the head of the company. With Sousa and the band leading the way, the teams and the political lions marched to the center-field flagpole, where Sousa's boys rendered the national anthem while the American flag was hoisted to the top of the mast.

"The big crowd," reported *The Times*, "let loose a roar that floated across the Harlem and far beyond."

To lend the finishing touch, Babe Ruth announced that he would give a year of his roistering life to hit the first home run in the park. And in the third inning, he did.

The Yankees went on to win 98 games that summer, and buried the Detroit Tigers by 16 games in the American League standings. The Giants, meanwhile, were winning 95 games and led the Cincinnati Reds by four and a half games when the season ended. And so, on October 10, there they were again for the third year in a row, two teams from New York grappling for the world championship. But this time they were grappling on the Yankees' turf in "the house that Ruth built."

The Times, drawing the lines of battle, got to the heart of the matter: "Ruth, win or lose, good or bad, is sure to attract more attention than any individual on either team. He was brimming over with the joy of living and playing the game. In this Series, as in the two others, Ruth will be the figure in the foreground. The figure in the background will be that of John J. McGraw."

And, in theatrical cadences on page one: "Will McGraw stop the greatest hitter in baseball? Will Ruth redeem his failure of 1922 and step forward as the outstanding star of the Yankees?"

They lined up by the thousands to pay $1.10 for a bleacher seat, $3.30 for the upper stand, $5.50 for the lower stand, and $6.60 for the boxes. By game time, a record crowd of 55,307 sat and roared as the third battle in the war unfolded.

For the third straight year, the Yankees struck first; and for the third straight year, Ruth did the early striking for them. He scored the first run in the Yankees' first time at bat behind a double by Bob Meusel, two more Yankees scored in the second inning, and suddenly pressure was being applied to the Giants' winning streak in the rivalry. They had won the last three games of the first city Series in 1921, they won all four in 1922, and they arrived with a seven-game streak in 1923.

But the Giants staged another of their revivals when they rallied with four runs in the third inning, lost the lead in the home half of the seventh when the Yankees came back with one run for a 4–4 tie, and then broke it in the top of the ninth in the least plausible way of all: Casey Stengel, who was thirty-three years old and slow, lined a clean "single" over the shortstop's head and started galloping around the bases as the ball skidded through a defense overshifted toward right field. The ball kept rolling to the deepest reaches of left-center field in the Yankees' immense new stadium, Whitey Witt and Bob Meusel kept chasing it, and old Casey kept puffing around second, then around third.

"It was Casey at the Bat all over again," reported *The Times* in a page one account of what it called "the greatest game of baseball ever played between championship teams."

"This time, though, the great Casey did not strike out. With one leg injured and the other not as young and spry as it used to be, Casey ran the race of his life. Out at the fences, Witt was gathering the ball in. He turned and flung it to Meusel, and Meusel turned and threw it to the plate.

"By now Stengel was rounding third, badly winded, but still going strong. It was a race between man and ball, but the man won, for Casey slid into the plate and up on one knee in a single motion. Then he waved a hand in a comical gesture that seemed to say, 'Well, there you are.' And the game was as good as over."

Half an inning later, in the bottom of the ninth, it was indeed over: 5–4, Giants. And now they had eight straight victories (and one tie) over their upstart neighbors in their three-year battle for the purse and the passion of Broadway.

But the die was cast, especially for any team that depended on Casey Stengel's bat to overpower Babe Ruth's bat. Nor could McGraw, flashing the signs endlessly from his dugout, stymie the strength of Ruth indefinitely. The press saluted the manager's "genius," but it was Ruth who rated the headlines just for showing up. Prominent boxes were printed every day to relate "What Babe Ruth Did at Bat in the First World Series Game." And so on, for all six games.

This was magic; this was mystique. This was the legacy that Ruth was creating with his big bat, big swing, big home runs. Even Casey Stengel, half a century later, long after he had shared the legacy as manager of the Yankees in the days of DiMaggio — even Stengel caught the essence of it when he was inducted into the baseball Hall of Fame and peered back through the imagery of his own career and said: "I chased the balls that Babe Ruth hit."

The balls that Babe Ruth hit and the cheers "that could be heard throughout the land" made an even greater impact on the public mind and mood because they were carried far beyond the ballparks by the radio waves that were revolutionizing the science of transmitting sound. They also were revolutionizing the *art* of transmitting sound, particularly after Grantland Rice was succeeded at the microphone by a young baritone named Graham McNamee.

He was born in Washington, D.C., on July 10, 1889, and he was making his way as a concert singer in the spring of 1923 after a measured debut at Aeolian Hall. The *New York Sun* said that "he sang with a justness, a care and style." Within two years, he was singing 150 times in one recital season and drawing notices like this one in *The Times:*

"Anyone who sings the air 'O Ruddier Than the Cherry' from Handel's 'Acis and Galatea' with such admirably flexible command over the 'divisions,' with such finished phrasing and such excellent enunciation as McNamee showed, is doing a difficult thing very well indeed."

In that spring of 1923, McNamee was growing a bit hungry to try that excellent enunciation on something more rewarding than "O Ruddier Than the Cherry." And he got his chance one day when he was serving on a jury in federal court in lower Manhattan, strolled up the street, and spotted a sign on the building at 195 Broadway that read: "Radio Station WEAF." He rode the elevator to the little two-room studio on the fourth floor and stepped into a new life.

Five months later, he was sitting behind the huge oval microphone in an open box at Yankee Stadium. He said later: "When Ruth batted, I was almost too engrossed to speak."

Not quite. From WEAF in New York to WJAR in Providence, Rhode Island, to WGY in Schenectady, and to other stations in other cities along the eastern seaboard, the excited but proper voice of Graham McNamee dramatized the Series for a rapidly expanding audience. He described Ruth turning the Series around when he hit two home runs in the second game and just missed hitting a third, and he described them with insight and emotion as the turning of the tide in the struggle between Ruth and McGraw. And his ad-lib oratory was matched by the classic sportswriters of the day, stars like Heywood Broun, who wrote in the *Sun:*

"The Babe flashed across the sky fiery portents which should have been sufficient to strike terror into the hearts of all infidels. But John McGraw clung to his heresy with a courage worthy of a better cause.

"In the fourth inning, after lunging at a fastball with almost comic ferocity and ineptitude, the *Bambino* hit the next pitch over the stands in right. In the fifth, Ruth was up again and by this time Jack Bentley was pitching. Snyder the catcher sneaked a look at the little logician in the dugout. McGraw blinked twice, pulled up his trousers, and thrust the forefinger of his right hand into his left eye. Snyder knew that he meant: 'Try the Big Bozo on a slow curve around the knees, and don't forget to throw to first if you happen to drop the third strike.' Ruth promptly poled the slow curve around the knees into the right-field seats.

"For the first time since coming to New York, Babe achieved his full brilliance in a World Series game. Before this he has varied between pretty good and simply awful, and yesterday he was magnificent."

Then Broun reached for the clincher, and wrote: "The Ruth is mighty and shall prevail."

He was mighty, all right. In successive innings, he had blasted holes in McGraw's tactical genius and had shaken McGraw's grip on the game itself. He was so mighty that his first shot even cleared the Polo Grounds roof and dropped into the parking lot on Manhattan Field outside, where a policeman stooped over, picked it up, and examined it as though he was examining some incredible fragment from space.

Even when Ruth made an out, McGraw winced. In his final turn at bat, in the ninth inning, there were two down and a Yankee runner on second base. McGraw had already put his foot in his mouth when he said before the game: "Why shouldn't we pitch to Ruth? I've said it before, and I'll say it again, we pitch to better hitters than Ruth in the National League."

So now in the ninth inning, Heywood Broun wrote, McGraw stood on the dugout step with "gritted teeth," signaled his catcher, "spelling out with the first three fingers of his right hand, 'The Old Guard dies but never surrenders,' which the catcher interpreted to mean: 'Pitch to the big bum if he hammers every ball in the park into the North River."

Ruth forthwith hammered a tremendous drive that almost became his third home run of the day. But it was run down and caught by Bill Cunningham just as it was about to carry past the center-field fence in front of the bleachers. *The Times*, endowing the performance with perspective, said the next morning: "Ruth showed that the Giant supremacy could be broken down. Leading the way himself, he showed that the Giants were not invincible, that their pitchers could be hit and that John J. McGraw's strategy, while superb, was not invincible."

The Series lasted six games, and the teams gave them even more of a theatrical tone by switching from the Polo Grounds to Yankee Stadium and back after each game. The Series was even after two games and after four games, but then the Yankees struck for an 8-1 victory in the fifth game and needed to win one more to win the championship. It was a memorable battle that began when Ruth whaled another home run in the first inning, his third of the Series. The Giants, though, charged back with single runs in the first, fourth, fifth, and sixth innings, and they were leading 4–1 with the Yankees batting in the eighth against Art Nehf, who had muzzled them three days earlier 1–0. But Nehf was tagged for two singles, then walked two pinch hitters on eight pitches and was gone while the crowd roared, Joe Dugan stepped to the plate, Babe Ruth moved into the on-deck circle, and Bob Meusel stood behind him, bat in hand.

"Away went Nehf to the showers," McNamee recalled later, his baseball idiom bristling. "Manager McGraw called in Rosy Ryan, a right-hander. But before he properly got under way, another pass was issued and another run scored.

"Then came the thrill of all time, all World Series and all sports. Babe Ruth stepped up to bat. One hit would mean victory for the Yanks, and for them the Series. It was another Casey at the Bat, and the stands rocked with terrific excitement.

"John McGraw took the biggest chance of his historic life. He ordered Ryan to pitch to Ruth. The crowd faded into a blurred background. Cheering became silence. Ruth lashed out at the first ball. Ruth hurled his bat and weight against the second. Ruth spun at the third. Ruth shuffled back to the dugout, head hung low. A picture of dejection."

"Ruth was so anxious to hit," McGraw said later, "that I knew he didn't have a chance. So, I ordered Ryan to throw him three pitches right in the dirt."

But fate played a cruel trick on the manager of the Giants just when he appeared to have trumped the ace played by Miller Huggins, the manager of the Yankees. In a spasm of new strategy, Huggins sent in *two* pinch-runners for the two pinch-hitters who had walked. Ruth was gone, but three Yankees were still on base waiting for the chance to score two runs and tie the game. They got three, and won the game.

Meusel set things in motion by hitting a high bouncing ball

over the head of Ryan, who had replaced the best fielding pitcher in the National League. The ball skipped over second base for a single, two runs crossed (yes, the pinch-runners), and the Giants' lead was gone. And when Cunningham fielded the ball in center field and unloosed a mighty throw past third base, trying to cut down the winning run, Joe Dugan sprinted the ninety feet home with the fifth Yankee run of the inning.

"But the biggest thrill," said McNamee, his emotions putting the ultimate test on his vocabulary, "the biggest thrill had passed when the great Babe fanned. Time's phantom flits into oblivion in moments like this. I was a dripping rag draped over the microphone when the 1923 diamond laurel finally graced the Yankee brow."

In the locker room, the Yankees exploded into shrieks and the champagne flowed until Babe Ruth bowled his way through the crowd to the center of the room and yelled for quiet. He pulled out a jeweler's box, and said:

"Boys, we've won the world championship, and we owe a lot of that accomplishment to the guiding hand of Mr. Huggins. We want to present you with this ring in token of the esteem we hold you in."

Huggins, who had been insulted and even persecuted by Ruth and his clubhouse cronies, was swept onto the shoulders of his troops, clutching his new diamond bauble as they tossed him around and shook the room with cheering.

The Yankees had won their first championship. They had arrived.

They hit .293 as a team in the Series, ninety points more than the year before. Ruth hit .368 with three home runs, eight walks, and eight runs. It was the first million-dollar Series, the first gate of 300,000, the first "network" broadcast of a Series, the first time a player would pocket as much as $6,143 for winning or $4,112 for losing.

Mostly, it was the first in a relentless run of pennants, championships, and epics. In 1925, they were joined by a serious young first baseman named Lou Gehrig, who had the physique of a fortress and the temperament of a saint. He got into the lineup on June 1 and stayed in it for 2,130 games without missing for the next thirteen years. In 1926, they won the pennant but lost the Series to the St. Louis Cardinals. In 1927, Ruth hit sixty home runs and they swept the Pittsburgh Pirates in the Series. In 1928, they swept the Cardinals in the Series. In 1932, with Joe McCarthy the manager, they swept the Chicago Cubs in the Series.

They ran their Series streak to three sweeps and twelve straight games won. It was also the tenth and last World Series that Babe Ruth played, and his seventh with a winning club. Yes, he hit two home runs, and he *may* have pointed toward the center-field flagpole in Wrigley Field, Chicago, before hammering one of them past the pole to prove his point. The point was that the Cubs were a bunch of cheapskates who had voted less than a full series share for their shortstop, Mark Koenig, a one-time member of the Yankees.

The larger point probably was that the Yankees were creating legends along with the pennants. They had won the Battle of Broadway in the twenties, and they were widening their horizons now in the thirties.

But after winning 107 games in 1932 and sweeping yet another World Series, they stopped winning for the next three years. Worse, the empire builder, the mighty Ruth, was gone after the 1934 season — and, with him, the memories of the time when "the cheers could be heard throughout the land."

So, it was almost on cue that Joe DiMaggio, the twenty-one-year-old rookie from San Francisco, appeared in their spring training camp on Tampa Bay on the morning of March 2, 1936, and Dan Daniel wrote, on whatever impulse: "Here is the replacement for Babe Ruth."

4

INSIDE THE
YANKEE YARD

IN STREET CLOTHES," Stanley Woodward observed, recording the grand arrival for the *New York Herald Tribune,* "he looks tall and slim, probably because his face is inordinately thin. His profile comes to a point at the end of his nose."

"He was a little timid," noticed Joe McCarthy, the manager of the Yankees. "He didn't bother anyone, and they didn't bother him. It would have been dangerous, and an injustice to the boy, to attempt to change him in any particular."

Colonel Jacob Ruppert, who had bought the Yankees in 1915 with his magnificently named partner, Colonel Tillinghast l'Hommedieu Huston, for $460,000 in cash, monitored the rookie's early moments with the team and said: "He seems to be very hard to get acquainted with."

Red Ruffing, the blocky and somewhat grizzled star pitcher, pierced the strain engulfing the arrival and said: "So you're the great DiMaggio."

The great DiMaggio nodded.

He was soon surrounded by fifteen newspaper writers, all of whom wanted to know how he liked New York, and he replied:

"I've never been in New York." When they pressed the point, he said: "I've never been east of the Rocky Mountains." When they demanded to know if he could hit big-league pitching, he said: "I don't know that yet."

Nobody was certain that his knee had healed, although he reported that Bill Essick had taken him "to a doctor in Los Angeles last winter, and the knee is cured."

Some people weren't even certain how to spell his name. One headline called him "Joe Demaggio, Coast Youngster." Another gave it a little space but still got it wrong: "Joe De Maggio, San Francisco." Another came right out and said: "It should be Di Maggio."

Well, they got that wrong, too. Some newspapers checked back with the old neighborhood in San Francisco, and learned that he had signed his contract with the Seals as "De Maggio." But his brother Tom, counselor and chaperone, signed *his* name as a witness to the signing as "Di Maggio." When Charlie Graham of the Seals asked how he wanted it, Joe said: "Spell it any old way."

For Tom DiMaggio, the main issue wasn't how you spelled your name exactly; it was more a matter of how you filled in the money line. And when Joe finally got to the Yankees and signed his first contract in the big leagues, he admonished Joe to drive a hard bargain, as he did in San Francisco under the same sort of prodding, and the bargaining brothers settled on the Olympian sum of $8,500. The contract was autographed "Di Maggio," with the space, but spelling still wasn't the issue.

Neither was the repaired knee or life in Manhattan or springtime in St. Petersburg. The only issue when he arrived in camp was whether bravura performances in the Pacific Coast League would play as magnificently in the American League, and whether he would play left field or right field or dislodge the talented Ben Chapman from center field, and whether he could hit to all fields or merely pull everything to left. And most of all, whether he was going to survive, to say nothing of succeed, as the bright new star who would light the way for the Yankees as they marshaled their resources to get back on top. You know, whether he was unmistakably "the replacement for Babe Ruth."

He certainly didn't arrive with Ruth's sparkle or with Ruth's gargantuan style. He was spare and silent, almost ascetic, maybe monastic, private and even remote.

As Jimmy Cannon phrased it later in one of his portraits in words: "He is more a spectator than a participant in any group. He is concealed and withdrawn."

He was concealed and withdrawn, all right. But he was by no means unknown and undiscovered. He didn't arrive in camp carrying any scrapbooks, probably because he didn't need them. He appeared on the scene with Lazzeri and Crosetti, but by any translation of the idiom, his fame had preceded him.

"Offhand," said Tommy Laird, the sports editor of the *San Francisco News,* heading the line of the West Coast bearers of testimony, "I would say there is only one finer ball player alive, and his name is Charley Gehringer."

"DiMaggio," wrote Gene Coughlin of the *Los Angeles Post-Record,* "is likely to kill an opposing infielder at any time."

"DiMaggio," sang Bob Cronin of the *Los Angeles Illustrated Daily News,* "has the strongest and most accurate arm since Long Bob Meusel."

"You've seldom seen a more accomplished flychaser," chorused Cliff Morrison of the *Seattle Star.*

"DiMaggio," reported Billy Tripp of the *Portland News-Telegram,* "plays ball with grim intensity."

"DiMaggio," said Harry Grayson, the syndicated columnist, "is so serious that they call him Dead Pan Joe in the Coast League. He is pictured as a ballplayer without nerves. He likes to play ball."

And in case that sounded too tame, he then cast DiMaggio in the company of other graduates of baseball at its best in California: "The Pacific Coast League has turned out some pretty good ones — Roger Peckinpaugh, Dave Bancroft, the Waners, Curt

Davis, Franklin Demaree, Stanley Hack, Bob Meusel, Earl Averill, Gus Suhr, Tony Lazzeri, Chic Gandil, Swede Risberg, to mention a few."

If there seemed something provincial in all this acclamation, the East Coast baseball writers quickly became enthralled, too. Dan Daniel, who took second place to no man in *les affaires* of the New York Yankees, unfurled some literary might when he reported from the training camp: "Writing about the 1936 Yankees is tantamount to being a Boswell for Joe DiMaggio."

And James M. Kahn, giving it the spin of history in *The New York Times,* invoked the image of the master, Babe Ruth, when he reported:

"The baseball fates, being as prankish as any others, may be preparing one of those bitter jokes for Lou Gehrig. A fine ballplayer in his own right, he was overshadowed through the more spectacular years of his career by the dominant figure of Babe Ruth. Now that the Babe has gone, leaving an opportunity for Lou to step out boldly on his own, a new figure, rookie Joe DiMaggio, is swinging up over the baseball horizon and threatening to obscure him again.

"With the Babe's passing last year, Lou ascended to the undisputed position of head man of the Yanks, but his elevation turned out to be an ironic anticlimax. He battled with jinxes and a hitting slump all last season and wound up with one of the most disappointing records of his career. This year, when he is in top trim, meeting the ball solidly, and appears to be off to a flying start, he finds a juvenile still to embark on his first major league pennant pursuit stealing most of the pre-season thunder."

A *juvenile,* indeed; and still to embark, indeed. Yet there was something about the way he made his stage entrance and took his cues, something about his silent presence, keeping his head when all about him were losing theirs (over him), something suggesting history still to be played out. He was six feet one inch tall and he weighed 187 pounds that spring, and he took his cuts in the batting cage with a strangely wide stance, simply lifting the front foot to shift his weight and taking a roundhouse swing that seemed to collar the ball.

In his first session of batting practice in the Yankee cage, surrounded by World Series veterans in Yankee uniforms and by swarms of writers covering the rookie's debut with full fury, he collared three pitches and hammered them past the fence in left field. No big deal; in batting practice, plenty of guys hit plenty of baseballs beyond plenty of fences. But to the headline writers back in New York, it was time to call for the big type, also the big stretch, as in this head that trumpeted the trivial: "Rookie Outfielder Blasts Three Homers in Debut."

Well, "homers" are baseballs that carry over fences, but not when the batting-practice pitcher is coming down the middle of the plate with tee-time speed. No matter: The "rookie" was making a clamorous "debut," and he was hitting "blasts" in St. Petersburg that would not exactly be "homers" in the Bronx. But who could quibble over terminology at a time like this?

One of the people impressed by the new player was the clubhouse attendant, Pete Sheehy, who served as valet, majordomo, and housekeeper for Yankee teams for more than half a century after that and who later was memorialized when the home locker room in Yankee Stadium was designated "the Pete Sheehy Clubhouse." He was short and wispy, firm with strangers but sweet with his locker-room family, and he had a spry sense of humor and a sure sense of history. And he extended both senses to DiMaggio.

His sense of humor told Sheehy that he could pierce Joe's shell, and probably *should*. Who else was going to horse around with the solemnity of DiMaggio? Besides, until Billy Martin came along fifteen years later, not many players or coaches or people in public life even tried to deflect the DiMaggio mood. He was austere, he was withdrawn, he was important. So he also was protected inside the Yankee circle. Pete Sheehy was one of the few who dared to mess with the deadpan of "Dead Pan Joe."

His sense of history proved just as sharp. When a new player joins a team in the big leagues, the clubhouse man customarily assigns him a uniform number that is no longer encumbered or otherwise claimed, preempted, or enshrined. When DiMaggio joined the Yankees that spring, Sheehy needed no prompting to recognize the elements of history that might be coming together. This was no ordinary busher; this was an extraordinary busher. And it seemed even sacrilegious to regard him as a minor-leaguer on trial. This one was anointed.

Sheehy accordingly fetched a highly respectable uniform number out of his storeroom of uniforms and other equipment: number 18, worn by Johnny Allen, the tempestuous pitcher, before he was traded to the Cleveland Indians.

But Sheehy was working on a grander design than that. He later switched DiMaggio to the uniform number that bestowed history on him, and did it in a way that appeared almost predestined. Babe Ruth had worn number 3 in the years when he was launching the empire; Lou Gehrig carried number 4 in the years when he was extending the empire. Joe DiMaggio inherited the only number that continued the line of succession: 5.

In later decades, Pete Sheehy stretched his sense of proportion even farther. The mighty Mickey Mantle, who arrived as DiMaggio was leaving in 1951, became renowned as number 7. Yogi Berra wore number 8 on *his* trip to the Hall of Fame. Roger Maris, hitting even more home runs in one season than Babe Ruth when he popped 61 of them in 1961, did it while wearing number 9.

"Around this club," Sheehy told me years after he had endowed DiMaggio with the only number that made historical justice, "you always had the feeling that great things would happen. It started with Ruth and kept going on. You didn't have to watch Joe DiMaggio play very long before you knew he was special. He was going to follow Ruth and Gehrig, and carry on their tradition. Even when he was a kid, he cut the figure of greatness."

Dan Daniel, one of the earliest converts, made no effort to soften the rapture when he wrote, not long after DiMaggio arrived in training: "Not only is DiMaggio furnishing most of the power on the New York club, but he has developed into a real attraction. Fans are coming out to see him. Each performance of the new star at the plate is the signal for a salvo of applause."

Then, rising to the occasion with language that soared, he added: "Never before in the history of the Yankees has a recruit fresh from the minors created the furore which DiMaggio has stirred up, or intrigued the fans so thoroughly with the magic of his bat and his possibilities in the American League."

John Kieran, the learned nature-lover and classical scholar of *The New York Times,* entered the rookie into his personal pantheon without the test of time.

"In lively fashion," he intoned, "DiMaggio is going about living up to all the advance notices about him from the California area. He is fast in the field, turns loose a good throwing arm and lines hits to all corners of the Florida ball parks."

One of the unanswered questions, however, was whether he could actually line hits to all corners anyplace else. But Dan Daniel, the disciple, attacked that question in the first three weeks.

"DiMaggio is very industrious," he wrote, "in his determination to break down the impression that he is a dead left-field hitter. In batting practice, he did not drive a ball to the right of second base. But in the early camp games, Giuseppe sent three hits into left, one into right and three into center.

"The fame of 'DiMag' is traveling abroad, and experts are coming in from alien camps to see the Italian in action, and write about his style and their reactions. He has become more quiet, more thoughtful. Perhaps he is beginning to feel the mental weight of striking achievement in the Big Show and the need for holding to a high standard."

Well, if *Giuseppe* the *Italian* felt the weight of history or of Daniel's prose, he didn't show it. In the Yankees' first intrasquad game in St. Petersburg on March 11, Daniel was the first to report:

"Joe DiMaggio, the expensive young outfielder who is expected to furnish the pennant punch for the New York Yankees this season, was the center of attention today as the Regulars beat the Yannigans, 5–1, in the first of the intra-club games.

"DiMaggio, who batted third, Babe Ruth's old position, got two hits and fielded his position in center field faultlessly."

Daniel also reported that Lou Gehrig had gone 0 for 5 in his debut, George Selkirk hit the only home run, and Roy Johnson had missed the game because his airplane from California "was forced down by a heavy fog in a remote region." Then, having covered the nuts and bolts, he turned his attention back to the man of the hour.

"DiMaggio," he wrote, "swings a bat which weighs forty ounces and is thirty-eight inches long. It may develop that Joe will have to cut down both on the size and weight of the bludgeon. He may not be able to bring the bat around fast enough against the type of fastball pitching he will see from Lefty Grove, Schoolboy Rowe, Mel Harder, Tommy Bridges and a few other lads in the American League.

"When Babe Ruth hit sixty home runs, he swung bats weighing more than fifty ounces. But since then, thirty-four ounces is regarded as plenty of wood for any hitter.

"DiMaggio is a peculiar batsman. He is not a long swinger, but a wrist swinger with a terrific pull on the ball. He will have to learn to punch that ball into right field, or he will run into a peck of trouble. The stadium in the Bronx is tough enough on a right-handed hitter even if he can smack an occasional ball into right. Neither Jimmie Foxx nor Al Simmons has a career average of .300 at the Yankee park.

"In stance, one foot from the plate, with feet twelve inches apart, DiMaggio reminds you of Joe Jackson. But in the application of power at the very last fraction of a second, Joe is more reminiscent of Tris Speaker. Earl Combs also had something of that knack. How DiMaggio gets so much power on the ball when it is right on top of him is amazing.

"In build, Joe is another Bob Meusel. The Italian lad has big strong arms, with tremendous wrists. His back muscles ripple in their sheaths.

"In temperament, DiMaggio is even and pleasant. He is not a mixer, for he sits too much by himself, thinking and looking out into the street. He is no reader of books."

Apart from the fact that it was doubtful "the Italian lad" really had back muscles that "ripple in their sheaths," and apart from the fact that not reading books would hardly make him distinctive in spring training or anyplace else that ballplayers lived, apart from the literary skyrockets, Dan Daniel certainly thrust the rookie under his microscope, didn't he? And there was more:

"DiMaggio looks like a youngster who rarely gets excited. In that respect, he closely resembles two other Italians on the Yankees, Tony Lazzeri and Frank Crosetti. That so-called hot Italian temper doesn't go with the three Romans of the Ruppert legion.

"Certainly, DiMaggio is no 'holler guy.' His feats may make him colorful, but his makeup promises no fanfare. The Yankees are sorely in need of what the ballplayers call a 'holler guy' — a man like Leo Durocher. Johnny Allen did considerable hollering, but he is gone. And not one of the newcomers — Roy Johnson and the additional pitching talent included — is known as a jockey of even lesser degree.

"DiMaggio came here with a reputation as a bashful boy. At first, he fostered that impression. But he can talk. In fact, he insists he knows he can make the grade."

There may have been more sweeping and total reports on the ethnic, personal, and workplace sides of a baseball player, but none comes to mind. Dan Daniel, though, caught in a frenzy of discovery, plunged forward from his "bashful boy" to the nitty-gritty of the playing field, and he lost no fervor getting there.

"The position DiMaggio should play," he announced, "is right field. He wants to play there, and that should be enough. But George Selkirk and Johnson also are right fielders. Placing Joe in the right spot is going to be no soft touch for McCarthy, and he admits it.

"While DiMaggio wonders about his destiny, McCarthy is pretty much on the spot with the lad, as he is with many other factors in the Yankee situation. DiMaggio has come here labeled 'a genuine wonder.' And it's up to McCarthy to give the fans what the label reads."

There is no other evidence that DiMaggio was wondering about his "destiny," and there is extensive evidence that he and most other people reasoned that he would settle one day soon into the only position and the only role great enough for his talent: center field. Joe McCarthy later said that he had started his prodigy in left field for a while, then moved him to right field for a while, but he knew, and DiMaggio knew, that he was only making brief stops on the road to center.

"I wanted to make sure he was comfortable before I put him in center field," McCarthy said. "He would never have become the great outfielder he was if I hadn't moved him there. He needed that room to roam in Yankee Stadium. Only the great ones can play out there. It was the toughest center field in baseball.

"He did what you're supposed to do. The idea is to catch the ball, not make catches that look exciting.

"He wasn't the fastest man alive. He just knew how to run bases better than anybody. He could have stolen 50 or 60 bases a year if I had let him."

There apparently wasn't much wrong with McCarthy's judgment or DiMaggio's destiny: In the first five games of the Yankees' exhibition season, the rookie went to bat twenty times, got twelve hits, didn't walk, didn't strike out, and was hitting .600 when he became an instant casualty. It happened in a game against the Boston Bees (née Braves), and it added one more line to a medical record that already had accompanied him east and that was fated to grow longer as his career grew longer.

He was on first base with his second hit in two innings when George Selkirk bounced a ground ball to the shortstop, who tossed it to second base for the force-out on DiMaggio. But as he came across the bag, the second baseman, Joe Coscarart, stepped on DiMaggio's foot as he wheeled toward first base trying for the double play.

"As I slid into the bag," Joe remembered, "Coscarart stepped on my left foot, and I figured I had been spiked. I took off my shoe, but when I found there was no cut, I played through the game. At night, though, the fun began. The foot swelled, and I remained up bathing it in Epsom salts."

The next morning, he put on his uniform and limped outside, but the pain was too strong. So he checked in with the Yankees' trainer, Doc Painter, who made a somewhat fateful decision.

He decided to treat the foot with short-wave diathermic heat, and kept it there for about twenty minutes. The length of time wasn't unusual, but DiMaggio's sensitivity was: When the heat was turned off, he had two immense blisters on the foot, and now he had a serious problem.

The attending physician, Dr. John Strickland, ordered him to stay in bed for forty-eight hours and suggested that he might not play again for ten days. By then, the Yankees would be headed north, playing the final exhibition games on the road to New York. The main medical concern was blood poisoning. And to avoid it, the Yankees were faced with the prospect of riding the rails through the eastern heartland of the country without the new player who had caused clamor throughout Florida.

So he opened his first season on the sidelines while the Yankees opened their season in Washington on April 14 without DiMaggio and without runs. They lost the opener to the Senators, 1–0. And, in fact, he stayed on the sidelines for the rest of the month of April, missing the chance to make a storybook arrival in New York and to show his new home fans what all the commotion had been about during the first weeks in St. Petersburg. No parades, no red carpets or keys to the city, no torchlight march down Broadway. He simply checked into the New Yorker Hotel and isolated himself from the multitudes below.

Except for the time when he was married to Dorothy Arnold and they set up house in an apartment on the West Side of Manhattan, he lived almost as a loner in hotels in midtown. He spent winters back home in San Francisco, anyway, and he spent two months in Florida in spring training and half the summer on the road — so, whether he was the toast of the town or not, he was still more of the itinerant in New York. As Eddie Lopat said later: "He's one of the loneliest guys I ever knew. And he leads the league in room service."

He showed no concerns over his job during that lost April, not even when the resident center fielder on the Yankees, Ben Chapman, finally ended his long salary holdout and joined the club on April 4. There was no doubt Chapman could play with the best of them. There also was no doubt he had worn out his welcome, and would soon be traded, which he was. But even after his place was taken by Jake Powell, a contentious redneck from the Washington Senators, it was clear that Joe was still ticketed for center field once he had served a kind of apprenticeship in left field.

Three days before the season opened, he got a new uniform number: no longer number 18, now number 9, but soon and eternally destined to become number 5. But he was still not in the lineup, by any number, and Ed Barrow, the general manager of the Yankees, sizzled "because a tremendous public interest had been built up in him, and I wanted to cash in on it at the gate."

He was still languishing at the New Yorker Hotel on the eve of the opening game when Frank Graham, one of the card-carrying New York writers, dropped by to see him and asked if he had seen anything of the city yet.

"I went out to my cousin's in the Bronx," he replied, misjudging the question. "I had a steak this big. It was too big for me."

Graham rephrased the question along these lines: Have you seen Yankee Stadium yet?

"Just from the outside," Joe said. "It looks like a big oval. I stood outside the left-field fence and looked up at those three decks of the stand. It looked pretty big."

This time, he meant the stadium, not the steak. Graham, still probing for reactions, then asked if he had formed any impression of New York in the first few days, and DiMaggio replied: "Right now, it looks a lot like San Francisco. This is our kind of weather. It makes me feel right at home. But, of course, the buildings are higher and better."

In danger of striking out, Graham groped for something to hit and asked: Do you think you'll get to like New York?

Joe, who seemed to be exceptionally amiable that day, rolling cheerfully from one piece of trivia to another, said: "I sure do. It may sound funny, but I always wanted to play with the Yankees. I guess maybe it was on account of Babe Ruth. Everybody was rooting for the Babe, and I was just like all the rest. I thought if I ever came up to the big leagues, I would like to play on the same team with him. I almost made it, at that, didn't I?"

Did he run into the Babe in St. Petersburg?

"No," he said. "I wish I had. The only place I've ever seen him was in the newsreels, taking batting practice or something. I was hoping to meet him in St. Petersburg, but I didn't. I wanted to meet him the worst way."

They came close one day, but it was the day when Joe was injured at second base and Ruth missed his chance to meet his own replacement, as it were. But he gave some free-swinging opinions about his old team, predicting the Yankees were not likely to win the pennant and also predicting that DiMaggio was not likely to become an instant success.

"He must first show something in the stadium," Ruth said. "Remember that left field is pretty tough on his type of hitter. He'll be nervous and pressing. Only one out of a hundred makes good, and they all look like a million dollars under a palm tree."

Well, nobody could blame Babe Ruth for talking the way he did everything, including swinging the bat: that is, freely. He was his own caricature, big and blustery and in every way the direct opposite of the guarded and private young man from San Francisco who supposedly was going to "replace" him. Babe Ruth was a "natural" in one way, in one primitive way; Joe DiMaggio was a natural in a measured, structured way. The Babe popped off; Joe seemed to have taken a vow of silence. Ruth spoke his mind, even if he gave the impression that he was criticizing or panning somebody; DiMaggio saw no evil, spoke no evil, heard no evil. At least if he did, he kept it to himself or stored it for future reference.

DiMaggio was closer in temperament to the superstar who arrived with Ruth and left with DiMaggio: the man who was portrayed unfairly as playing second fiddle to both, Lou Gehrig, who was truly the strong, silent type, not boisterous like Ruth and also not arid or antiseptic in manner like DiMaggio. Gehrig was shy because he came from a poor background (as they did), and he was forced onto the public stage because he could play sports with exceptional skill and strength. He was more comfortable, to say the least, socking a baseball into a crowd than trying to dance with a young lady, or even talk to her.

The young lady he talked to the most was the smart and spirited Eleanor Twitchell of Chicago, who grew up in the roaring decade of the twenties and who cruised down the fast lane of society, ranging in easy and untroubled contacts from Johnny Torrio to Mike the Greek to the Grabiner sisters, whose family ran the Chicago White Sox. They introduced her to big-league baseball and, when the New York Yankees came to town with the traveling circus of stars, they even introduced her to shy, solid Lou Gehrig.

"This was the postwar golden age of sports," she told me when we were compiling her memoirs in the 1970s. "And Babe Ruth was the eighteen-carat center of the golden age. He was a huge, good-natured lummox who called everybody 'Kid' or 'Joe' because he couldn't remember their real names. He had an incredible flamboyance, with the talent to back it up.

"Some of the players resented him. He was a one-man gang who didn't pay much attention to anybody else's feelings. He was also getting more money than anybody else in baseball, and more than twice as much as anybody on the Yankees. But he was worth every penny of it. He brought in two dollars through the turnstiles for every dollar Ruppert paid him.

"Lou admired Babe as a ballplayer. You had to, he was superb. Lou liked him as a man, too, and got a kick out of his shenanigans — even though he didn't want to copy them, and couldn't. For a time, they were even roommates. Before that, Babe's roommates had been selected by the team in the hope that they might exert some good influence on him; instead, he exerted some of his own rousing influence on them. No curfew and no set of training rules were invented that could hold Babe down."

Eleanor Gehrig also had an unobstructed view of the dynamics of the batting order.

"In 1927," she said, "Ruth set his home-run record of sixty and he got plenty of support from the fact that he batted number three in the lineup with Lou batting number four. Whenever Babe went to the plate, the pitcher had two possibilities: walk him or pitch to him. If he chose to pitch, Babe might strike out — or he might knock the ball out of sight. But after Lou started to bat after him, the pitchers faced double jeopardy. If they chose to walk Ruth intentionally, they'd face Gehrig with Ruth on base. They were some pair."

They were some pair, all right. Ruth set the record for home runs that year with 60, Gehrig hit 47 for a combined total of 107, they knocked in 339 runs, and Gehrig was voted the most valuable player in the American League.

Now it was 1936, just nine years later, and the Yankees still were dealing in depth. If you pitched to DiMaggio, he might hammer one out of there or deliver the hit that could trigger a burst of runs. If you walked him, you faced Gehrig. And if you walked *him,* you got Bill Dickey.

They hadn't won the pennant since 1932, when Ruth was still

the artillery captain; they lost the race to the Washington Senators once and the Detroit Tigers twice. But here they were now, finding and perhaps forging the link from the era of Ruth to the era of DiMaggio. All that DiMaggio had to do, at the age of twenty-one, with no experience in the major leagues, was to step in and establish his era. It was as simple, and as unthinkable, as that.

He didn't even get into the lineup until May 3, but he did it with fanfare and flourishes.

"Joseph Paul DiMaggio Jr.," wrote Dan Daniel the day before, "the Yankee outfielder who has yet to play in the Yankee outfield in the American League, finally is ready to return to the wars. The New York club has announced that DiMaggio will start in left field against the St. Louis Browns in the Stadium tomorrow.

"Never before has there been so much interest in a new player at the Stadium. The Yankees' front office has had at least 100 telephone inquiries each day for the last fortnight, and the question has been: When will DiMaggio play?"

They finally got the answer that day in May. He was living with a bunch of other Yankees in the Concourse Plaza hotel, a few blocks from the ballpark, and he walked to work that morning with full regard for the fact that this was it. And a few hours later, after Pete Sheehy had served him several cups of coffee, he trotted out to left field for the first time. He was, as billed, number three in the lineup; Gehrig was number four; the pitcher for the Browns was a large right-hander from Texas named John Henry Knott.

He went to the plate for the first time in the home half of the first inning and, wasting no time or anxiety over the setting and his role in it, he lined Knott's second pitch into left field for a single. It was the first of the 2,214 hits that he would deliver in the career being launched that afternoon, and it was followed by another single the next time he went to bat. Then he grounded out — yes, they finally got him out — but he promptly atoned by whacking a triple to deep left-center.

Before the curtain fell on the performance, he popped up, closing the show with three hits in six times at bat. The Yankees, who picked on the Browns relentlessly in those days, won the game, 14–5.

The New York Times seized the moment but didn't lose its sense of proportion. Under a one-column headline, it reported: "DIMAGGIO'S 3 HITS HELP YANKS SCORE," and the subhead said: "Joe Plays Brilliantly in His Big League Debut as Browns are Beaten by 14 to 5."

The story by Kingsley Childs recorded the great event with some literary overkill but with remarkable underkill involving the point of it all: DiMaggio wasn't mentioned until the third paragraph. He put it this way:

"Considerably more proficient in frequently smashing timely hits of various dimensions in virtually every corner of the ball park, the Yankees climbed back into the winning column yesterday as the Browns invaded the Stadium for the opener of a three-game series.

"Although the rival batters furnished the opposing pitchers with anything but sweet music, they provided plenty of harmony for the 25,000 customers, the vast majority of whom were delighted in the 14-to-5 victory recorded by the McCarthymen.

"Joe DiMaggio, making his American League debut, fared well and got a big hand from the fans. He clouted a triple and two singles in six turns at bat and was the only Yankee to get a hit from Russ Van Atta, who pitched the eighth."

How's that for a sense of history? DiMaggio was the only Yankee to get a hit off Van Atta in the eighth inning of a 14–5 game, which doesn't seem worth noticing. But 25,000 fans showed up for a game against the Browns, which *does* seem worth noticing, especially if they were drawn by the first appearance by Joe DiMaggio on the great stage.

One week later, on May 10, a crowd of 32,004 showed up, and nobody missed the milestone that time. In the first inning, Red Rolfe drew a walk from George Turbeville of the Philadelphia Athletics, a strapping right-hander with good speed and good breaking pitches, who should have been more careful not to walk anybody in front of the power train of the Yankees.

He paid the price when DiMaggio took the full-arc swing at the first pitch, a fastball on the outside part of the plate, and whaled it to the opposite field into the bleachers in right. It was the first of the 361 home runs he would eventually hit, and it gave new thrust to the Yankees' drive into first place, which they took while winning ten of the twelve games on the home stand — ten of the first twelve games DiMaggio played.

He was hitting .322 for his first two weeks when the Yankees made their first road trip, taking him by train to St. Louis, where he got seven hits in fourteen times at bat in three games. In five games against St. Louis pitching at home and away, he now had thirteen hits in twenty-five times at bat. And, like a dominant team that mauls bad teams, he was already dominant against bad pitching and clearly dangerous to the best pitching.

Four of the hits were unloaded on the final day in St. Louis, and then the Yankees went to Chicago for the rookie's first visit there and he got three more hits, giving him seven in consecutive games, 10 for 19 in his first four games on the road and a batting average of .420 for his first two and a half weeks in the league.

Next stop: Cleveland, and the Yankees ran their new winning streak to five games and for the first time found themselves targeted for special treatment, and for the first time found that the particular target was their streaking rookie.

He ran into the line of fire in the ninth inning, when the Indians were chafing, probably because they were three outs from losing their fifth straight to the Yankees in little more than a month. DiMaggio led off the ninth with his second hit, and Gehrig followed with a sharp grounder to shortstop. DiMaggio slid into the bag at second, trying to break up the double play or at least to complicate it. And Billy Knickerbocker aimed the relay squarely at DiMaggio's cap, missed, and threw the ball away.

Tony Lazzeri and Joe McCarthy led the charge from the visiting dugout, and both teams went into battle formation. The umpires quickly moved in and kept the war from breaking out. But the Yankees got the message: When you're becoming the big team in the business, you will be surrounded by assassins. The other teams got the message, too: When you target DiMaggio, you target the whole club.

The caravan made it to Detroit, where Joe got his first chance to test "the hitter's park" against one of the professional aces of the game, Schoolboy Rowe, the tall and talented right-hander who ranked with the best pitchers in the business. It was one more learning experience in DiMaggio's first swing around the league.

Twice in the late innings he had the chance to tie the game, which already was becoming one of those small classics of pitching by Rowe for the Tigers and Ruffing for the Yankees. In the eighth inning, with the tying run on second, he struck out. In the tenth inning, with Ruffing on third after the Yankees had tied the game in the ninth, he struck out again.

This was unusual in itself because in his first fifteen games in the big leagues he had been struck out just four times: by Vernon Wilshere, George Blaeholder, Earl Caldwell, and Ted Lyons. He was already the rarest of rare birds in baseball: the power hitter who didn't strike out. He had either the instincts or the reactions or the measured swings. He didn't flail at the ball. He didn't turn his head from the ball. He didn't guess what was coming and then shoot the works. He watched, and waited.

By the time he left the scene fifteen years later, he had gone to bat 6,821 times and struck out 369 times. He struck out about as often as he hit a home run. Lou Gehrig went to bat 8,001 times and struck out 789 times. Babe Ruth went to bat 8,399 times and struck out 1,330 times.

"It's phenomenal," Ralph Kiner said later. "It's phenomenal any time you strike out only as often as you hit a home run. Joe didn't lunge at the ball. He didn't commit himself. He stayed back. He also didn't stride into it and get out in front. He barely lifted his front foot off the ground, held his arms and hands back and waited till the last second before pulling the trigger."

Kiner, who won seven home run titles in ten years in the big leagues, spoke with all the insight of a man who has served in the front trenches. He went to the plate 5,205 times in his career, hit 369 home runs and struck out 749 times.

But even when he was victimized by a pitcher like Schoolboy Rowe, there always seemed to be a moment of redemption for DiMaggio. He may have been struck out twice by curveballs, but when Rowe tried to slip the fastball past him during another time at bat, he nailed it and hammered a 370-foot shot off the iron fencing of the new upper deck in right-center field. Don't tread on me.

"He's a real good hitter," said Mickey Cochrane, the catcher and manager of the Tigers, the two-time defending champions of the league. "I've never seen a hitter with a nicer free swing than that kid has."

Harry Heilmann, who hit .342 during seventeen seasons as one of the best right-handed hitters in the game, most of them with the Tigers, said the rookie was simply "marvelous."

"He's just great," the old hero of Detroit said. "Why, he looked better to me striking out twice against Rowe than he did hitting that home run. Why? Because of the way he swung at the stuff Rowe was throwing. Rowe got him out with outside curves; they were honeys.

"You're telling me Rogers Hornsby says an outside curve is going to stop DiMaggio. Well, tell me what hitter a real good curve, kept low and outside, won't fool. That's the pitch they're all suckers on."

From Detroit, where he survived his first encounter with Schoolboy Rowe and even tagged him for a memorable home run, his second in the majors, DiMaggio rumbled into Philadelphia. The master on the mound there was Lefty Grove, who set standards of excellence five years earlier when he won thirty-one games and lost four. He muzzled Joe the first three times, but the rookie finally struck on his fourth trip to the plate with a line-drive single for two runs that tied the game.

They moved to Boston, and DiMaggio hit a triple in the twelfth inning that beat the Red Sox, 5-4. They went home for Memorial Day, and 71,754 fans went through the turnstiles to watch the Yankees sweep two games from Philadelphia. DiMaggio hit three doubles in a row. And by then he was hitting .381 and was riding a fourteen-game hitting streak that was casting silent shadows into the future.

The Yankees also were four games on top of the league by then, and 200,000 fans ahead of their attendance of the year before. And a few weeks later, on June 24, they put on another show of force in Chicago. They manhandled the White Sox, 18-11, with Gehrig contributing four hits (for a season's total of 101) and the Yankees crashing five home runs. Two of them were hit in the same inning by DiMaggio, who also hit two doubles.

Life isn't perfect, and he was reminded of it every now and then when the fates and the pitchers conspired. So there was probably some poetic justice to his first coast-to-coast, fall-on-your-face embarrassment. It happened two weeks later in Fenway Park. Seven Yankees had made the American League All-Star team, including the rookie celebrity, who promptly bombed in Boston.

In the first inning, facing the great Dizzy Dean of the St. Louis Cardinals, he hit into a double play. In the ninth inning, with the tying run on second base, he popped up. In right field, he misplayed a line drive into a triple, and he made an error that allowed Billy Herman to advance to second base, from where he later scored the winning run.

One week later, though, he was restored to the good graces of the public: He made the cover of *Time* magazine, which was usually reserved for people who saved, threatened, or shook the world. For any baseball player to make the cover, especially a rookie who had played only two months or so, was editorially and socially unthinkable.

If New York was looking for a revival of its baseball fortunes that year, that's what it got. At the close of the season, the Yankees were nineteen and a half games in front of the second-place Tigers with a record of 102 victories and 61 defeats. They had won thirteen more games than the year before. And they did it with exceptional range: Gehrig, the Most Valuable Player in the league, hit .354 with 49 home runs and knocked in 152 runs. Tony Lazzeri hit .287 with 14 home runs and drove in 109 runs. George Selkirk: batting average of .308 with 18 home runs and 107 runs batted in. Bill Dickey hit .362 with 22 home runs and knocked in 107. Red Rolfe batted .309 and hit ten home runs. Frank Crosetti hit 15.

And the rookie closed with straight A's: He batted .323, hit 29 home runs, and drove in 125 runs. They didn't lead the league; they blitzed the league.

They also found that the best was yet to come. In the World Series, they shook down the thunder from the Battle of Broadway when they were confronted by the New York Giants, who won the National League pennant under Bill Terry, the successor to the great Mr. McGraw. For the first time in thirteen years, since the battles between Babe Ruth and John McGraw, the stage was set for high theater.

The Giants were no sloths, either. Terry was still playing first base, Mel Ott was supplying the home-run stroke and playing right field, Dick Bartell anchored the infield at shortstop, and King Carl Hubbell remained the club pro of the pitching staff, backed by Hal Schumacher and Fred Fitzsimmons. And they promptly stopped the march of the Yankees in the opening game, 6–1, with Hubbell outpitching Ruffing.

But that was the last time in the Series that the Yankees were subdued; the last time in several Series, in fact. They came crashing back the next day in the Polo Grounds with seventeen hits, including a grand slam by Lazzeri and a double and two singles by DiMaggio, and buried Schumacher and the Giants, 18–4.

The 43,543 spectators included a superstar of world class, President Franklin D. Roosevelt, who was running for re-election; one month later, he swept forty-six of the forty-eight states from Alf Landon. And with one out to go in the bottom of the ninth inning, the public-address announcer asked the crowd to stay in their seats until after the President had made an exit across the field in his special car.

The words were still echoing when Hank Lieber exploded the last pitch of the day from Lefty Gomez, driving it high and deep to the remote reaches of center field. DiMaggio turned, tracked the ball on the run, and caught it in the farthest part of the old horseshoe stadium, almost at the point where the outfield ended and steep stairs led through the bleachers to the locker rooms beyond.

"I didn't know whether I should just keep running up the steps to the clubhouse," he said later. "But I saw the rest of the guys standing still, as they were asked to do, and I stopped short and did the same."

As he did, Roosevelt's convertible glided past and the President seemed to nod or wave to the rookie outfielder. Joe said that he believed the President was really waving to the crowd in the bleachers.

Within the week, the Yankees rolled on to win the Series, four games to two. Joe got nine hits in twenty-six times at bat for an average of .346, and Bill Terry minced no words: "I've always heard that one player could make the difference between a losing team and a winner, and I never believed it. Now I know it's true."

True or not, DiMaggio played thirteen seasons with the Yankees and got to the World Series ten times.

James C. Isaminger, the dean of Philadelphia sportswriters, observed that the season had proved two things about DiMaggio: "It proved that he can cover center field like Tris Speaker. It proved that, as a drawing card, he approaches Babe Ruth."

"It was the year," Eleanor Gehrig remembered, putting it in a few short words, "when Joe DiMaggio arrived from San Francisco and the Yankees began another phase of their long reign."

Reign, indeed. But before resuming the reign, one month or so short of his twenty-second birthday, he headed home for San Francisco after one tumultuous year away. He had rave reviews and a World Series winner's check for $6,430.55.

"Instead of being the second Babe Ruth," wrote James M. Kahn in *The New York Times*, "here is a young man who is going to be the first Joe DiMaggio."

5

THE TOAST
OF THE TOWN

THE FIRST THING that "the first Joe DiMaggio" did after collecting his senses, his baggage, and his check from the World Series was to go home — for the first time in eight months. He guessed that he would have "a bunch of stories to tell the old gang at Columbus Avenue and Taylor." But before he got to the corner and to the old gang, he was steered instead into the high road, into the paths of glory where he returned as the native son who came, saw, and conquered New York.

He rode in an open convertible with Mayor Rossi and other civic lions in San Francisco, he promptly moved his mother and father and half a dozen of his brothers and sisters from the crowded apartment on Taylor Street into a handsome and solid stone house on Beach Street in the Marina district, and he invested in Joe DiMaggio's Grotto on Fisherman's Wharf, a restaurant that Tom ran and Joe visited. He also helped Mike buy a boat to expand his fishing fleet, and he accepted all huzzahs. He had left town as a rookie, maybe a prodigy, and came back as a hero.

He didn't know it at the time, but he also was embroidering the legend, or at least the libretto, that accompanies instant success on the public stage. He was even being interviewed by celebrity columnists who rarely watched him play ball but who increasingly watched him grow into a headline star on Page One.

Dorothy Kilgallen, the syndicated queen of the press and a star in her own right, reported after her first meeting with him that "Joe DiMaggio has wonderful brown eyes." And she added: "Gentlemen, he's divine."

DiMaggio demonstrated the basic elements of the game to her with bat and ball, and said, ball in hand: "This is what we call the stitched potato, or the apricot, whatever you like." And she replied: "I like you."

"He has black hair that grows to a widow's peak like Robert Taylor's," she wrote, embroidering the libretto herself, "and quizzical eyebrows, to say nothing of eyelashes a yard long.

"He says he gets a lot of fan mail from little boys, and offhand I could name a few little girls who would be very glad to write him a line, too."

"He says he is an outfielder," she went on, gushing slyly, "and I think it's a shame to put him away out there where nobody can see him."

For the finishing touch, Kilgallen reported: "In his spare time, Joe eats steaks, sleeps and goes to the movies. He likes watching movies but not being in them. He just likes to play ball."

"And," Joe replied, taking the last shot, "I don't dance."

You can often judge a celebrity by the tonnage of trivia he generates. It's one thing to be analyzed and lionized as a man who hits home runs for the New York Yankees; it's probably more of a status symbol to be analyzed as a man who goes to the movies and sleeps a lot but doesn't dance. In the winter of 1936–37, after his first summer hitting home runs in the big leagues, DiMaggio now was making copy because he had beguiling brown eyes.

He also was receiving twenty fan letters a day, which may have set another record for a rookie who actually tried to duck the spotlight if it cast beams toward his personal life.

On the other hand, nudged by his private finance minister, his brother Tom, he stayed stubborn in money matters and skirmished publicly with Ed Barrow and even Jake Ruppert every winter. The country was still mired in the Great Depression, many people were working for fourteen dollars a week, and baseball players holding out for three hundred or more a week were considered greedy and almost unpatriotic.

Ruppert wasn't dissuaded by the fact that the Yankees had just won the World Series and looked as though they had a good chance to keep winning it. In fact, he disclosed that DiMaggio was just one of five star players who were demanding more money than he had offered: DiMaggio reportedly wanted a more than 100 percent raise from $8,500 to $17,500; Lou Gehrig was offered $31,000 but wanted $50,000; Red Ruffing was offered a raise of $3,000 to $15,000 but wanted $30,000; Lefty Gomez sent back a $7,500 contract without comment but was known to be looking for at least $12,500, and Jake Powell also was offered $7,500 but was demanding $14,000.

"I'll put a ball club on the field this spring, no matter what happens," Ruppert said. "I've taken a definite stand on this, and will see it through."

Ruppert, taking a deflection shot at Tom DiMaggio, said that Joe was "ill-advised." Joe said nothing, but he also stayed away from the spring training camp until March 12, the day before the first exhibition game, and then he appeared in camp and signed his contract. The Yankees, not wanting to seem too generous, said that he had agreed to $15,000; Joe later suggested that the figure was closer to the $17,500 he had been demanding.

The following winter, after he had led the league in home runs and led the Yankees to their second straight championship, Ruppert offered him the same money, but he told them that he expected $40,000. Then, after keeping him waiting for forty-five minutes at Ruppert's brewery in New York, they argued it out and Barrow said: "What would you say if I told you Lou Gehrig, who's been a star for fifteen years, doesn't make $40,000 himself?"

And DiMaggio replied: "I'd say, Mr. Barrow, that Gehrig is grossly underpaid."

Ruppert then intervened and offered $25,000, and said it would "make you the highest-salaried third-year man in baseball history." Joe said $40,000.

Then he shook hands and flew back home to San Francisco, helped Tom run the restaurant, worked out with the Seals in Hanford, California, and waited. It was March 12 again before Gehrig agreed to a $3,000 raise and ended his holdout at $39,000, his highest salary on the Yankees. (Ruppert felt that going to $40,000 would sound too big and round and might trigger a volley of demands from other players.) Then Ruppert rode his private Pullman car to St. Petersburg, where he persuaded Joe McCarthy to say: "The Yankees can get along without DiMaggio. That 25 is final."

From San Francisco, where he was sheltered from the cruel world once more, DiMaggio replied: "Maybe McCarthy knows what he's talking about and maybe he doesn't. That contract for $25,000 is gone with the wind. The Yankees are going to pay my price, or else."

From Ruppert's railroad car, as the Yankees closed the Florida phase of training and headed north, came the reply to the reply: "Presidents go into eclipse. Kings have their thrones moved from under them. Great ballplayers pass on. If DiMaggio isn't out there, we have Myril Hoag for center field."

Hoag hit .352 that spring, and he was playing center field when the regular season opened. But when DiMaggio arrived two weeks later and signed for the $25,000 offered, Hoag relinquished the territory. It was April 30, and the fans and the press alike took it hard: DiMaggio was berated and booed, even though he hit two home runs inside three days. He also had a narrow escape in his first game when he and Joe Gordon collided chasing a pop fly behind second base, and both went to the hospital for examination. Neither was hurt, but the press intimated that it might never have happened if DiMaggio hadn't missed spring training.

Even Rogers Hornsby sniped away. He said that $25,000 was enough for DiMaggio, and added: "DiMaggio has been up here only two years. I'd rather have Joe Medwick of the Cards. He's showed he can stay there."

The salary struggle of 1938 haunted DiMaggio for much of his career, but the struggle was renewed nearly every winter. Even after he hit in fifty-six straight games in 1941, he was asked to take a $5,000 cut by Barrow, who said: "Don't you know there's a war on?" And DiMaggio, who was getting good at the infighting and repartee of contract jousting, replied in one word that time: "Preposterous."

But along the way, the wounds of the contract wars pained him so much that he became a casualty of his own strategy. The Depression starved people both literally and figuratively and, while the man in the street might find fantasy in the ballpark, and even might find some relief from the hopelessness at home, he was just as certain to find arrogance in the behavior of a baseball star "holding out" for money that seemed sinful — holding out his talent from the hard-pressed public that paid the sinful money. The player had no agent, no lawyer, no free-agent window. All he could do was withhold his talent, or at least his presence, and hope to bring economic pressure on the owner of the team.

But Ruppert was one owner who didn't flinch, not even when he was beating down national heroes like Lou Gehrig and Joe DiMaggio. In their epic struggle in the winter and spring of 1938, Ruppert paid no homage to DiMaggio's standing in the community, not even when DiMaggio capitulated after the third game of the season.

He capitulated in a telegram to Ruppert that the owner took pleasure in releasing to the public as a kind of unconditional surrender. It read simply: "Your terms accepted. Leave at 2:40 P.M. Arrive Saturday morning."

Not content with total victory, Ruppert even made it known that DiMaggio's salary wouldn't be paid until he was ready to start playing. And he added: "Until he is in condition, if he wants to travel with the Yankees, he'll have to pay his own way."

The cost was eleven days' pay, or about $1,500. But DiMaggio always said that the cost was far greater: He was portrayed as a greedy, self-centered prima donna, and he was harpooned in the newspapers and jeered in the grandstand.

"All I was trying to do," he said, "was to get as much as I could. Is that so terrible? I had a great season and some of my friends said I ought to be worth $40,000 to a team like the Yankees. I guess they were wrong. I know I was wrong holding out as long as I did.

"I hear the boos, and I read in the papers that the cheers offset them, but you can't prove that by me. All I ever hear is boos. Pretty soon, I got the idea the only reason people come to a game at all was to boo DiMaggio. And the mail. You would have thought I had kidnapped the Lindbergh baby, the way some of the letters read."

When he said some of his friends had goaded him to go for it, he was telling the truth. But he didn't appreciate that this particular truth sharpened the public resentment because his friends also struck people as crude or even sinister. He lived in a series of hotels in midtown Manhattan: the New Yorker, the Madison, the Edison. And he was soon surrounded by an entourage of partisans who seemed to him to rank high in the smart set of the Great White Way. Or they seemed to him to rank high in the legions of people clamoring for the chance to dote on the great DiMaggio, and he loved it.

His sycophants were led by Toots Shor, the onetime speakeasy bouncer who now presided over his own "joint," as he termed it, a watering-hole mecca for the sports and newspaper crowd where Joe would nestle into a seat in the sheltered corner, safe from the thundering herd of tourists and customers but enthroned for the regulars to behold and even approach. Shor was a large, abrasive man — actually, a fat abrasive man — who put conversations at a low level where he could deal with things on his own terms, and he usually did that by addressing people in insulting ways. But with DiMaggio, he was possessive and patronizing, and Joe loved that, too.

The byline writers and columnists would flock there, too, absolutely certain that they would find DiMaggio in residence, and he was worth a few lines every time, even if he didn't say much but more often provided name-value for the next day's column. Walter Winchell was there, and Bob Considine, two of the syndicated titans of the press; later, Jimmy Cannon, who became a close friend of DiMaggio and who even lived near him in the Edison Hotel for a time.

Nobody got closer to him, though, than the short and stocky little ticket broker George Solotaire, who ran the Adelphi Theatre Ticket Agency and who liked to say that the Astors and Vanderbilts were his steady clients but Joe DiMaggio was his hero. Solotaire not only lived *near* him for long stretches of time but also lived *with* him; they were an odd couple separated by a generation in time but joined by forces of life on the town, or at least by life *in* the town where DiMaggio quickly became the crown prince and Solotaire resolutely became the prince's page.

Solotaire had a wife, but in DiMaggio he had an idol. They often took meals at the Stage Deli, they shared an apartment, they made the nightspots. Some people also suspected that Solotaire lined up girls for his idol. Not that Joe needed help; but he was either lazy or imperious in such matters, and he accepted favors as royal "perks."

"George Solotaire did things for Joe all the time," Pat Lynch remembered. "A real hanger-on. A gopher. He talked a lot about women, but I don't know that he had much to do with women himself. But he couldn't do enough for Joe.

"He was a short, stumpy guy, he wore eyeglasses and he was the 'other' half of an *odd couple* with his hero, Joe D. The only way they could have got together in the first place was because they both lived and hung out in midtown Manhattan, and they did it during the time just before and just after World War Two when New York was a night-life town and Manhattan was the heart of it. Solotaire could line up tickets to all the sporting events and Broadway shows for you. And if he liked you more than that, he could line up Broadway show-girls for you, too. Joe inspired hero worship, and George worshipped him.

"At Shor's many nights after the Yankee games, Joe would come in and head straight for the corner booth where he always liked to sit with Toots alongside him and maybe one or two of the big sports columnists. You know, Bob Considine or Jimmy Cannon in those times, and Red Smith later on."

Pat Lynch was one of the sportswriters himself, one of the stars on Hearst's *New York Journal-American,* back in the days when newspapers carried the word to the masses without competition from television or from computers or communications superhighways. If you spent the evening lounging at Toots Shor's place, and if you were seen *by* Walter Winchell, you had a good chance of being mentioned in his column the next day. If you were seen there *with* Walter Winchell, you had a good chance of being mentioned in his column a lot of days.

"Joe would go to other places at times," Pat Lynch recalled. "He'd go to Leon and Eddie's. A ha-ha club. You know, laughs. But Shor's was the big joint. No music, no clowning, no entertainment. Just the sports crowd, and particularly guys like Joe DiMaggio and his entourage of columnists and gophers like George Solotaire."

Herschel Waxman, one of the regulars in Broadway show business in later years, remembered that Solotaire was a kind of legend in his own right as the main man in one of the two big ticket agencies on Broadway.

"But he got to be bigger than life," Waxman said, "because of his closeness to Joe DiMaggio. He lined up tickets, women, whatever you wanted."

Roger Kahn, who created *The Boys of Summer* for baseball history, put it a little more directly in his book *The Era* when he wrote that George Solotaire "sent out Joe DiMaggio's laundry," ran to the Stage Deli to fetch sandwiches for him, and got show-girls to meet him.

Kahn also suggests that Toots Shor orchestrated "the legend" of Joe DiMaggio to some extent by surrounding Joe with the big Broadway columnists, who became infatuated with "the Yankee Clipper" and sang his praises forevermore.

"Toots acted kind of mopish," Pat Lynch said, "but he had a quick mind. And he grew more and more possessive of Joe."

Like the literary Round Table at the Algonquin Hotel a few blocks from Shor's place, the sporting circle at Shor's had a life of its own in the playtime and professional community. Some of the members even *lived* a few steps away.

"A bunch of us lived at the Elysée Hotel on East Fifty-fourth Street before the war," Lynch said. "Frank Conniff, who was a columnist on *The Journal.* Tallulah Bankhead lived there. Joe lived there. Even *I* lived there.

"Baseball was played almost entirely in the afternoon then. There were only a few night games, and they were more like novelties. So, there was plenty of time for a full evening on the town. Joe's favorite evening seemed to be spent sitting in his booth with Toots shielding him from the world and with the big columnists talking the night away with him and with the cheer-leaders like George Solotaire on the fringes."

Solotaire didn't have to commute very far in order to take up his station as the captain of the palace guard flanking DiMaggio. He worked out of his ticket office in the Claridge Hotel on the southeast corner of Broadway and Forty-fourth Street. So he was a familiar figure along Tin Pan Alley and beyond.

"It's interesting," Pat Lynch said, "this state of mind that feeds on public heroes, especially sports heroes. Joe DiMaggio came along about the same time as Eddie Arcaro in horse racing. They're even a year or two apart in age, and their careers were parallel. It's strange how parallel they were, in time and style both.

"Both epitomized grace. Eddie was a tremendously graceful man riding a horse. He even would stroke the horse with his stick *in rhythm*. And Joe was all style at bat. Every kid playing sports imitated them. Grown men tried to wait on them and ingratiate themselves.

"But loyalty was always Joe DiMaggio's top priority. And because of it, he eventually fell out with many of his circle of sycophants, including George Solotaire and Toots Shor.

"It wouldn't take much to set Joe off. He never brought other ballplayers or women with him to Shor's. He was a solo there, a loner in a crowd of loyalists. You couldn't tell what was going on inside him by the look on his face. I think pride was his thing, more than the shyness that he showed when he got to New York. Some people still think he was just dull; he didn't have anything to say in conversation. But I think pride was the main thing, and if you stopped being loyal to him, or if he imagined that you had stopped being loyal to him, then his pride exploded and you were gone.

"As tight as Joe and George Solotaire were, even sharing a hotel apartment at one time, they eventually fell out. Nobody seems to know why. But you can bet that George did or said something that struck Joe as a betrayal. That's all it took with Joe. If he sensed disloyalty, you were gone from his life.

"He fell out with Toots years later over a remark Toots made about Dorothy Arnold, who was Joe's first wife. Toots said something crude about her, and Joe flared, and Toots said: 'Well, you're divorced, so what does it matter?' And Joe snapped: 'She's still the mother of my son.' "

Even in later years, after his career had closed and the circle of sweet-talkers had been dispersed, DiMaggio preferred the company of a few tight friends who guarded his privacy. His favorite was Edward Bennett Williams, the legendary lawyer, who even induced Joe to accept a seat on the board of directors of the Baltimore Orioles after Williams bought the team.

But Williams was a rare one: He was one of the few people DiMaggio seemed to *need*. At least, he was one of the few people DiMaggio craved far above the level of stroking or flattering. When Williams came to New York, which was often, he stayed frequently at the Madison Hotel, where DiMaggio also stayed many times. They would make the customary run on Shor's place, or at Joe and Rose's Italian restaurant on the East Side, or the Harwyn Club, one of the nightspots in midtown.

"Nobody had the instant identification Joe had," Williams said later.

But nobody in Joe's circle had the enduring respect that Edward Bennett Williams had. It took a while, but DiMaggio eventually elevated his social sights from the circle at Shor's to the professionalism and insight of Ed Williams. And when Williams died after a long fight against cancer, the hero of Toots Shor's lost a hero of his own.

But by then the era of the cheerleading circle at Shor's had come to an end with appropriate irony. George Solotaire, who had been dropped by DiMaggio, and Toots Shor, who had been dropped by DiMaggio, finally dropped each other. They split, their friends suspected, because of their creeping jealousy over the other guy's claim on DiMaggio's affections.

One final act remained to be played, and it was played the night Shor's joint ran out of money and closed its doors for good.

A few of the Old Guard appeared for the lowering of the flag. Bob Considine was there, and Pat Lynch, and a small herd of the others from the DiMaggio era. They were sitting there with Toots, drinking a few final toasts, when Sammy Renick came in.

Sammy had been one of the ranking jockeys in the country and a longtime running mate of Eddie Arcaro, as well as a dapper presence in the Stork Club, the 21 Club, and other oases of Manhattan nightlife. He went straight to Shor, and said: "I was here the night you opened, so it seemed fitting for me to be here the night you closed."

And Shor, quick and crude to the end, replied without hesitating: "You little shithead, where were you in between?"

If there was any doubt that DiMaggio had become the toast of the town, all you had to do was glance at the mammoth billboard propped over Times Square with the picture of the man smoking a cigarette alongside the printed words: "Heavy-hitting baseball star Joe DiMaggio feels the same way about Camels as so many millions of smokers do. Says Joe: 'When I need a lift in energy, Camels is the cigarette for me. I stick to Camels. They don't irritate my throat or get my nerves jumpy. Ballplayers really go for Camels in a big way.' "

Leaving aside for the moment the literary quality of that ghostwritten testimonial, it was at least true that he smoked cigarettes regularly, just as he drank coffee relentlessly in the locker room before games. But it was also true that the endorsing of cigarettes by athletes or any other celebrities would become obsolete later in the century. But one famous athlete or entertainer after another adorned the big billboard overlooking Times Square, just as the center fielder for the Yankees did when he assured his disciples that "they don't irritate my throat."

But if DiMaggio was reigning in a Manhattan kingdom filled with star-struck subjects, he was reigning with contrasting styles. In a baseball uniform, he was dignified and noble; in a double-breasted suit beneath pomaded hair, he was aloof and self-serving. Also, judging from his circle of fawning friends, either naive or so spoiled that he courted the company of cheerleaders and loyal followers. Toots Shor wined and dined him. Walter Winchell stroked him. Jimmy Cannon romanticized him. George Solotaire even drove him to the airport.

"Babe Ruth and Jack Dempsey used to hang around the joint a lot," Shor remembered. "Dempsey was the greatest American hero of all time. Nobody was bigger, not Lindbergh, not the

President. I'll tell you who could have been bigger than Dempsey, only one man. If Joe DiMaggio had stayed in New York
every winter instead of going back to San Francisco, Joe DiMaggio would have been bigger.

"As it is, he probably is second greatest only behind Jack
Dempsey. They can halt business on Fifth Avenue by walking
down the street. How many guys can do that?"

But once a year, it seemed, DiMaggio quarreled with the Yankees about money and lost favor with the multitudes, and his
skyrocketing stature was set back the most when he missed
opening day in 1938 and then surrendered. When he finally
headed for New York to join the team and to wave the white flag
in front of Ruppert, dozens of newspaper writers crowded the
platform at Pennsylvania Station. But he avoided them by getting
off the train at the Newark station, where he was met by one of
the charter members of the entourage, Joe Gould, who also was
one of the mistakes of the entourage.

Joe Gould lived for a time at the Mayflower Hotel on Central
Park at Sixty-first Street, which was where DiMaggio also lived
for a time in his perennial game of revolving hotels. Gould was
the manager of James J. Braddock, who won the heavyweight
title in 1935 when he went the distance with Max Baer, only to
lose it two years later when he didn't go the distance with Joe
Louis. He went eight rounds before Louis flattened him.

Toots Shor recalled that he was still working as a maître d' at
Billy LaHiff's joint in 1936, before setting up his own joint, when
he met DiMaggio for the first time.

"Braddock came over to lunch with Jack Dempsey," he said,
"and he brought the kid, DiMaggio, along. That's how I met him.
He was very humble, very shy."

But DiMaggio was outgrowing his humble stage two years
later when he grappled with Ruppert over his contract and was
met at the Newark depot by Joe Gould, who by then had become a member of the inner circle. In fact, Gould was reported
to be his chief financial adviser, at least on the East Coast, where

Tom DiMaggio did not normally stray. And he was further reported to be collecting twelve and a half percent of whatever salary DiMaggio wrested from the Yankees.

It took a while for the implications of this alliance to trouble the conscience of Kenesaw Mountain Landis, the former federal judge who became commissioner of baseball in 1920 with the mission of rescuing the game from the Chicago Black Sox scandal the year before. But when Landis realized that here was a star player rocking the boat by negotiating his contract with the help of an agent or business manager, he wasted no more time rescuing the game again. He summoned DiMaggio and his field manager, Joe McCarthy, to his headquarters in May of 1940 and confronted them with his findings, or at least with his suspicions.

Ed Barrow, when he was asked about the radical notion that a player might arrive with an agent, said flatly that he would probably throw both of them out of his office. And Bob Considine wrote in his column: "The reason the average owner wants no part of a player's agent or manager is that it would cost the owner more money."

That was blunt enough, and true enough. In those days, the "owner" owned the team and the players. But in DiMaggio's case, there was another problem: Joe Gould also was a betting man. So DiMaggio ran the risk of appearing not only greedy in his salary disputes and holdouts but also reckless in his choice of cronies.

After hassling the two Yankees for an hour, Landis ruled that DiMaggio had not really paid for professional help before signing his contract, which let him off the hook. But DiMaggio, in turn, as his part of the plea-bargain, issued a statement saying "my salary never has been and never will be shared with a manager or agent." After that, DiMaggio lost his zest for salary contests, but in his first five years in the major leagues he had fallen into five fights with the Yankees over money, and it took him years to live down the public impression that he was one more grasping, greedy bastard.

It usually took some extraordinary achievements on the field to tone down the booing that always accompanied the holdouts. Fortunately, the extraordinary achievements eventually showed up. In 1937, for example, following his first contract dispute, he countered the booing most effectively by hitting a grand-slam home run on July 4. And *The New York Times* reported the reaction this way:

"The stands shook with shouts and stomping, a deafening crescendo of shrieks, cheers, whistling and hand-clapping. At the plate, there began a demonstration of affectionate mobbing that continued on the bench as every player pummeled and thumped the youth."

One month later, in August of 1937, "the youth" went to the Biograph Studios on 175th Street in the Bronx to play a spot role in a film titled *Manhattan Merry-Go-Round.* For cash, yes; but he had to report at seven o'clock in the morning to earn it. He also had to recite three lines that wouldn't tax him, even at seven o'clock in the morning: "Well, I'm here." And, "What?" And finally, "But I'm . . ."

He mastered the lines, and also mastered his first encounter with a blond bit player from Minnesota named Arnoldine Olson, now known (or unknown) as Dorothy Arnold for her minor movie career. She told a columnist later that "I fell in love with him before I even knew who he was."

Before he left the set, DiMaggio made a date with her and learned some genealogy: She was born in Duluth, one of four daughters of a railroad official named V. A. Olson. She hit the road when she was only fifteen to travel on the Balaban & Katz vaudeville circuit, singing and dancing. Three years later, she reached New York. She sang in clubs and on the radio, signed a low-level contract with Universal Pictures for somewhere between fifty and seventy-five dollars a week, and made a modest debut as one of the unspoken ladies in the cast of *Manhattan Merry-Go-Round* on the morning she met but did not recognize Joe DiMaggio.

It took two years for something more solemn to develop, but it did. After the World Series in 1939, he took her home to San Francisco to meet his parents and his four sisters and three brothers. Dorothy even began taking instructions to convert to Catholicism, and then they took the town by storm on Sunday, November 19.

It was a landmark event in San Francisco, the day the horsey hero graduated from the ranks of the bachelors and walked down the aisle for the first time. But before either one of them could walk down the aisle, they had to fight their way through a throng of 10,000 and maybe 30,000 people jamming the streets surrounding the Cathedral of St. Peter and St. Paul in the old neighborhood. The groom arrived with a police escort and a personal escort of his two baseball brothers, Vince, who had played in the National League for three years and who already had led the league in striking out, and Dominic, who had just been sold to the Boston Red Sox for $50,000. For a while, the brothers got trapped in the crowd, and they couldn't work their way inside until two o'clock, just when the wedding was supposed to be starting.

Part of the crowd inside the cathedral consisted of plain-clothesmen planted there by Mayor Rossi, who was taking no chances with his civic star. But the deed was done, and then the wedding party fought its way back outside and boarded limousines for the trip to a photo studio, and eventually to Joe DiMaggio's Grotto for the reception. That's right, not the Fairmont or Mark Hopkins, but Joe DiMaggio's Grotto. The maître d' duly reported later that they had served twelve turkeys, eight hams, fifteen chickens, and four sides of beef.

Back in New York, for a time at least, DiMaggio abdicated the life of a hotel hermit and set up housekeeping. They lived at 400 West End Avenue, and they quickly became a foursome with Yankee pitcher Lefty Gomez and his wife, June O'Dea, who had been a musical-comedy star when they met.

"Joe and I would go to the stadium early," Gomez remembered, "and the girls would come up later for the game. I lived on Ninety-first Street on the West Side, and Joe lived eight blocks away in this big penthouse near Eighty-third Street. He didn't like to drive, so I'd pick him up every morning. He never got to like driving. And in those days, anyway, he hated playing golf. He used to say it was bad for your baseball swing."

They made a stylish quartet around town, two of the headline heroes of the Yankees and the actresses they had married. But marriage can be a severe test, especially when it imposes a radically new lifestyle on one of the partners, or on both, as DiMaggio would discover soon — and again fifteen years later. And while he gained a good-looking wife, he lost the daily devotion of his entourage. He gave the impression of a romantic dreamer who loved the idea of being in love but who felt uncomfortable with the details and the limitations it demanded.

Three years after they married, she took up residence in Reno, complaining that he was cold and independent.

Jimmy Cannon once asked Joe DiMaggio why he played so hard on the field, and he replied: "Because there might be somebody out there who's never seen me play before."

It sounded sanctimonious, but it was indisputable that he played with the drive of a perfectionist and established himself as the virtuoso of his generation during his first four seasons in the big leagues. And the Yankees, during that time, had one of the great runs of success in baseball history.

In 1936, when he was a rookie, they won 102 games, lost 51, and won the pennant by nineteen and a half games over Detroit. Then they won the World Series in six games over the Giants. The rookie in center field hit .323 with 206 hits and 29 home runs, and knocked in 125 runs.

In 1937, the Yankees won 102 games, lost 52, and won the pennant by 13 games over Detroit. Then they overpowered the Giants in the Series in five games. The sophomore in center field hit .346 with 215 hits, drove in 167 runs and led the league with 46 home runs.

In 1938, they won 99 games, lost 53, and outran Boston by nine and a half games. In the Series, they swept the Chicago Cubs in four games. DiMaggio batted .324 with 194 hits and 32 home runs, and knocked in 140 runs.

In 1939, they won 106 games, lost 45, and blitzed Boston by 17 games in the standings. In the Series, they swept the Cincinnati Reds in four games. DiMaggio won the batting title with an average of .381, hit 30 home runs, and drove in 126 runs.

So in four years of dominating the business the Yankees won four pennants by a combined total of 59 games and won four World Series, sixteen games to three. If that wasn't a dynasty, it certainly was a monopoly.

Before the 1937 season, Ty Cobb paid a visit to St. Petersburg in spring training and, with all the impunity of a man who hit .367 during twenty-four years as the hellcat of baseball, offered some words of wisdom. DiMaggio took the advice gracefully.

"In the first place," he reported, "I cannot go through the season swinging a forty-ounce bat. I intend to start with a forty, but after August First, I intend to switch to a thirty-seven or thirty-six ouncer. Last summer, I found myself getting tired lugging that heavy stick through August and September. In the last two weeks, I got so fagged out that I fell off eighteen points in my hitting.

"Another thing I must do is lay off those bad balls I went after with the count three-and-two. I was too anxious. Now I appreciate that the percentage is altogether with me. The pitcher must satisfy me because right behind me he sees Lou Gehrig, and behind him Bill Dickey."

Then he nodded verbally toward Ty Cobb, who must have loosened his tongue as well as his batting stance.

"Cobb wised me up to another trick," he said. "He told me that after August First, a good outfielder is crazy to spend fifteen minutes shagging flies. He said to me, 'Joe, the trick of conserving your energy and pacing yourself is one of the most important things a young fellow has to master. Don't spend your hitting energy chasing flies. Grab a few, and then sit down in a cool, shady spot. The flies you catch in practice never show in the records or the salary because the fans don't pay to see that sort of thing."

The Yankees didn't have much trouble treating their fans that spring: They played twelve exhibition games in St. Petersburg and won all twelve. They lost three games on the road, and headed north playing .800 ball. But they also headed north with DiMaggio fretting over a throwing arm that lacked strength and, when the doctors decided that the problem originated in his tonsils, which were infected, he returned to New York and had them removed.

It was the second straight time that he missed the opening of the season. He had missed the first seventeen games in 1936, but this time he rejoined the team in Washington one week into the season and promptly pinch-hit a double to center field.

He did even better a few weeks later when the Yankees played a tumultuous doubleheader in St. Louis and won the opening game, 16–9, by simply scoring seven runs in the ninth inning. Then, in the second game, DiMaggio hit three home runs in three times at bat and, with the score tied at an untidy 8–8, the game was called so that the Yankees could catch a train.

If there was anything more remarkable than his playing record, it was probably his medical record. In 1939, he managed to avoid injuries in spring training and he actually made an opening day. But two weeks later, on April 29, Bobby Estalella of the Washington Senators lined a single to left-center at Yankee Stadium, and DiMaggio cut to his right on the wet grass, caught his spikes, and fell down.

"I heard a loud crack," he said. "I thought my bone was gone."

It wasn't, but he was sidelined again and didn't play until

June. In fact, he was resting his ankle in Lenox Hill Hospital in New York on May 2 and missed one of the milestones in baseball history: Lou Gehrig went to Joe McCarthy in Detroit, removed himself from the lineup because he was clearly hurting — and, as he said, hurting the team — and ended his endurance streak at 2,130 games.

When DiMaggio got back to work, he was already high on the list of hitters in the American League, and by September he was leading the league at .408. And just when he had a chance to make some history himself, he came down with an inflammation in the left eye. He still won the batting title, but his average dropped 27 points in the final days and he finished at .381. He didn't complain until years later, when he remembered how he had kept playing but didn't really know why.

"Something was really wrong with my left eye," he said. "I could hardly see out of it. But Joe McCarthy didn't believe in cheese champions, so he kept me playing every day. He knew the agony I was going through, and I'll never understand why he didn't give me a couple of days off. But he didn't, and I paid the price. You played in those days with anything short of a broken leg."

One year later, he reverted to the old pattern and missed the opening of the season, one more time. Wrenched knee, this time. And the Yankees got off to a slow start, chased Detroit and Cleveland all summer, gained on them in the home stretch — and just missed. They finished two games behind the Tigers, one behind the Indians, and by the most slender of margins ended their string of championships. Having swept four pennants in a row by fifty-nine games, they missed by just two.

If there was one knock on the Yankees in those days, it was that they were mechanical and dull. They weren't rowdy like the St. Louis Cardinals. They weren't whacky like the Brooklyn Dodgers. McCarthy pressed the DiMaggio button, people said, and he'd get a home run. He would press the Gomez button, and he'd get a shutout. They were so automatically powerful that they inspired a cry that lived in the language: "Break up the Yankees."

Nobody did. They recoiled from their near miss in 1939 and came back to win again in 1941 and 1942, and that made it six pennants in seven years and exactly two games shy of dominating the business seven years in a row. But even when they lost, they contended, and they contended for forty-five years from the day when Babe Ruth arrived in 1920.

In his column in the *Washington Post* one day, Shirley Povich isolated the odd trait of dullness and centered it on DiMaggio, who apparently led the team in all things, including sullen looks. The heading on the column got right to the point: "DiMaggio Can Hit, But He Has No Color."

"Joe DiMaggio, with his free swing and solid stance," Povich wrote, "may conceivably displace Babe Ruth as the all-time home run champion of the big leagues, but Giuseppe never will make the turnstiles click as merrily as did the Babe.

"Because DiMaggio is news only when he hits a home run. Modesty may be a virtue in other walks of life, but in the big leagues they pay off on braggadocio, color and showmanship. In that league, DiMaggio couldn't hit .029.

"The Yankees' young Italian boy is seemingly too goldarned content to hit his home runs and those long triples, and let it go at that. He has none of Ruth's flourish and gusto, and none of Dizzy Dean's self-admiration. And because of that, he will set no salary records no matter how many slugging records fall before the power of his bat."

Colorless or not, with or without flourish and gusto, there was no doubt that DiMaggio both led and typified the new generation of baseball stars as the game turned into the 1940s and the epochal changes at hand. They were *not* exactly like Babe Ruth and Dizzy Dean and certainly not like Ty Cobb or John McGraw. But they could play, and DiMaggio was the ranking member of the original cast.

He was 21 years old when he joined the Yankees in 1936 and delivered 206 hits, 29 home runs, 125 runs batted in, and an average of .323. Bob Feller was 18 that year when he came off the family farm in Van Meter, Iowa, and joined the Cleveland Indians with his strikeout speed. Two years later, Feller opened a four-year rampage during which he won 93 games and struck out 1,007 batters. Then he went off to war.

DiMaggio and Feller had been in the league for three seasons when Ted Williams of San Diego arrived with the Red Sox in 1939 and hit thirty-one home runs and batted .327. One year later, he hit .344 with twenty-three home runs. One year after that, he hit .406. One year after that, he went off to war, too.

Nobody could have known at the time, but 1942 was the final year they would appear onstage together until after World War II. They were gone for a group total of ten years — one decade.

But at least they gave people something to remember. In that valedictory summer of '41, Feller won 25 games and lost 13. Williams hit his remarkable .406. And DiMaggio got at least one hit a game for two months.

Later, Williams looked back on their time together and said: "It is probably my misfortune that I have been and inevitably will be compared with Joe DiMaggio. We were of the same era. We were the top two players in our league. In my heart, I always felt I was a better hitter than Joe. But I have to say: He was the greatest baseball player of our time. He could do it all."

6

THE STREAK

I managed for 24 years in the Pacific Coast League. In 1935, I had Joe DiMaggio in right field and we won the pennant. He hit .398. Sold him to the Yankees over the winter, and the next year we finished next to last.

— *Lefty O'Doul*

He didn't care who was pitching — Feller, Grove, any of them. He just hit them. He just hit the ball, not the pitcher.

— *Joe McCarthy*

I was always conscious of the *other* guy. Usually the guy was Joe DiMaggio.

— *Ted Williams*

That's like in 1944, when I was playing with the Yankees. I finished up my career with them. Some fans in the bleachers yelled at me: "Hey, Paul, how come you're in the outfield for the Yankees?"
    "Because," I said, "Joe DiMaggio's in the Army."

— *Paul Waner*

IT WAS a hazy Thursday afternoon in Yankee Stadium on May 15, 1941, when it began. In four times at bat against the Chicago White Sox, he hit one single. The next day, he hit a triple and a home run. Two weeks later, he was suffering from a swollen neck, but still hit three singles and a home run in Washington. Nobody noticed it particularly, but Joe DiMaggio was launching The Streak.

In sports, as in life, doing things in streaks can be decisive, magnificent, or fickle.

Rube Marquard won nineteen straight games in 1912 for the New York Giants from opening day through July 3, then won only seven more in the second half of the season. The Giants rode with the momentum of his early heroics, won a total of 103 games, lost just 48, and won the National League pennant by eleven and a half games. But in the World Series, with Christy Mathewson pitching to protect a 2-1 lead in the bottom of the ninth inning and needing three outs to nail it down, Fred Snodgrass muffed a lazy fly ball to center field, the Boston Red Sox jammed two unthinkable runs across the plate, and John

McGraw watched in disbelief and distemper as the championship careened away, four games to three.

Four years later, the Giants opened the 1916 season by *losing*
eight straight games. McGraw began moving bodies around like
chess pieces, and even traded his personal hero and old friend
Mathewson to the Cincinnati Reds, ostensibly to enhance
Matty's ambition to become a manager. The Giants suddenly
won seventeen games in a row, all of them *on the road.*

But for sheer, fickle fate, nothing prepared John McGraw for
what happened in the final month of his strangely streaking season. On September 7, having trailed the Brooklyn Dodgers, Philadelphia Phillies, and Boston Braves all summer, the Giants
launched a blockbuster: They defeated the Dodgers that afternoon, and kept winning for twenty-six straight games to the end
of the month.

They had winning streaks of seventeen games in a row and
twenty-six games in a row — and still finished *fourth* in an eight-
team league.

If the Giants were a streaky team, for better or worse, DiMaggio was the super-streak player of all time. When he was eighteen years old, in 1933, in his first season in professional
baseball, he got at least one hit a game from May 28 to July 26 in
the Pacific Coast League, one notch below the major leagues.
Sixty-one games in a row.

For brinkmanship, nobody came close. In both games of one
doubleheader with the Seals, he didn't get a hit until his last time
at bat. In his forty-first game, with big-league scouts swarming to
watch, he went hitless into the ninth inning. The pitcher was
Tom Sheehan of the Hollywood Stars, the catcher Johnny
Bassler, who called for three curveballs in a row. They all missed
and, at three balls and no strikes, DiMaggio was one pitch away
from forfeiting his streak.

Bassler gave the sign for another curve, and Sheehan shook
him off. So the catcher went out to the mound, where Sheehan
said with non-negotiable firmness:

"Look, I'm as anxious to horsecollar this kid as you are. But I ain't going to walk him his last time at bat. These fans would swarm on the field and hang me from the flagpole."

Bassler subsided, Sheehan fired a high fastball around the shoulders, and DiMaggio whistled a double to deep left field.

"I've got to hand it to him," Sheehan said later. "He had the guts to lay off the curve and wait for a fastball. And what I mean, he waited. He all but hit it out of Bassler's glove."

When the streak reached fifty, Bobo Newsom bragged that he was going to stop "this guy," and he came armed with the fastest fastball in the league. Joe nailed him for two doubles and a home run. In the sixty-first game of the streak, he went 0 for 4 and didn't figure to get another shot. But the Seals staged a monumental rally in the ninth inning, he got an extra chance to swing — and he lined a single to center off Lou McEvoy.

In the very next game, he faced Ed Walsh Jr., the son of the onetime ace of the Chicago White Sox, and Joe remembered: "He threw bullets. The next time I faced him, I was 3 for 5. But this day, I could do nothing with him."

They went to the ninth, the score tied, one out and a runner on third. Last chance, one more time.

"Jim Poole was in right for Oakland," he recalled years later. "They pulled the infield and outfield in for a play at the plate. I hit a long one to right. Poole went way back and made a great one-handed catch."

And that's how the streak ended at sixty-one: He went 0 for 5. But the ending was decisive, magnificent, and fickle at the same time: The runner on third tagged up and scored after the catch, and scored the winning run on DiMaggio's fifth *out* of the game.

In his rookie season with the Yankees three years later, he hit in eighteen straight games. The next season, in twenty-two. And the season after that, in twenty-three. Then in 1941, he hit safely in the final nineteen games in spring training and in eight more games after the season opened. They didn't all count, but that still added up to twenty-seven games in a row.

So when he singled off Edgar Smith of the White Sox on that hazy afternoon of May 15, he was firing the first salvo in something that he had done regularly in the past: hit in streaks.

There was no clue, of course, that this was the start of something special. And nobody cared much at first because the Yankees had other cares: They had dropped into third place in 1940 after dominating the game for four straight years, which was a memorable streak in itself. Now, one year later, they were still struggling to restore the empire. Beyond that, the rookie Phil Rizzuto had replaced Frank Crosetti at shortstop (Crosetti then came back and replaced Rizzuto at shortstop), Bill Dickey was hitting in seventeen games in a row, several other Yankees were launching streaks of their own, and Lou Gehrig, the very symbol of the empire, lay dying at his home in Riverdale, losing his long struggle against amyotrophic lateral sclerosis.

The New York newspapers didn't particularly chronicle anybody's streak until May 28, and did it then mostly because Johnny Sturm had hit in eleven games in a row and the rejuvenated Crosetti in ten. DiMaggio said later that he hadn't started to notice his own streak until it reached thirty-three games, but he would have been the most isolated and unaware person in America if that were true. Everybody else was getting involved before then, and for good reason: The streak was supporting an identical Yankee streak in the direction of first place.

The setting was rich, too, in a season of bravura performances in baseball. Lefty Grove won his 300th game, Mel Ott hit his 400th home run. Ted Williams was building a batting average of .406. Bob Feller, who won 24 games in 1939 and then won 27 for an encore in 1940, was on his way to winning 25 in 1941. Those were the days, my friends. Williams and Feller were both 22 years old, DiMaggio was 26, and all three were reaching peaks of performance before interrupting their careers and disappearing onto a world stage already teeming with history and brutal war: Adolf Hitler was storming across Europe, the Germans were invading Yugoslavia and Greece, the British were girding to attack Rommel at El Alamein, the Japanese were plotting to attack Pearl Harbor.

But at Yankee Stadium, before 9,040 fans on that Thursday afternoon of May 15, small things seemed to be taking place. In the home half of the first inning Phil Rizzuto doubled, and with two down DiMaggio singled to center field for the run. It was the only hit he got, the Yankees went on to lose to the White Sox 13-1, and they then had a streak of their own going: five straight defeats.

The next afternoon, the Yankees held Ladies Day but counted only 1,483 cash customers. In a way, that was unfortunate because they played a classic thriller against Chicago. The tone was set in the third inning when DiMaggio hit a titanic home run into the bleachers in left-center field, where only Hank Greenberg of the Detroit Tigers had hit one before (and he was already in the Army as part of baseball's advance guard).

Still, the Yankees were losing 5-4 when they reached the ninth inning, with the left-handed Thornton Lee pitching for the White Sox and trying to prevent any uprising. No such luck. DiMaggio triggered things by driving a triple off the bleacher wall in left-center, about 415 feet down-range, and Joe Gordon lined a triple to the same spot.

Jimmy Dykes, the manager of the White Sox, then ordered Lee to walk the bases loaded and hope for the best. But the Yankees countered by sending up Red Ruffing as a pinch-hitter. And Ruffing, a pitcher who hit like a hitter, and who ended the season with a batting average of .303, delivered a single and won the game, 6-5.

The day after that, the Yankees managed only five hits off John Rigney, but one of them was a second-inning single by DiMaggio, and the silent streak crept past game number three. He wasn't picking on easy targets exactly: Smith, Lee, Rigney, Ted Lyons, and the rest of the Chicago staff pitched 106 complete games that season, the most in the big leagues since Cy Young and the rest of the Boston Red Sox staff pitched 148 complete games out of 154 in 1904, which was unbelievable in itself.

There were 30,109 fans inside the stadium the next day, which was not only Sunday but also "I Am an American Day" across the country. It did nothing to dampen the day for New York when the old patsies, the St. Louis Browns, showed up and took the prescribed hammering, 12–2. DiMaggio went 3 for 3.

The day after that, Denny Galehouse muzzled the Yankee bats on four hits and the Browns put it to them, 5–1. But one of the four hits was a two-out double to left field in the seventh inning by Joe DiMaggio. Unsung, the streak reached five. Bill Dickey, meanwhile, hit a home run and ran *his* streak to twenty.

Streaks always reach an emotional point and escalate from there. The Detroit Tigers once lost nineteen games in a row, and by then people were surrounding them with outrageous emotional support, engulfing them with prayer cards, rosary beads, amulets, tokens, and good-luck charms — as though the fate of millions was at stake. On the flip side of streaks, when Gabe Paul was running the Cincinnati Reds, the Cleveland Indians, or the New York Yankees, he liked to invoke the baseball adage: "When you're on a winning streak, even the food tastes better."

The emotional responses to the various streaks that were hatched in the spring of 1941 seemed rather slow in hatching, perhaps because of the gravity and urgency of world events. And that was certainly understandable, even when world-class athletes like Williams and DiMaggio were doing the streaking.

Coincidentally, almost incredibly, their streaks started on parallel tracks and stayed there for a while. They both got hits for the sixth game in a row on May 20, but Joe cut it close. He was hitless going to the bottom of the eighth inning against St. Louis in Yankee Stadium, trying to solve the mystery of Elden Auker's underhanded whip, known to the public as the "submarine" pitch and hated by the hitters because it started traveling like a submarine but darted upward and down like an airplane.

It was a tantalizing situation, especially since DiMaggio had already managed to hit one pitch hard, shooting a low bullet to the right of first base in the fifth inning. But Harlond Clift somehow knocked it down while performing a dazzling pirouette and came spinning out of it with a perfect throw to second base for the force-out on Tommy Henrich.

In the eighth, though, neither brooding nor begging, DiMaggio got his final look at Auker's submarine pitch and lined it to center field for a single.

The Detroit Tigers followed the Browns into the stadium the next afternoon, and this time the pitching problem was Schoolboy Rowe. But this time, no late heroics. Joe singled and knocked in a run in the first inning, and came back with a single in the ninth that tied the game against Al Benton. One inning later, the Yankees scored the tiebreaker and won, 5-4.

The day after that, DiMaggio went to the seventh inning in the rain without a hit. Then he singled off Archie McKain, thought about stretching it into a double, promptly thought better of it, and slid back into first base in the mud, evading the tag by Rudy York. The final was 6-5, Yankees, and the streak stood at eight.

Next came the Boston Red Sox for a Ladies Day on a Friday afternoon, May 23, and they battled until dark deadlocked at 9-9. Then the umpires called the game, which didn't count in the standings. But the players' statistics did count, including DiMaggio's single off Dick Newsome in the home eighth.

People may not have developed any sense of a streak yet, but they had no trouble sensing that the Yankees had started to gather momentum. When DiMaggio launched it on May 15 with his undistinguished single off Edgar Smith, the Yankees were in fourth place, five and a half games back. They were being nagged about their drift, and DiMaggio was being nagged about his annual holdout for more money. But, as Swinburne fancied, "Blossom by blossom the spring begins." And inning by inning, the recovery was beginning.

It continued on Saturday, May 24, when they scored four times in the bottom of the seventh and defeated the Red Sox again, 7–6. But Joe had another close call: In the sixth inning, he hit a long fly to center that was misplayed by his brother Dominic. In the press box, Dan Daniel, probably the leading partisan of the DiMaggio mystique, ruled as the official scorer that it was a three-base error.

But with two down in the seventh, Joe singled off the left-handed Earl Johnson, got Daniel off the hook, and kept the streak alive at ten games.

He kept it alive at eleven the next day when he singled off Lefty Grove in the first inning before 36,461 spectators in the stadium as the Yankees closed a home stand that later would be viewed as a prelude to some baseball history. But the rave performances were achieved by the Red Sox: The relentless Williams cashed four hits and raised his batting average to .404. And the 41-year-old master Lefty Grove pitched his 296th victory en route to a career record of 300 and 141.

One of the bizarre footnotes to the annals of power hitting in the rivalry between the Yankees and Red Sox was supplied by Charlie Keller, who resembled a gorilla in terms of muscled force. During the game, he hit an inside-the-park home run to the monuments, 457 feet from home plate in the remote reaches of center field. That was neat in itself, especially for a man who customarily drove baseballs past fences. But it was particularly neat because it was the second home run in ten days that Keller had outrun inside the stadium.

Leaving the friendly confines after their revival at home, the Yankees stopped off in Norfolk the next day, en route to a series in Washington, and played their farm club. DiMaggio popped out twice and walked, and he left in the seventh inning. The Norfolk farm team was the only team that kept him from getting at least one hit during his remarkable run.

It didn't count, of course. But after taking a steamboat up Chesapeake Bay to Washington, the Yankees aimed their firepower at the Senators. And as if to atone for his tame work against the minor league pitchers the day before, DiMaggio went 4 for 5 in Griffith Stadium and scored three runs. The hits were no cheapies: three singles and a three-run home run that carried 425 feet to left field.

In the next game, a dimension was added to the challenge of streaking: It was the first night game ever played in Griffith Stadium. It had been six years since Larry MacPhail had introduced night baseball to Crosley Field in Cincinnati, in 1935, a revolution that reached Ebbets Field in Brooklyn in 1938, Shibe Park in Philadelphia in 1939, and the Polo Grounds in New York, Comiskey Park in Chicago, Municipal Stadium in Cleveland, and Sportsman's Park in St. Louis in 1940.

To deepen the tone of history, the venerable strikeout star Walter Johnson threw out the first pitch. It tripped an electric beam that in turn threw on the lights. It took the Yankees until the eighth inning to adjust to the lights, and they were trailing then by 3–1. But DiMaggio, going to the brink one more time, spared himself and his streak by whacking Sid Hudson for a triple. Before the inning ended, George Selkirk pinch-hit a grand slam, five runs crossed, and the Yankees won the Capital's first night game, 6–5.

In the cold light of the next day, the teams shadow-boxed to a tie at 2–2, and DiMaggio lived through yet another close call. He got a hit off Steve Sundra when he hammered a pitch squarely off home plate and the ball bounced high into the air toward third base. He beat the throw by an eyelash. It was the kind of carom shot renowned as the "Baltimore chop" back in the days when John McGraw and Willie Keeler were inventing "Oriole baseball" in the 1890s. The "butcher boy" bounce, Casey Stengel called it years later. But by any name, it extended the string to fourteen games, and counting.

Now it was Friday, May 30, and time for the big Memorial Day doubleheader in Boston, where 34,500 fans jammed Fenway Park and 25,000 were turned back at the gates. It was the first of six doubleheaders played during the streak, and the Yankees swept all of them except this one. They won the opener, 4–3, but lost the second one, 13–0. And DiMaggio even dropped a fly ball in center field for an error. But with the Red Sox leading by 3–1 going to the ninth, the cannonading began.

It began with another pinch-hitting appearance by Ruffing, a right-handed pitcher and batter, who replaced the left-handed Henrich and lined a single off the great green wall in left field. Next came DiMaggio, who had two walks but no hits so far, and he promptly lined a single to right field. Fifteen games in a row. Eventually, the Yankees loaded the bases, Keller walked to force home one run, Crosetti singled for two more (stretching *his* streak to twelve games), and the Red Sox blew the lead, 4–3.

In the second game of the holiday doubleheader, DiMaggio was suffering with a stiff neck and shoulder and showed it. He didn't come up with a ground single by Williams, he threw two other balls away, and he closed the performance with a total of *four* errors for what was clearly and almost unthinkably the worst day of his career in the field, where he usually reigned.

With all that, though, and still favoring his neck and shoulder, he got one break when Pete Fox lost his fifth-inning fly to right field in the sun and it fell for a gift double.

Then it was on to Cleveland, where their Saturday game was rained out. But on Sunday, June 1, they swept another doubleheader before a crowd of 52,081. Ruffing pitched the opener and won, 2–1; Lefty Gomez pitched the second game and won, 5–3. DiMaggio, still hurting, managed a two-out single in the third inning of the opener off Al Milnar. Then he went to the eighth inning of the second game before he skimmed a hard one down the third-base line, it ticked Ken Keltner's glove and carried down the left-field line, and the streak reached eighteen. Ken Keltner, of all people.

Mel Harder was a mild-looking man from Nebraska who wore eyeglasses and a concerned expression but who had a granite physique and slanting speed that conceded nothing to good hitters. To Joe DiMaggio, he was always ranked first on the list of "pitchers who gave me the most trouble." Harder did it for as long as they played for their teams, too. He pitched twenty years in the big leagues, all of them for Cleveland, and he won 223 games. On May 14, the day before the streak started, he faced DiMaggio four times and got him out four times.

While all this was going on in Cleveland, meanwhile, Ted Williams was getting four hits in Detroit, running his average to .430 and his streak to nineteen.

When you follow Mel Harder with Bob Feller, you're probably being unfair to the other team. But it happened all the time, and it happened to the Yankees in the last game in Cleveland. Not only that, but Feller had a streak of his own blooming: thirty scoreless innings in a row.

That is, they were scoreless until the Yankees got to him in the second inning. They went on to lose the game, 7–5, but DiMaggio reached the fireballing Feller for a single and double, and now he stood at nineteen games, too.

"When I was a kid," Feller said later, remembering the wars, "I had two separate fastballs I threw to Joe. One had this big hop and rose up and in on him. The other jumped away from him. He hit them both."

After the game, the Yankees took the train for the short run to Detroit, where they were met on their arrival by the news they had dreaded for two years: Lou Gehrig, the captain, the Iron Horse, the Eagle Scout, had died back home in Riverdale. He was seventeen days short of his thirty-eighth birthday. And in terms of streaks, he was still the king: 2,130 games without missing.

Before the game in Briggs Stadium the next day, the teams lined up in front of their dugouts in silence for Gehrig. Then they went out and played to a decision in ninety-nine minutes, with Dizzy Trout pitching the Tigers to a 4–2 victory. But DiMaggio led off the fourth inning with a home run, and the streak reached twenty.

Joe McCarthy and Bill Dickey left the team and returned to

New York to attend Gehrig's funeral. And after rain forced cancellation of the game the next day, the Yankees faced one more power pitcher, Hal Newhouser, and they didn't win that one, either. But in the sixth inning, DiMaggio tripled into the left-field corner and that made it twenty-one games in a row.

At the other end of the star wars, Ted Williams was getting five hits in Cleveland that day, his batting average reached the stratosphere at .434, and his batting streak reached twenty-two games.

After all that great pitching, the Yankees probably rated a reward of sorts, and they got it when they arrived in St. Louis and started swinging at the Browns.

In the opening game of the series, DiMaggio got three singles, they scored five runs in the ninth, and they whacked the Browns, 11–7. The next day, in a Sunday doubleheader on June 8, he hit two home runs in the first game and a double and home run in the second, knocking in seven runs on the day. The Yankees swept, 9–3 and 8–3.

Meanwhile, in a doubleheader in Chicago that day, Ted Lyons and Thornton Lee stopped Ted Williams at twenty-three games. But he hit .487 during his streak, which was more of a reign of terror, and it seemed doubtful that any hitter in history had a better month at bat, anywhere, anytime.

Williams struck many people as self-centered and immobile, but he admitted later that he was far from detached about the streaking DiMaggio.

"Left field in Fenway Park," he said, "is where the scoreboard is. I got to be buddies with the guy who operated it, Bill Daley. He'd give me the word on what was going on around the league, all the scores and everything. When DiMaggio was on his hitting streak, Bill would keep track. He'd call out to me from his window in the scoreboard and say: 'Joe just got a double,' and I'd pass it on to Dom DiMaggio in center field."

Then, in a kind of soul-searching confession, he admitted: "I was always conscious of the *other* guy. Usually the guy was Joe DiMaggio."

But the man in the scoreboard wasn't the only person picking up on DiMaggio's day-to-day performance. As the streak and the Yankees both kept rolling, they began to attract newspaper and radio coverage in every city they visited. It was gradual, but it was steady, and even the other players on other teams started to notice that number 5 on the New York Yankees was building something extraordinary in its consistency and class.

They kept rolling on Monday, June 9, before a tiny crowd of 2,832 in Comiskey Park in Chicago. The Yankees got complete-game pitching from the rookie Steve Peek, who survived five hits and three runs in the home half of the ninth, mainly because the rest of the lineup had provided him with an eight-run lead. DiMaggio, meanwhile, survived yet another close call. He went without a hit into the seventh inning, then slammed a hard grounder toward third base, where it was stopped but not handled or thrown by Dario Lodigiani, an old family friend from San Francisco. The official scorer decided that the ball was too tough to handle, and the streak reached 25.

Then they took the show under the lights in Comiskey Park before a crowd of 27,102, and DiMaggio indulged in no suspense this time. He opened the fourth inning against Thornton Lee with a sharp single to left field, and that was that. The Yankees, however, needed some late drama to stay in the game, and they got it in the ninth when the remarkable Red Ruffing went to the plate once more as a pinch-hitter and promptly whacked a double off the left-field wall to tie the game.

It was still tied with two down in the tenth when DiMaggio went to bat and did the only thing any red-blooded American power hitter would do: He nailed Lee for a home run and a 3–2 victory for the Yankees.

Three days and two rainouts later, they opened in New York with two streaks on the line: Joe needed to hit in three more games to match the Yankees' club record of twenty-nine in a row, which was shared by Earl Combs and Roger Peckinpaugh, now the manager of the Indians. And the Yankees also had a home-run streak going: at least one a game for the last nine games.

Not only that, but Cleveland was fighting to hold first place against the New York streaks of all kinds, and they led with the ace, Bob Feller. For flourishes, the Indians opened the series with six straight victories, the Yankees with five.

All this was drama enough for the public, which responded with a crowd of 44,161 for the opener. And the teams responded with a bristling game that the Yankees won, 4–1. Beating Bob Feller was always one of life's milestone events, especially since he started the game with thirteen victories and three losses and with a streak of his own: eight straight. But in the third inning, DiMaggio glanced a double to right field, driving in a run and advancing his streak to twenty-seven.

Joe McCarthy, applying all the tactical advantage that he could apply against Feller, watched the count rise to three balls and no strikes and then flashed the "hit" sign to DiMaggio, who did exactly that.

It was the only hit he would deliver during the streak off Feller, who said later: "If it's not 3-and-0, he gets nothing fast from me. I put it over the plate to get a strike — and he hit the cripple."

The next day, a throng of 43,962 saw the Yankees win another close one, this time by 3–2, putting them within two games of first place and extending everybody's streak. Their winning streak rose to seven, DiMaggio's streak rose to twenty-eight when he hit a home run into the upper deck in left field in the third inning, and he also nudged the team's home-run streak to eleven games.

On the next day, DiMaggio doubled off Al Milnar in the fifth inning, tying Combs (who was coaching at first base for the Yankees) and Peckinpaugh (who was managing in the dugout for the Indians). The Yankees also hit a home run for the twelfth game in a row and won for the eighth game in a row, and closed the performance just one game behind the Indians in the pennant race.

The whole deck almost collapsed the next afternoon when the Chicago White Sox came to town and rallied to beat the Yankees, 8–7, ending their winning streak at eight games. They almost ended DiMaggio's streak, too. He was stopped cold by John Rigney and the streak seemed to be broken in the bottom of the seventh when he topped a ground ball toward shortstop straight at the senior picket, Luke Appling. But just as Appling reached for the ball, it took a bad hop and skipped off his shoulder into left field.

The 10,442 fans, both teams, and probably even the umpires turned and looked up at the press box, where the official scorer again was Dan Daniel. He and everybody else knew that this was it: either an error on Appling that would end the streak or a bad-hop single that would prolong it. Daniel deliberated a moment, held up his right index finger, and DiMaggio had a single, a club record, and thirty games in a row.

He kept it alive the next day with a bloop single just beyond Appling's lunge, and the day after that with a single off Edgar Smith, and the day after that with three singles and a double. By then, he had seven hits in a row in two days, including the last two in the same inning, and he also made a spectacular catch of a 450-foot drive to center field by Rudy York of the Detroit Tigers.

"I didn't really warm up about this thing," Joe said later, "until the thirty-third game."

Well, *that* was the thirty-third game, and they all started to seem memorable after that. The next day, June 21, he looped a single over York's head behind first base, and for the third straight day got a hit in his first time at bat. He also matched the 1938 streak of thirty-four games in a row by George McQuinn of the St. Louis Browns. And Phil Rizzuto hit a home run that carried the Yankees' long-ball streak to seventeen games, tying the major-league record set the year before by the Tigers.

They went to the brink again the next day, June 22, when they outscored and outlasted the Tigers, 5–4. DiMaggio didn't get a hit until the sixth inning, when Newhouser fired an outside fastball that he drove 370 feet to right-center for a home run. It was the thirty-fifth game in his hitting streak and the eighteenth game in the Yankees' home-run streak.

The Tigers still led Red Ruffing 4–3 with two down in the bottom of the ninth, but Red Rolfe hit a home run for a tie. And one inning into overtime, Bobo Newsom hit Henrich with a pitch, DiMaggio doubled into the left-field corner, Bill Dickey was walked intentionally to load the bases, and Newsom unintentionally walked Charlie Keller and forced home the winning run.

Two days later, the St. Louis Browns came to town and were muzzled by Lefty Gomez, 9–1. But DiMaggio meanwhile was being muzzled by Bob Muncrief. In the first inning, he grounded out lightly to Harlond Clift at third base. In the third, he fouled out to the catcher, Rick Ferrell. In the fifth, he took Muncrief deep to left-center, where Roy Cullenbine ran down the ball 450 feet from home plate.

They went to the home half of the eighth, and the Bronx Bombers did some late bombing, starting with a home run by Henrich. Then came DiMaggio, the streak on the line. He fouled off an inside pitch, took an inside ball, and then drilled a curveball over the head of Johnny Berardino at shortstop into left field.

Afterward, Joe was asked if it would "jinx" him to talk about the close call, and he said: "Heck, no. Voodoo isn't going to stop me. A pitcher will."

Luke Sewell, the manager of the Browns, went up to Muncrief afterward and asked: "Why didn't you walk DiMaggio the last time up to stop him?" And Muncrief replied: "That wouldn't have been fair. To him or to me. Hell, he's the greatest ballplayer I've ever seen."

DiMaggio made fast work of game number thirty-seven the following afternoon when he hit a two-run home run off Denny

Galehouse in the fourth inning. It was his sixteenth home run of the season and his eleventh in the thirty-seven games in the streak, and he also stretched the team's home-run string to twenty games. But more than that, he now had his gun sights directly trained on George Sisler's modern record of forty-one games in a row, and he seemed to be closing in.

But first he had to survive the closest call of all. It was Thursday, June 26, and Eldon Auker was snapping the submarine ball in and around and up and down. He got DiMaggio on a fly to left in the second inning. He got him on a grounder that Berardino booted at shortstop in the fourth. He got him again on a grounder in the sixth. And then they went to the eighth, with the Yankees leading 3–1, and it looked for all the world that he wouldn't get another chance to hit.

It looked even worse when Sturm popped out. But Rolfe worked Auker for a walk, Henrich went to bat, and DiMaggio walked to the on-deck circle, bat in hand. It was no secret to anybody in the stadium that if Henrich hit into a double play, the strcak would end.

Henrich, who knew this better than anybody, walked back to the dugout to consult Manager McCarthy, and got the green light to bunt. He promptly did, sending Rolfe to second and DiMaggio to the plate. Auker fired the sinker on the first pitch, and Joe lined it past Clift's dive at third base into the left-field corner for a last-gasp double.

Marius Russo, who was pitching for the Yankees that day, put things into perspective when he said: "I was pitching a no-hitter into the seventh inning. But nobody cared. They cared only for one thing: to see Joe get the hit."

Reprieved, DiMaggio quickly racked up No. 39 the next day with a first-pitch single in the first inning and later added a home run, his seventeenth, extending the team's streak to twenty-two games. And the day after that, he doubled off Johnny Babich in Philadelphia in the fourth inning and drew to within one game of Sisler's record.

Some sweet revenge spiced the day. Babich, who had beaten the Yankees *five* times the year before, had been quoted as saying he would give Joe nothing but "junk" to swing at. This was the same Johnny Babich who had grappled with Joe during his sixty-one-game streak in the Pacific Coast League eight years earlier. This time, he went to three balls and no strikes, DiMaggio got the green light from Art Fletcher, coaching at third base, and he rammed the next pitch past Babich's crotch into right-center for the double. Take *that.*

So the stage was set for high drama: two games in Griffith Stadium, Washington, D.C., on Sunday, June 29. One to tie Sisler, two to pass Sisler. And 31,000 fans crammed the old ballpark along with armies of writers straining to record some baseball history.

To make matters even stickier, Dutch Leonard was fluttering knuckleballs toward the Yankees, and he was unpredictable, pitch for pitch.

In the second inning, DiMaggio lined out to Roger Cramer in center. In the fourth, he went to 3 and 0 and got the green light again, but this time popped out to third base. But in the sixth, he went to one ball and one strike and then Leonard tried to sneak a rare fastball past him and Joe hammered it into left-center between Cramer and George Case, the ball skipping 422 feet to the bleacher fence for a double and a piece of Sisler's record.

It was a record Sisler had set as the first baseman for the St. Louis Browns in 1922, when he hit .459 in his forty-one games en route to hitting .420 for the full season.

Having caught Sisler at forty-one games, DiMaggio rested briefly between halves of the doubleheader and then walked into the dugout for the second game and found his "streak" bat missing from the rack along the box-seat railings next to the dugout. The bat was a thirty-six-inch, thirty-six-ounce Louisville Slugger with an ink mark on the bottom of the knob, and it was easy to spot because it was racked in the number four slot in the rack, which was arranged for each game in the same sequence as the batting order. He prized it the way King Arthur prized his cherished sword Excalibur.

Tommy Henrich, who had borrowed one of DiMaggio's "heavy" bats five weeks earlier, promptly gave it back now so that he would not be going to the plate fretting over the loss of his war club. But Joe was fretting even more after going without a hit the first three times he went to bat. The fourth time, in the seventh inning, against the right-handed Red Anderson, he took a brushback pitch high and tight for ball one, then got a fastball out over the plate and lined it to left field for a single and a baseball record: forty-two games in a row.

He often managed to sound trite or even obvious on landmark occasions, and he did it this time, too, saying to the assembled press corps: "Sure, I'm tickled. It's the most excitement I guess I've known since I came into the majors."

The Yankees then boarded the train for New York and celebrated in small ways: DiMaggio ordered beer for the entourage and said, without offering great insight: "I wanted that record." And George Sisler stayed in the same low-keyed mode when he was asked for his reaction and said: "I'm glad a real hitter broke it."

Almost eclipsed in the focus on the streak was the incidental achievement that the Yankees had now hit home runs in twenty-five games in a row. And because of all their streaks, individual and collective, after sweeping the doubleheader in Washington they moved one and a half games in front of the Indians in first place.

The next target was Willie Keeler's more or less ancient record of hitting in forty-four games in a row, which he set in 1897 with the Baltimore Orioles. If his strategy was truly to "hit 'em where they ain't," Keeler must have hit a lot of balls where they weren't that year: He got 239 hits and closed the season at .424.

Keeler's streak was more or less hidden in the folds of time because the playing rules had been revised dramatically since then and it would have been inexact, to say the least, to carry records over into the next century. But once the baseball archivists found the Keeler record, people accepted it as the next challenge and wasted no time getting obsessed with it. In fact, when the Yankees opened at home on Tuesday, July 1, they were greeted by a crowd of 52,832 fans *and* the mayor of the city, Fiorello H. La Guardia. And this was a Tuesday afternoon.

The afternoon featured two games with Boston and one more exercise in brinkmanship by DiMaggio. He went hitless into the fifth inning, then hit a grounder to third base, where Jim Tabor somehow couldn't pick it up cleanly and Joe outran the late throw. Guess who was calling the plays as the official scorer? That's right, Dan Daniel of the *World-Telegram,* who came through with a decision that saved the streak but offended the purists. He later wrote that "DiMaggio pasted that ball with every ounce of his strength." But his vehemence told some people that he was trying to build a case supporting his own decision.

However, not pleading for any favors at a time like this, DiMaggio got his old disciple off the hook again by delivering a clean single the next time he went to bat.

One streak died that day: the team's home-run roll ended at twenty-five games. But during the twenty-five games, DiMaggio had led the charge by hitting ten home runs himself.

In the second game of the doubleheader, rain ended things after five innings. But the Yankees were in front 9–2 by then, and DiMaggio had singled off Jack Wilson in the first inning, tying Wee Willie Keeler at forty-four games.

So, the record went on the line the next afternoon with 8,682 fans in Yankee Stadium and Lefty Gomez pitching against Dick Newsome, filling in for Lefty Grove, the senior eminence and pitching wizard, who had been weakened by the heat.

DiMaggio seemed to be settling the issue early, when he hit a line drive to deep right-center in the home half of the first inning, but Stan Spence made a remarkably gaudy catch for the out. The next time he went to bat, Joe grounded out to third. But in the fifth inning, he worked the count in his favor at two balls and no strikes and then smacked a high fastball over the fence in left field.

Gomez, the class wit, nodded a salute to Willie Keeler and quipped: "Joe hit one today where they ain't." And Joe McCarthy, giving a more solemn appraisal, said: "I don't believe anybody but a ballplayer is in a position to appreciate just what it means to hit safely in forty-five straight games."

The Yankees also were in a position to appreciate the fact that they had won six straight games now and led the league by three. And the next afternoon, DiMaggio punctuated his record by hitting a home run off Phil Marchildon of Philadelphia, and the Yankees roared on to make it seven straight and 21 of their last 25.

The clubhouse telephone rang the next day with a call for DiMaggio from an unidentified man who said: "I'm from Newark, New Jersey, and I know where your bat is. One of our guys pulled it from the rack for a souvenir. He didn't mean no harm. He loves you, Joe."

DiMaggio, not swept off his feet, replied: "I want it back." And he got it back with the help of an intermediary, his friend Jim Ceres, who was generally understood to have bought it back from the fan who "loves you, Joe."

Not that he needed any rejuvenation, but DiMaggio went out before 60,948 fans on Sunday, July 6, and joined his teammates and the Yankee family in the unveiling of a center-field monument to Lou Gehrig. Then he attacked Philadelphia pitching with three singles and a double in the first game of a doubleheader and later tripled and doubled in the second game. For the Yankees, the winning streak reached nine; for their leading man, the hitting streak reached forty-eight.

He was going so good by then that he even got a hit in the All-Star Game in Detroit later that week, a double in the eighth inning off Claude Passeau. It didn't count, of course. But it did count the next day in St. Louis when he hit three singles and a home run, his twentieth of the season.

The next day, he doubled off Eldon Auker. The day after that, he singled twice off Ted Lyons in Chicago. Then he singled off Ted Lyons in the first game of a doubleheader and singled off Thornton Lee in the second. The Yankees won their fourteenth straight, and his hitting streak reached fifty-three straight. And the day after that, he broke his prized bat on a pop fly but later swung a clone bat and singled. Then he singled in the next game off Edgar Smith and headed for Cleveland with the streak at fifty-five.

The series opened in the old League Park, where the Indians still played some of their games, and Joe singled hard off Al Milnar in the first inning. In the third, he looped a single to center field off Milnar. In the fourth, he doubled off Joe Krakauskas, the ninety-first hit in the streak, which stood now on a pinnacle at fifty-six games in a row.

The night it ended was Thursday, July 17, with a crowd of 67,468 watching in Municipal Stadium and with Joe's roommate Lefty Gomez pitching against lefty Al Smith. It was the largest crowd ever to see a night game in the major leagues, and they were witnesses to baseball drama and baseball history.

The drama began in the first inning when DiMaggio pulled a low inside curveball down the third-base line. It was a rocket, but Ken Keltner made a backhand stab behind the bag and fired long across the infield and threw him out. It was close at first base, but the ball won.

"He wasn't deep," DiMaggio remembered years later. "He was standing in left field. And I couldn't get out of the box quickly because it had rained the day before."

The second time up, Smith walked him — and the huge crowd booed. But the next time, in the seventh inning, Keltner was still playing in short left field, guarding the line and leaving open territory between himself and the shortstop, Lou Boudreau. If ever there was a "prevent" defense in baseball, this was it. And if ever there was a crossroads in baseball, DiMaggio was standing at one with his streak dangling.

The left-hander threw, and he pulled the ball with another roundhouse swing, rifling it where he had rifled it in the first inning: deep down the line, behind third base. But Keltner was there one more time, and he reached across his body, trapped it backhand on the short hop, and gunned him down by a step, one more time.

Was that it? Not quite. The fates, after smiling for two months, had one more perverse moment to inflict. And they inflicted it in the top of the eighth inning after the Yankees had scored two runs for a 4–1 lead and still had the bases loaded with one out, the right-handed Jim Bagby pitching and DiMaggio batting.

The count went to two balls and one strike, and Bagby threw a fastball that DiMaggio hit hard to deep shortstop. It was his third shot of the game to the left side of the infield, and this one even took a treacherous bounce as Boudreau lunged for it. But he somehow fielded it, cleanly and fatally for the streak, fired it to Ray Mack at second, Mack wheeled and fired to Oscar Grimes at first for a double play — and The Streak ended at fifty-six games.

"Well," DiMaggio said after the game, "I'm glad it's over."

So was the rest of the American League. During the streak, the Yankees won 41 games and lost 13 with two ties, charged from fourth place to first, went on to win 101 games and led the Red Sox on the final day of the season by 17 games while the Indians subsided to fourth place.

But the tumultuous events of that July 17 had a life of their own, John Drebinger wrote in *The New York Times:* "Tonight in Cleveland's Municipal Stadium, the great DiMag was held hitless for the first time in more than two months."

This is the story of The Streak in sheer numbers:

* It started on May 15 and ended two months later, on July 17, after 56 games.
* DiMaggio went to bat 223 times.

* He got 91 hits, including 16 doubles, 4 triples, and 15 home runs.
* He batted .408.
* He walked 21 times and was hit by pitches twice.
* He struck out only 7 times. (For the entire season, he went to bat 541 times and struck out 13 times.)
* He scored 56 runs in 56 games.
* He knocked in 55 runs in 56 games.
* When it started, the Yankees were fourth in the American League, five and a half games back. When it ended, they were first by six.

Bill Dickey, the Yankees' catcher, judged it this way: "He gave the most consistent performance under pressure I have ever seen."

"Joe was like Charley Gehringer," said Hank Greenberg. "He never seemed to have a bad day."

"I believe there isn't a record in the books that will be harder to break," said Ted Williams. "It may be the greatest batting achievement of all."

7

WAR AND PEACE

THE ONLY SANE THING to do after they stop your hitting streak, the only noble thing to do, is to start another streak. And that's precisely what DiMaggio did the day after he had been finally collared by Smith, Bagby, and Keltner. The very next afternoon, just a few hours after the clamorous night in Municipal Stadium, he showed that he still had the batting eye in focus when he singled and doubled off Bob Feller.

Cleveland actually won the game, and Feller won for the nineteenth time in a season in which he ultimately won twenty-five games. But DiMaggio kept hitting, with no sign of being spent or bored or jaded after his siege of two months, and he pieced together a mini-streak of sixteen more games until August 3, when he was stopped royally by the St. Louis Browns, of all teams. He went 0 for 4 in the first game of a doubleheader and 0 for 4 in the second game. When the Browns got you out eight times in a row, you simply had a lost afternoon. But he still had hit in seventy-two of his last seventy-three games, and there was nothing shabby about that.

"It was terrific, the reaction of the fans and all," he said years later, retracing his steps into the baseball history books. "But the thing that touched me even more deeply was what happened at the Shoreham Hotel in Washington, D.C., a month or so after the streak had come to an end in Cleveland.

"I was getting spruced up for dinner in my hotel room, and Lefty Gomez, my roommate, was shining his shoes.

" 'Hey, Joe,' he hollered across the room, 'I'm tired of tagging around with you to all those banquets you're invited to. Tonight you're going where I want, okay?'

" 'Okay,' I said, 'but shake a leg. I'm starved.'

"I've never seen Lefty go through so many wind-ups getting dressed as he did that evening. His shine took fifteen minutes alone. Finally, he was ready and we got in the elevator. But instead of going down to the lobby, we got off at the fourth floor. He said we'd stop and pick up George Selkirk for dinner and a movie. We walked down the hall and Lefty opened the door to a big suite of rooms and told me to go in.

"The whole team was gathered there waiting for me. I was surprised speechless. A testimonial to one player from all his teammates in midseason doesn't happen more than once in a lifetime. But they were all there waiting, and they gave me a beautiful silver Tiffany humidor with a gold figure of me batting on the lid, and the signature of every member of the team engraved inside. They also had gotten permission from Joe McCarthy and the owners of the club for each of us to drink one glass of champagne. And they all lifted their glasses to me and sang, 'For He's a Jolly Good Fellow.'

"I stumbled through a speech of thanks. But it didn't seem to say exactly what was in my heart: that the Yankee club was my home, and every man in that room was more than my teammate. He was my friend and brother."

If this reaction seemed more eloquent than usual for a silent and almost Sphinx-like person, it was prompted by a far more eloquent gesture than usual from the Yankees. Beneath the gold figure of Joe swinging the bat, the number "56" was engraved in the silver, and below that the inscription: "Presented to Joe DiMaggio by his fellow players on the New York Yankees to express their admiration for his consecutive-game hitting streak, 1941."

By the time they rang down the curtain on the season, the Yankees were seventeen full lengths in front of the Boston Red Sox, and the other numbers were just as extravagant. DiMaggio had 30 home runs, he led both major leagues by driving in 125 runs, and he closed with a batting average of .357. And for the pièce de résistance, he also outpolled Ted Williams in the annual vote by the baseball writers and was elected the league's Most Valuable Player.

Not everybody agreed with that, especially since Williams closed with a batting average of .406 with 37 home runs and 120 runs batted in. And on the final day of the season, he gave one of the great professional performances in the annals of the sport.

He went into the final day with an average that carried out to .39955. So he could have sat out the doubleheader scheduled that day and settled for a rounded-off batting mark of .400. But Williams was a perfectionist in the science of hitting, and he was obsessed with the need to put his theories to the only proof that mattered, so he insisted on playing in both games.

They were in Philadelphia that closing day, and old Connie Mack rose to the occasion with a fine feel for the history that might be unfolding. The Athletics were first in the hearts of their countrymen, at least their countrymen in Philadelphia, but they were last in the American League with a record of 64 victories and 90 defeats. They won thirty-seven fewer games that year than the Yankees.

Tom Ferrick, who won eight games for Mr. Mack that season as a card-carrying, scar-carrying member of a pitching staff under constant attack, remembered years afterward how they had approached the confrontation with Ted Williams and his personal rendezvous with history.

"Mr. Mack got us together in the locker room before the doubleheader," Ferrick told me, sounding like a Desert Rat who had marched with Montgomery and the British Eighth Army. "And he told us very seriously: 'Gentleman, there is a man on the Boston club who has a chance to hit .400 for the season. Give him your best stuff. But don't walk him. Give him a fair chance to do what he has to do.'

"We gave him a fair chance, all right, and that was a fatal mistake. We all pitched to him the best we could. But we never saw so many line drives crashing all over Shibe Park. We did our damndest, and Ted got six hits."

He got six hits, all right. Four hits in the opener, two in the second game. Four singles, one double, one home run. He nailed everything we threw up there."

And he raised his batting average six points with his six hits, and closed his own season's performance at .406.

If Ted Williams was outraged that these lavish numbers earned him only second place in the voting for postseason honors, he didn't go public with his outrage. In fact, in seven years' time, he lost three elections to the Yankees for Most Valuable Player. But he still was able to look back on those lost causes with unusual clinical detachment.

"In 1941, when I hit .406," he remembered, "Joe DiMaggio was named the MVP and I didn't feel robbed or cheated because DiMaggio had that 56-game hitting streak and he was a great player on a great team that won the pennant.

"Funny it should work out that way, but it was pointed out to me later that over that same 56-game period, Joe hit .408 and I hit .412."

The ballots for personal honors must be cast immediately after the close of the regular season, so nothing that happens in the World Series counts in those elections. But the Yankees in those days did few things in the Series to tarnish the memory of what they did in the regular season. And that was dramatically true in 1941.

DiMaggio batted only .263, but nothing he did could tarnish the memory of his season of streaks. And the Yankees collectively handled the Brooklyn Dodgers with a kind of mastery. They held the Dodgers to a team batting average of .182, and their leading hitter, Joe Medwick, to .235. Pete Reiser was the only member of the Dodgers who hit a home run. Joe Gordon, meanwhile, was hitting an even .500 for the Yankees.

In the opening game, he hit a home run and knocked in two runs as Ruffing outpitched Curt Davis, 3–2. There was a pause while the Dodgers were rebounding to take the second game by the same score, with Dolph Camilli driving in Dixie Walker with a single for the winning run and Whitlow Wyatt outpitching Spud Chandler. But after that, the Dodgers self-destructed with spectacular flair.

In the third game, they held the Yankees in the grip of a scoreless game into the eighth inning, with Fred Fitzsimmons pitching against Marius Russo. But in the top of the eighth at Ebbets Field, the Yankees broke the grip: DiMaggio and Keller singled in two quick runs for the ball game. And in the fourth game, the Dodgers carried a 4–3 lead into the ninth inning with Hugh Casey protecting it in relief, and then came unraveled in one of baseball's least likely and most theatrical revivals.

With two down in the ninth and nobody on base, and the crowd starting to stream toward the exits, Casey went to three balls and two strikes on Tommy Henrich and then fired a breaking ball that Henrich flailed at but didn't touch. Many baseball people still aren't certain whether the ball was wet or dry, but all baseball people are certain it was a swinging strike three. And it would have ended the game and tied the Series if Mickey Owen, the catcher, had caught it. But he didn't, and he chased the ball toward the box seats while Henrich alertly ran to first base — a strikeout victim reprieved by a passed ball that lives in Dodger infamy.

The Dodgers still could have spared themselves the ultimate red face by getting somebody to hit a ground ball or pop fly for the *final* final out. But before they got anybody else out, the Yankees struck like a typhoon: DiMaggio lined a single to left field, Keller whipped a double off the wall in right for two runs and the lead, Dickey walked, Gordon doubled for two more runs, and the toll mounted to 7-4 as the Dodgers paid the full price for not catching their maddeningly elusive third strike.

The next day, Ernie Bonham outpitched Wyatt, 3-1, and the Dodgers suffered the last full measure of self-sacrifice.

The New York Times turned to the ace of its writing staff, Meyer Berger, to etch the fourth game into history. And he responded with a parody of "Casey at the Bat" under the heading "Casey in the Box — 1941." It opened with these verses:

The prospects all seemed rosy for the Dodger nine that day.
Four to three the score stood, with one man left to play.
And so, when Sturm died and Rolfe the Red went out,
In the tall weeds in Canarsie, you could hear the Dodgers shout.

Half a dozen stanzas below, Mike Berger depicted Casey firing the fateful pitch for strike three, and in these words roared to a crescendo:

But Mickey Owen missed this strike. The ball rolled far behind,
And Henrich speeded to first base, like Clipper on the wind.
Upon the stricken multitude, grim melancholy perched.
Dark disbelief bowed Hughie's head. It seemed as if he lurched.

DiMaggio got a single. Keller sent one to the wall.
Two runs came pounding o'er the disk, and all this wasn't all.
For Dickey walked and Gordon a resounding double smashed.
And Dodger fans were sickened. All Dodger hopes were bashed.

Oh, somewhere north of Harlem, the sun is shining bright.
Bands are playing in the Bronx, and up there hearts are light.
In Hunts Point, men are laughing. On the Concourse, children shout.
But there is no joy in Flatbush. Fate has knocked their Casey out.

* * *

But satire didn't dominate the mood for very long. Momentous events were taking shape, and they gave a tumultuous ending to a year that was already tumultuous enough.

The DiMaggios were then living at 400 West End Avenue on the Upper West Side of Manhattan before moving to another apartment at 241 Central Park West. It was the first time since he left San Francisco that Joe had not lived in a hotel. And his new role as a family man took on a new dimension two weeks after the Series, on October 23, when Dorothy gave birth to Joseph Paul DiMaggio Jr., his namesake and only heir.

Six weeks later, Japanese warplanes attacked Pearl Harbor, the Far East and Pacific basin exploded into combat, the United States declared war on both Japan and Germany — and Mickey Owen's muffed third strike didn't seem so memorable or meaningful, after all.

DiMaggio's draft board back in San Francisco bestowed a 3-A rating on him in view of his family status, which meant that he was not likely to be inducted in the immediate future. But the war made quick inroads into his life, as it did into millions of lives, and baseball suddenly lost all of its frolic and most of its fantasy.

His mother and father took out their first papers for citizenship in February 1942 but were not actually naturalized until after the war had ended three years later. Meanwhile, the fishing fleet in San Francisco was effectively beached by a War Department edict that ordered no fishing boat to venture outside the Golden Gate. And business at the family restaurant, Joe DiMaggio's Grotto on Fisherman's Wharf, was dwindling as travel and tourism kept dwindling. His brother Tom, still the supervisor of the family finances, wrote to Joe that business was slowing to a standstill.

Joe didn't say much about his draft status or his next contract, but he did say that he had bought five thousand dollars' worth of war bonds, "and I intend to go right on buying them as the pay checks come in."

He also didn't say much about the paychecks, either, probably because he was girding for the perennial battle of wits with Ed Barrow of the Yankees, who had signed him the year before for $37,500 and who now faced the problem of signing him again after a season of runaway success for both the team and the star in center field.

To the naked eye, even with a world war shattering lives and values, it might seem that DiMaggio confronted Barrow with some extraordinary credentials. Not only had he been voted the league's Most Valuable Player for the second time in three years, but he had outpolled Williams, Feller, and Thornton Lee in that order, and the only other Yankees who finished in the top ten were Charlie Keller and Joe Gordon.

But he even transcended that distinction when the year-end reviews were made public and he led the Associated Press poll for outstanding athlete of 1941 in any sport, and he led it by a two-to-one margin over Williams. In the two previous years, the college football stars Tommy Harmon of Michigan and Nile Kinnick of Iowa had won. But baseball held center stage this year, and its two virtuoso performers won top billing.

After DiMaggio and Williams, the ranking went like this: Joe Louis, the heavyweight champion; Craig Wood, the U.S. Open golf champion; Don Hutson, the legendary pass-catching end of the Green Bay Packers; Bruce Smith, the all-American running back from the University of Minnesota; Cornelius Warmerdam, the world record holder in the pole vault; and then Frank Sinkwich, Bill Dudley, and Coach Frank Leahy of Notre Dame in football. And if there was any doubt about the preeminence of DiMaggio and Williams during a season of stratospheric success, they ran far in front of Joe Louis even though he had defended his title *seven* times during the year.

"The strain of the streak was terrific," DiMaggio admitted later. "When I hit in 61 games in a row my first year with San Francisco, nothing bothered me in those days. Besides, it happened in the minor leagues, and nobody paid much attention to

Joe DiMaggio's mother and father, Giuseppe Paolo and Rosalie, who came to America from Italy at the turn of the century, toast what they had wrought: nine children, three major-league baseball players, and the last American knight.

But Joe looked more like a dude when he arrived with the New York Yankees in 1936. (*The New York Times*)

He also arrived with a counselor: brother Tom DiMaggio, who counseled Joe into confrontations with Col. Jacob Ruppert, owner of the Yankees. The issue: money. (Ernest Sisto, *The New York Times*)

Above, left: Showgirl Dorothy Arnold, whom Joe married in 1939, became a decorative addition to Yankee Stadium and, in 1941, the mother of Joe Jr.

Above: It was 1936, and the Empire Days were flourishing, from the missing Babe Ruth to the aging Lou Gehrig to the youthful Joe DiMaggio.

Left: And, armed with a steady supply of talented players, like the power-hitting Charlie Keller, the Yankees rolled on to new heights. (*The New York Times*)

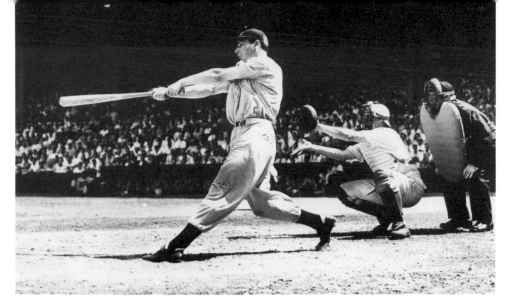

1941 was the year of The Streak, when Joe hit in fifty-six games in a row, including this home run against the Philadelphia Athletics. (The Associated Press)

During the streak, the Yankees rose from fourth place to first, and kept going. It finally ended on the night of July 17 in Cleveland, mainly because Ken Keltner made two dazzling plays at third base. (*The New York Times*)

Man of the hour: Joe and the Yankees salute The Streak, from Frank Crosetti, left, to manager Joe McCarthy, right. (United Press International)

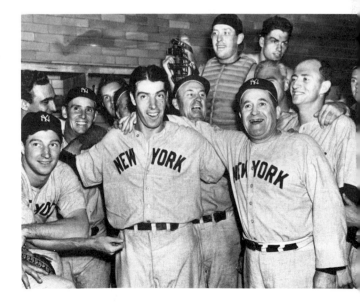

But something else happened in 1941:
Pearl Harbor. And early in 1943, DiMaggio
raised his right hand in San Francisco and
joined the Army Air Forces.
(The Associated Press)

Back to the ballpark with Ted Williams,
the pride of Fenway Park and Joe's
archrival. (The Associated Press)

In 1948, Joe underwent heel surgery at
Johns Hopkins and didn't recover until the
middle of the 1949 season. Then he
recovered with a roar, leading the Yankees
to a dramatic confrontation with the
Boston Red Sox. They were down by one
game with two to play, but everybody
stopped to pay tribute to the Yankee
Clipper: his mother, his son, his brother
Dominic, center fielder for the Red Sox.
The Yankees won the final two, and won
the pennant.

Casey Stengel, who won 10 pennants in 12
years as manager of the Yankees, and Joe
DiMaggio, who won 10 pennants in 13
years as master of the Yankees. Despite
the success and the smiles, their
relationship was strained. (Ernest Sisto,
The New York Times)

Marilyn Monroe entered DiMaggio's life after he retired. They were married for nine months in 1954, but Joe was never comfortable with Marilyn's role in life. The marriage unraveled after the famous subway-grating scene was shot for the film *The Seven Year Itch.* (United Press International)

But in later years, whenever Marilyn needed support against the demons of Hollywood and her world, she turned to Joe—and he responded, as in 1961 at the Yankee spring training camp in St. Petersburg, Florida. (United Press International)

He responded with his greatest gallantry and grief after her death in 1962, when he took charge of her funeral. The marine at the far right: Joe DiMaggio Jr. (The Associated Press)

Back in the embrace of baseball with fellow Hall of Fame stars from the Yankee years: Mickey Mantle, Yogi Berra, Whitey Ford, and Casey Stengel. (The Associated Press)

Or back with his brothers, where it all began: Vince, Joe, and Dominic of the San Francisco Seals. (The Associated Press)

For a while, Joe even served as a coach with the Oakland Athletics, where he shared the wisdom of the ages with Reggie Jackson. (United Press International)

He also tried to share the wisdom of the ages with Joe Jr., who was a nineteen-year-old freshman at Yale. (The Associated Press)

In cap and gown of Columbia blue, looking pleased but wary, DiMaggio gets an honorary degree and great attention. (Chester Higgins, *The New York Times*)

Where have you gone, Joe DiMaggio? The Bowery Savings Bank found out, and revived his career by making him the star of its TV commercials. Yes, kids with gloves at Yankee Stadium. (Ernest Sisto, *The New York Times*)

Joe DiMaggio takes a final curtain call: a man and his memories.
(Vic DiLucia, *The New York Times*)

me. There were no big crowds, no fans waiting outside the park, no writers interviewing me every day."

He reflected a moment on the "next" time he kept hitting for two months, and said: "If I say it myself, that fifty-six-game streak was a good trick. That's one job the boys are not going to beat while I'm around."

But neither streak nor success nor World Series comebacks could stay the tight fist of Ed Barrow, who pinched pennies with the zeal of a man on a mission during a time when the dynamics of finance in professional sports was as primitive and one-sided as it later became complex and many-sided. So, surrounded by the spoils of his grandest season, and persuaded that a $12,500 raise to the nice round level of $50,000 would not be irrational, DiMaggio was stunned when his new contract arrived in the mail and he read that Barrow was offering him a *cut* of $5,000 in his pay.

Ed Barrow was a tall, tailored, bushy-browed man who won a pennant in his first year as manager of the Boston Red Sox in 1918 and who then followed his prize pupil Babe Ruth to the Yankees two years later as business manager. He brought with him to New York the sense of urgency in money matters that had grown over the years in Boston: Every time Harry Frazee, the owner of the Red Sox, invested in another Broadway musical comedy, there was a pretty good chance that another crisis was developing. He solved the ultimate crisis by selling his ultimate player, Babe Ruth, to the Yankees. And the watchdog of the treasury soon followed.

Barrow opened his unlikely skirmishing with DiMaggio that winter by issuing a release to the newspapers expressing his disdain that his number one player wanted "a big raise while American soldiers are making $21 a month." In other words, if there was anything bigger than Joe DiMaggio, it was the war. He was right about that, of course, but he was wrong to invoke the war to stack the deck so bluntly.

One generation later, it would have been unthinkable for a

team to play hardball with its preeminent player after a career
year that included a fifty-six-game hitting streak, a pennant, victory in the World Series, and the Most Valuable Player Award.
But until 1975, when the players won the right to become free
agents, they were "reserved" from one year to another by the
"reserve clause" in their contracts: Even if they didn't agree to
sign the next contract, they and their services were "reserved"
in perpetuity to their team. You could hold out, and not report
for work; you also could sit home and not be paid.

DiMaggio even agreed years later that if he had been playing
with the immense leverage of the free-agent system, he could
have walked into the front office and announced to George Stein-
brenner, the freewheeling owner: "Hello, partner." But lacking
that ultimate weapon in his public tilting with Ed Barrow, especially at a time when other ballplayers were already enlisting in
the military forces, he settled the argument and signed for a raise
of $5,000 for 1942.

But 1942 proved to be a difficult and even fateful year. It was
his seventh as a member of the Yankees, and it was his last until
the war ended three years later. So it marked the end of the
beginning of his baseball career; and, unfortunately, the beginning of the end of his marriage to Dorothy Arnold.

He was twenty-eight years old now and he was hitting thirty-
one home runs a year on the average and batting .339, recognized as the best talent on a team crammed with talent. He also
seemed one of the more vulnerable talents on the team: In those
seven seasons, he had missed ninety-seven games.

But in 1942, as the curtain came down on the first half of his
career, he played in all 154 games for the first time. And, although he didn't ring as many bells or set as many memorable
marks as he did the year before, he still hit .305 with 21 home
runs and drove in 114 runs. The performance totals were notice-
ably below his peaks, but the Yankees had plenty of firepower
and won the pennant by nine games over the Red Sox, and then
careened into yet another World Series.

They had won seven Series in seven appearances in fifteen years, and they didn't particularly expect to end that streak of success against the St. Louis Cardinals, who had to win 106 games to win the National League pennant over the Brooklyn Dodgers, who won 104 and still finished second. But the Cardinals came with a full cast of professionals led by the rookie Stan Musial, Enos Slaughter, Marty Marion, Walker Cooper, his brother Morton Cooper, Whitey Kurowski, Terry Moore, Johnny Beazley, Howie Pollet, and Max Lanier. The manager was Billy Southworth, and the Cardinals showed no sign of intimidation or even reasonable respect as they dethroned the Yankees in five games. They were the first team to beat the Yankees in the Series since old Grover Cleveland Alexander and the rest of the Cardinals did it in 1926.

Two months after the Series, on December 3, his life took the inevitable turn when he enlisted in the Army Air Forces in San Francisco. But an even bigger turn was taking shape in his life: His wife had engaged a lawyer.

They cared for each other, and they showed it during several attempts at a reconciliation. They even shared the tugging pressure of their son, "Little Joe" to the public, barely thirteen months old. But they also shared the strain of DiMaggio's priorities: He was devoted but distracted.

"We had a home," Dorothy said later. "I wanted to make it a nice home. But he was never there."

For all these reasons, military and domestic and professional, DiMaggio was showing a kind of malaise that had surfaced during the baseball season. He even showed signs of shortness with writers from home. Prescott Sullivan of the *San Francisco Examiner,* who went on to become one of the wry titans of life in the city on the Bay, buttonholed him the day after the Yankees announced they would not hold spring training in St. Petersburg because of wartime restrictions on travel.

Sullivan started to ask how the Yankees would be affected if they didn't take the customary training in Florida, and DiMaggio replied: "It won't concern me next year." Sullivan asked more questions, and Joe also didn't answer them directly. Finally, Sullivan popped the big question: Are you trying to have a reconciliation with your wife. And DiMaggio snapped: "It's none of your business."

"Joe was kind of a cold guy, everybody knows that," Tommy Henrich told Maury Allen years later, analyzing his old teammate's moods. "He never asked me to go out to dinner alone in all the years I was with the Yankees.

"There was never anything wrong between us. We would ride in a cab to the ball park together or dress next to each other, or sit down on the train together, but we never really kidded around a lot. Joe wasn't the type you kidded around with. He roomed with Gomez, and Gomez was the only person I ever saw who could get away with it. Lefty would make fun of him or call him a silly name, and Joe would just laugh. Nobody else could get away with that. Nobody else would try."

One other person would try, and he always got away with it: Pete Sheehy, the majordomo of the clubhouse. He kept DiMaggio supplied with cups of coffee, almost nonstop, and served loyally as valet and aide-de-camp. He was a partisan, and he set and enforced the pecking order in the locker room with all the impunity of a man who was there before *they* arrived and who would still be there after they left. He may have run errands, as he did for Ruth and Gehrig in the early years and for Mantle and Maris in the later years. But he didn't run scared. It was his clubhouse, and DiMaggio was the star tenant.

DiMaggio once had a red mark on his backside and was examining it on the bench near his locker. He called out to Sheehy, his jack-of-all-trades: "Hey, Pete, take a look at this. Is there a bruise there?" And Sheehy, not cringing before the gods, said smartly: "Sure there is, Joe. It's from all those people kissing your ass."

Lefty Gomez, who dared to tweak the great DiMaggio on a higher social plane, as it were, remembered his running mate as a reclusive youngster who arrived on the team with personal mystery and who pretty much stayed that way over the seasons.

"He was just a kid from San Francisco, as I was," Gomez said, "and we stayed together. We called Lazzeri 'Big Dago,' and Crosetti 'Little Dago.' When Joe came to the club in 1936, we called him just 'Dago.'

"You remember the sports broadcaster Arch McDonald? He began calling Joe 'the Yankee Clipper,' and it stuck.

"Everybody knew that Joe didn't talk much. We took a two-week road trip once to Chicago, Cleveland, Detroit and St. Louis, and I swear he didn't say one word. He'd carry one of those small radios and listen to the big-band music and those old quiz shows. He'd read the sports pages in the newspaper, nothing more, and he'd even read *Superman* comics.

"Mostly, he was quiet. Sort of mysterious. You never knew what he was thinking."

But Gomez had the charm and the daring, merry nature to probe the mystery, and he did it regularly.

"Joe loved to play a shallow center field," he said. "He knew he could go back and run down the ball. But he always played too shallow — especially when I was pitching.

"Once, he was playing just behind second base on Rudy York, who could hit as deep as anybody, and I kept telling Joe to play back. He'd say don't worry, he was the new Tris Speaker, just like the newspapers were saying. And don't you know, late in the game York bombs one like a shot off the golf tee. DiMaggio gets a great jump on the ball, but it carries way over his head and rolls to the fence, and we lost the game.

"He finally comes over to me and says, 'Lefty, I'm sorry about that ball. I know I should have caught it. But I'm still going to make them forget Tris Speaker.'

" 'You keep playing shallow like that,' I told him, 'and you'll make them forget Lefty Gomez.' "

But banter was not one of DiMaggio's specialties, even though he tolerated it from compulsive wits like Gomez. He remained more of "the cold guy" remembered by Henrich, and Charlie Keller confirmed the image of aloof privacy.

"Joe and I never really went around together," he said. "We'd have an occasional beer and sandwich after a game, but he went his way and I went mine. The relationship with Joe and the other guys wasn't close. He was a solid guy and, if anybody needed help or advice, Joe was there. But the relationship wasn't close."

Unfortunately, neither was Joe's relationship with his wife. On January 13, 1943, they met the press together in Reno, where she had gone to establish residency for a divorce suit. Joe joined her and their son, went to great lengths to patch their problems, and then announced: "We had a few differences of a personal nature. That's all behind us now."

It seemed like a fair assessment when he reported to the Army reception center at Santa Clara Army Air Field in southern California one month later. It was February 17, and the pressure was now squarely on the marriage as it teetered. Dorothy and Joe Jr. moved to Los Angeles "so we can see each other frequently." But time was running out.

Eight months later, on October 11, she finally filed for divorce in Los Angeles, asking $500 a month in alimony and $150 in child support. She told the court that she estimated his income at $50,000 in 1942 and at $12,000 in 1943 when he was in the Army. She charged cruelty, specifically that he had ruined their marriage by "cruel indifference" and had "never acted like a married man." She added that she had hoped their son's birth would have made him "realize his responsibilities as a married man" but concluded that "even the baby's arrival did not change him."

DiMaggio, who by now was suffering from stomachaches and even the onset of ulcers, did not contest the divorce. And after four and a half years of marriage, the breakup was made official early in 1944. She was back in court eight years later asking for more child support, but the judge denied the request and even berated her, saying she had "made a mistake" divorcing him in the first place.

That was easy for the judge to say, of course, but he might have had a hard time proving his point. DiMaggio could be gallant in manner, courtly, even noble. But he also became set in his bachelor ways, did not yield them gracefully, and apparently tried to maintain them despite his marriage. He cherished the notion of being married, especially to a beautiful actress, but he wasn't much for detail. And he also cherished his independence, his lifestyle, his circle, and his role as the toast of the town.

The Air Force, which was then still a branch of the Army, might have intruded even more on his style of living. But after his draft board in North Beach announced that he was enlisting in the Air Force in February 1943, he was treated with all due respect as a celebrity who might just hit a few home runs for God and country.

In fact, he played briefly for the Santa Ana baseball team, then shipped out to Honolulu as a staff sergeant and, to put it bluntly, as the center fielder for the Seventh Air Force team, which had been assembled with precision by Brig. Gen. William Flood, a commanding officer and baseball zealot of the first rank.

The general also conscripted Mike McCormick of the Cincinnati Reds, Walt Judnich of the St. Louis Browns, Gerry Priddy of the Washington Senators, and Ferris Fain and Charlie Silvera, who were apprentices headed for the major leagues.

Generals and admirals all over the world were handpicking baseball and football teams in those days with the kind of care and intensity that they might exert in handpicking a commando unit. Ted Williams played at the Pensacola Naval Air Station in Florida, although he made more significant contributions to the war effort as a pilot — in both World War II and the Korean War. The Great Lakes Naval Air Station fielded one of the best football teams on any front. And tens of thousands of Air Force cadets passed through Maxwell Field in Montgomery, Alabama, where they underwent long and arduous tests to determine who should be classified as pilots or bombardiers or navigators — but only nine made the starting lineup of the all-star baseball team that had been gathered and classified by the commanding general with similar zeal. At the height of the war, Maxwell Field faced its baseball enemies with this starting pitching rotation: Royce Lint, who would pitch for the Pittsburgh Pirates after the war; Mel Parnell, who would pitch for the Boston Red Sox after the war; Bill McCahan, who would pitch a no-hitter for the Philadelphia Athletics after the war, and George Turbeville, who had already made some history as the man who pitched the ball that Joe DiMaggio hit for his first home run as a rookie back in 1936.

The Seventh Air Force team was so good that it drew a crowd of 20,000 when it played a game against a Navy team in June of 1944, and the Navy team arrived with artillery, too. It had Johnny Mize at first base and Pee Wee Reese at shortstop. But the man in the spotlight was DiMaggio, who responded by whacking a home run that traveled 450 feet, at least according to people who were watching (and hoping that DiMaggio would hit one 450 feet).

Years later, I remember asking Pee Wee Reese when he had first heard of Jackie Robinson, and he said: "I was coming home from the war, sitting on the deck of the big transport ship, coming back from the Pacific, and I was reading a newspaper, maybe *Stars and Stripes.* They had this article about college baseball stars, and they said the best of them was this guy from UCLA named Jackie Robinson. He was an all-around athlete, he was a Negro, he was headed for the Brooklyn Dodgers — *my* team — and he played shortstop — *my* position."

When Robinson arrived in Brooklyn two years later and made major history as the first black player in the major leagues, the Dodgers counted their blessings, played their new star at second base and third, and kept Reese where he belonged at shortstop.

Honolulu wasn't exactly New York, and the Seventh Air Force wasn't exactly the American League, but the military life (even the military baseball life) still put pressure on DiMaggio, and especially on DiMaggio's stomach. It was already six months after his divorce, but he was still pining for his wife and son. He was trapped: He was a romantic slave who had neither his wife nor his freedom, nor the lifestyle that made his wife incompatible with his freedom.

His stomach sent the first signals, and in August he was admitted to a military hospital in Hawaii with a recurrence of the ulcers that had flared during his first rounds of hassling with Dorothy Arnold. One month later, he was reassigned to the Air Transport Command, which ferried troops and supplies all over the world and in this part of the world ran a shuttle service between California and Honolulu. But the change of assignment did nothing to change his mood, and in October he was sent to the Fourth Air Force Hospital in California for more treatment.

Three weeks later, he still had the pain, but he also had a three-week furlough. And he used it to fly east and pursue Dorothy and Joe Jr. in New York, where they were living again, and to return to Toots Shor's and the other Manhattan shrines where he had ruled as the resident god. Things could hardly get better, but they did: Next he was assigned to something called the Redistribution Center in Atlantic City, where, by the most remarkable (and suspicious) coincidence and intervention of the supreme powers, the Yankees were booked into spring training in 1945. And Joe spent the next six months there in the physical training section with sergeant's stripes on his sleeve and often with a baseball bat in his hands.

The ulcers didn't improve much, but his good fortune kept improving as the war in Europe ended and the war in the Pacific wound down. As it was ending in August, he received one more assignment *de luxe*. He was sent to the most splendid treatment center of all, the pink palace on St. Petersburg Beach in Florida named the Don Cesar, once the palatial hotel home of the rich and famous in the 1920s and later the spring-training home away from home for the New York Yankees. They were sequestered there ostensibly for isolation from the temptations of downtown

St. Pete, but isolating the Yankees in their glory days was no simple task, even though nobody was allowed to drive a car (except Babe Ruth) and nobody was allowed to travel with his wife on the team train (except Babe Ruth).

You know, war is hell. But DiMaggio's war, such as it was, now was counting down. On September 14, he was discharged. On November 20, he was back in New York signing his first baseball contract in three years. He was almost thirty-one years old and home at last, back on the block.

But the block had undergone major landscaping since the boys went marching off and later came back as wiser, sadder, and slower men. Even the owners of the Yankees were new. The club now was in the hands of a triumvirate that was as strange and flamboyant as old Colonel Ruppert had been dated and dull. They were Dan Topping, the stereotype of "the sportsman," once married to the ice-skating star Sonja Henie and now, in 1946, married for the fourth time; Del Webb, the stereotype of "the developer," who developed communities as well as buildings and who held memberships in fourteen golf clubs, and Larry MacPhail, the stereotype of "the impresario," who led a mission impossible to capture the Kaiser Wilhelm in Germany during World War I and who later succeeded in creating tumult as the baseball Barnum in Cincinnati and Brooklyn before whirling on to the Yankees.

They welcomed DiMaggio home with open arms and open checkbooks, but the transition from war to peace quickly proved to be bumpy as all sixteen teams in the big leagues greeted their returning players and wondered if they could still play. In the Yankees' case, the answer was mixed. DiMaggio was promptly restored as the team's titan, but he had missed three summers and showed it. He hit twenty home runs in the first forty-one games, and only five for the rest of the season. He also hit only .290, which was low for him, and missed twenty-two games with a series of injuries. The most telling injury came when he sprained his knee sliding into second base in Philadelphia just before the All-Star Game, and he also began to feel pain in his right heel. It was caused by calcium deposits, and it forced him to take something off his controlled fury both at bat and in the field, and it even forced him to take something off his line-drive throws.

"They conceded him perfection," Jimmy Cannon wrote, "but they took it out on him when they detected a temporary flaw in his skill."

"I'm tired of being called a sourpuss," Joe said, reacting to the early signs of criticism or, at least, of murmuring. "I'm learning to take all that stuff, and I guess maybe, if I could relax and smile a little more, it would be better all around."

But he was finding it hard to relax and smile at anything. In the second month of the season, Joe McCarthy, his only manager since his rookie season ten years before, resigned to escape the nagging from MacPhail, who said indelicately that the manager was "drinking too much." Then Bill Dickey took over the team, and when Dickey decided it was a bad fit, Johnny Neun became the third man to manage the Yankees that season. But the departure of McCarthy rocked the empire the most. "He was," DiMaggio lamented, "like a father to most of us."

The father was long since gone by the time the Yankees straggled home in third place behind Boston and Detroit. Two years later, adding to the tension and the rivalry between the teams, he made a dramatic switch and became manager of the Red Sox. But for now he was one of the prominent victims of baseball's uneven transition to the postwar era.

But if DiMaggio's spirit was wounded by the tide of changes, his body was wounded even more as the seasons rolled past. In 1947, he signed for $43,750, the same money he had received the year before. But a few days later, on January 7, he was back in the hospital for surgery to remove a three-inch bone spur from his left heel, the "other" heel. And when the heel didn't mend by the time the Yankees went to spring training, another operation was performed on March 11. In that one, to enhance his recovery, a patch of skin was grafted from his right leg onto his right heel. Time was starting to take its toll.

The Yankees opened the 1947 season with another new manager, Bucky Harris, their fourth in little more than a year. He rested DiMaggio for the first four days to give the heel more time to mend, then Joe got into the lineup and hit a home run in his first time at bat. But by the close of the season, his personal totals were once more below his prewar peaks: 20 home runs, an average of .315, and 97 runs batted in. However, he made only one error in 141 games in the field, and was elected the league's Most Valuable Player for the third time over Ted Williams, who hit 32 home runs, knocked in 114 runs, and won the batting championship at .343. But the Yankees won the pennant, the Red Sox ran third, and that was the difference.

The Yankees were filling the old cast with a generation of new players by now: Yogi Berra, Bobby Brown, Vic Raschi, and Allie Reynolds, the Oklahoma Indian who was acquired from Cleveland on DiMaggio's advice in a trade for Joe Gordon. And then there was Joe Page, the tall left-handed relief pitcher whose runaway personal life was as adventurous as his wild ways on the mound.

Joe Page became a kind of protégé of the senior star, and even shared a hotel room with him on road trips. They were the odd couple, and the *odd* quality of their alliance reflected DiMaggio's strange fondness for people who ranked below him on the social or celebrity scale. Page was unbridled, bellicose, frequently drunk. DiMaggio was measured, withdrawn, and sober. Yet he supported and even lectured Page, who in turn idolized him.

But DiMaggio's avuncular side had limits, too. Page came back to the hotel late and looped one night in Boston and was berated and scolded by DiMaggio, who warned him about the evils of self-destruction and braced him on the virtues of commitment to the team. But after that, DiMaggio invoked his executive privilege and paid extra to assure himself of a single room on the road.

The 1947 season became one of the landmark seasons in baseball history: Jackie Robinson arrived, Leo Durocher left (suspended for the year by Commissioner Happy Chandler for associating with some high rollers), and the Yankees played and won a memorable World Series against their natural enemies, the Brooklyn Dodgers. The dramatic high came in Game Four when Floyd (Bill) Bevens of the Yankees pitched no-hit ball for eight and two-thirds innings and needed only one more out to finish the job. But Cookie Lavagetto doubled off the right-field wall at Ebbets Field for two runs to win the game and shatter the no-hitter.

DiMaggio batted only .231 in the Series, but he won the fifth game with a home run and he hit a ball 415 feet with two men on base in the sixth game when the Yankees needed three runs for a tie. But he was foiled when Al Gionfriddo, a five-foot-six sliver of a man in left field, tracked the drive to the bullpen gate and hauled it down with a leaping catch that *The Times* called "breathtaking." DiMaggio was such an Olympian figure by then that every movement or gesture he made tended to be magnified for posterity. And when he kicked the dirt near second base in sheer frustration, he created footnotes to history.

It was, the chronicles said, the only time he had ever betrayed steep emotion on the field. It was, John Drebinger wrote in *The Times,* the kind of storybook catch that "stunned the proud Bombers and jarred even the usually imperturbable DiMaggio."

Like the years after World War I, these were years when the public clamored for its heroes. And the heroes responded. The Yankees and Red Sox staged one sizzling pennant race after another in the American League; the Dodgers and Cardinals did the same in the National League. And the Yankees and Dodgers were the crosstown arch-rivals in the World Series. Behind the microphones in the broadcasting booths sat two of the classic baseball announcers of their time: Mel Allen for the Yankees and Red Barber for the Dodgers. They tracked "the Ballantine blasts," placed "the ducks on the pond," and kept things stirring "in the pea patch," and they described the exploits of the characters on stage with Southern charm and Southern idioms.

Mel Allen remembered later how DiMaggio had pictured the hazards of playing the outfield in the Series.

"The shadows are tough here in the fall," Joe told him, "and it's always worse when there's a big crowd and you get all that smoke hanging over the ball field. The combination of the sun and the shadows and the smoke is really tough."

How come it didn't bother him? DiMaggio, perhaps conceding the erosion of time and age and the breakdown of relationships, but too proud to mourn the erosion, replied stoically:

"You aren't going to start worrying about the old boy now, are you?"

8

THE SECOND DYNASTY

THE OLD BOY came limping into the locker room after the second game of the doubleheader and flopped down, staring and sipping a beer supplied instantly by Pete Sheehy and wincing because the pain in his right heel had become a fact of life. Somehow, he had played through the pain for both games, so he wasn't amused when young Yogi Berra started joking around on the bench in front of his. He wasn't amused because Berra had begged off catching the second game.

"You're twenty-three years old," DiMaggio finally said, his voice rising with resentment, "and you can't catch a double-header? *My ass.*"

Eddie Lopat, the left-handed pitcher who had joined the Yankees that year from the Chicago White Sox, remembered later that "Joe chewed out his ass for twenty minutes, and after that, Yogi caught more games than any other catcher."

Yogi Berra, like Joe Page, felt the fury of the senior member of the cast because DiMaggio was growing and maturing and even aging, and he was becoming the voice of the Yankees and even the conscience of the Yankees, the "presence" who could keep order and also keep the team's traditions secure from young players who at times might get flip. All teams operate under rules of decorum, implied or stated; or, in the case of bad teams, neither implied nor stated. On a team with the continuity of the Yankees, there was always a strong cadre of veterans and longtime stars to impose the rules. And when the imposing might be done by Joe DiMaggio, especially as he grew older and touchier, the young and the wayward steered clear.

"Just one stare from Joe DiMaggio was worth a thousand words," Whitey Ford told me years later. "That's the way it was when you tried to make a club as established as the Yankees were then. We young guys were more or less afraid of the older guys like Gene Woodling and Ralph Houk and Joe D. You know, Vic Raschi or Eddie Lopat would say something, and we'd listen. That's the way it was when the older guys told you to 'act like a Yankee.'"

"Joe DiMaggio was my hero," Mickey Mantle said, "but he couldn't talk to me after I arrived on the club because I wouldn't even look at him. I'd duck my head and pass by."

"I remember once," Ford said, "Joe Page and I went out one night when I was a rookie. I couldn't help feeling excited that here was Joe Page asking me to go to dinner with him in Chicago. We went to a real nice restaurant, and then we went to watch the fights in a place like Madison Square Garden back home, and then we went bouncing around town and before we knew it, it got pretty late.

"But Joe Page knew a place where they'd still let us in, it was called the Airline Club or something. The front door was closed, but Joe knocked on the window and the owner comes and looks out and says, 'You can't come in.' And Joe is telling him, 'It's me, Joe Page.' And the guy says, 'I know, but you can't come in.' By this time, I guess it must've been about two-thirty or three o'clock in the morning, and we got shut out just like that.

"The next afternoon, I'm running in the outfield with Eddie

Lopat before the game, and he says, 'What time did you get home last night?' So, I said, 'Oh, I was in bed around eleven,' as though I'm a monk or something. But Lopat right away says, 'You're a goddamned liar, that's what you are. I was inside that bar when you and Page showed up around two-thirty or three in the morning and tried to get in. I was the guy who told the owner not to let you two characters in. So, don't give me that stuff about being in bed by eleven, you bastard, I was there."

Ford and the other mischief-makers had no illusions about the rationale: The older guys, the watchdogs, had more than manners and morals in mind.

"If a guy blew a play or a game," he said, "because he came to work late after a long night of drinking or bouncing around, that's when somebody like Hank Bauer settled it in a hurry. He'd grab you in the dugout and look you right in the eyes and growl: 'Don't fuck around with my money.' And that's maybe the main thing that kept the guys straight, the idea that you're not only screwing yourself but you're also taking money out of everybody else's pocket if you screw up."

In DiMaggio's case, one stare and you cringed, and that obviously was because he wasn't just looking down from Olympus; he was still backing it up on the field. He played in 153 games in a 154-game season in 1948 when he was 33 years old, and he led the league with 39 home runs and 155 runs batted in. He also hit .320 and led the league in total bases, and when he hit his 300th home run late in the season, he became only the tenth player in baseball history to reach that level. And no active player in the American League had more.

But the bone spur in his right heel kept growing and hurting, and he tried all sorts of shoe pads and adjustments in the shoes themselves. He even tried walking and running in a different style to take some pressure off the heel. When his friend Jimmy Cannon caught him walking tentatively down the staircase of the hotel in Manhattan where they both were living, DiMaggio made him promise not to write anything about it in his column until the season ended. But to a few of his intimates, he admitted that the pain felt like "someone's driving an ice pick into my heel."

Still, he played the part and didn't retreat into pity. In fact, when Bucky Harris told him that he didn't have to stay in the lineup for the final series of the season in Boston because the Yankees were no longer alive in the pennant race, DiMaggio declined the offer. He said that he didn't want to give anybody the impression that he was trying to do any favors for the Red Sox. They were locked in a tight race with the Cleveland Indians and his brother Dominic was playing center field for the Red Sox. So, on the last two days of the season, with their father watching and rooting for Dominic's team, Joe got three hits in one game (including a home run) and four more hits in five times at bat in the final game.

His last hit that day — his last, as it turned out, until the following June — bounced off the wall in left field, but he barely limped to first base and then allowed Harris to take him out of the game. The crowd in Fenway Park stood and cheered, but later he remembered mostly the pain. "I hobbled off the field," he said, "on my bum gam."

The ovation was particularly telling because the Fenway fans loved to hate the Yankees, and they were watching the Red Sox closing the season deadlocked for first place with the Cleveland Indians, with the Yankees in third place, two and a half games back.

It was the end of a long and solemn season for the Yankees, who even lost the symbol of their first dynasty six weeks earlier when Babe Ruth died of cancer on August 16.

It wasn't just that Ruth had dominated the sport for most of his twenty-two years in it. Nor that he had played in 2,503 major-league games, gone to bat 8,399 times, made 2,837 hits, scored 2,174 runs and closed his career with a batting average of .342. Nor that he had excelled as a pitcher before becoming a great hitter. Nor that he had rescued the game from the disaster of the Black Sox scandal of the 1919 World Series. Nor that he had "built" Yankee Stadium and the modern Yankees.

Ruth's real role was even broader than all that: By hitting 714 home runs and revolutionizing the image of baseball, he had elevated the game itself, raised the sights and salaries of all players along with his own, raised the revenues of all clubs — and captured the public's imagination with the style and stuff of legends.

So the Yankees were losing more than a pennant that year. They were losing a mammoth part of their past. And as DiMaggio limped off the field in Fenway Park on the final day, they seemed in danger of also losing a mammoth part of their future. And to steepen their losses, the Cleveland club was enjoying a renaissance under Bill Veeck, the promotional wizard, who energized Cleveland with so many stunts (and so many good players) that the team performed before an average of more than 40,000 persons every time it appeared in Municipal Stadium that year.

The Indians' magic touch lasted into the final hours of the season, and then beyond the final hours into a tumultuous playoff for the pennant, which they won from the Red Sox, and then into the World Series, which they won from the Boston Braves. They did it under the direction of Lou Boudreau, the shortstop and "boy manager," and they brought home Cleveland's first championship since Tris Speaker's team had defeated the Brooklyn Dodgers twenty-eight years earlier.

It was a difficult act to follow. But the day after the Indians won the World Series, the Yankees followed it.

It was a cloudy, rainy day, October 12, and the World Series was still dominating the front pages, although Allison Danzig wrote in *The New York Times* that "now that the World Series has come to an end, football holds the center of the stage for a run through November." He meant college football, as in Columbia against Pennsylvania, and he may have been stretching the point.

At the St. James Theatre off Times Square, not far from where the Yankees were unveiling their new manager, Ray Bolger had just opened in *Where's Charley?* and Brooks Atkinson noted that the dancer made "a mediocre show seem thoroughly enjoyable." Tony Pastor and his orchestra were holding the fort at the Paramount, with a new singing star, Vic Damone. On the political front, Vito Marcantonio was running for a seventh term in the House of Representatives, and *The Times* asked in an editorial whether the electorate would "vote Russian or vote American."

Harry S. Truman was whistle-stopping his way across the country in his campaign against Thomas E. Dewey, while George C. Marshall headed for the opening of the United Nations General Assembly meeting in Paris, saying the country was "completely united" in foreign policy — though the presidential campaign indicated otherwise. And Great Britain at that hour was asking for a censure of the Soviet Union over Andrie Y. Vishinsky's disarmament proposals, charging that Vishinsky actually was obstructing disarmament.

The Alger Hiss–Whitaker Chambers controversy was at its height, too. And stylists were reporting that Persian lamb collars on women's coats were about to make a solid "bow" for the fall season. It was Columbus Day. Yom Kippur began at sundown. And at the 21 Club, one of the toniest oases in town, Dan Topping stood before a phalanx of microphones in the glare of spotlights raised by the photographers and television cameramen and introduced the new manager of the Yankees.

"Meet the new manager of the Yankees," John Drebinger wrote in *The Times.* "Charles Dillon (Casey) Stengel, onetime hard-hitting outfielder, manager of both major and minor league clubs, sage, wit, raconteur as glib with the wisecracks as the late Johnny Walker."

True, but the man brought 2,700 miles from his home in

Glendale, California, to take over the American League's most traditional club had never played, coached, or managed for a single inning in the American League. He had been a player, coach, or manager on seventeen professional baseball teams. He had been traded four times as a left-handed outfielder in the major leagues. He had been dropped or relieved three times as a manager in the big leagues. He had even been paid twice for *not* managing.

He owned oil wells in Texas, was vice president of a bank in California, and controlled real estate that made him a millionaire. His face was heavily wrinkled, his ears were floppy, his voice was guttural, his endurance beyond belief. Like Mickey Mouse and Charles de Gaulle, to say nothing of Joe DiMaggio, he was a household figure of towering identification.

The Yankee high command, which now was being directed by George Weiss, had spirited their man into New York under cover of the World Series in two other cities, booked him into the Waldorf-Astoria, signed him to a two-year contract, and now, thirty-six hours later, put him on display as the successor to Bucky Harris, who had been just as summarily dismissed.

To present a united front, especially since Casey Stengel was considered in some circles as something of a comic, and maybe even a has-been, they also put Joe DiMaggio on display alongside Stengel. They did that for two reasons: to endow Stengel with the trappings of Yankee success and to deflect the occasional rumors that DiMaggio harbored a secret ambition to become manager of the Yankees himself. It was only a few days before he was scheduled to visit Johns Hopkins in Baltimore for a medical checkup to determine whether an operation was needed on the right heel, and the vultures were already circling his playing career.

"You know me, boys," Joe said indulgently, turning aside the questions. "I'm just a ballplayer with one ambition, and that is to give it all I've got to help my ball club win. I've never played any other way."

Clarence (Brick) Laws, the owner of the Oakland club in the Pacific Coast League and Stengel's most recent employer, also stood in the front ranks in another show of force and unity. He acknowledged that he had released Stengel from his commitment to Oakland so that he could accept the Yankees' offer, which had been made only a few days before despite speculation about it on the West Coast for nearly a month.

But none of the stage-setting overcame the fact that the Yankees had reached out into left field, so to speak, for a celebrated clown as their field leader, and not even Stengel could find the words to dispel the misgivings that settled over the ceremony.

In fact, with the first words he uttered to accept the cudgels, he fell on his face. With tape recorders, microphones, and cameras all switched on from a common cue, the man of the hour said: "I want first of all to thank Mr. Bob Topping for this opportunity."

That was all right, except that he should have thanked Mr. Dan Topping for this opportunity instead of his brother Bob, whose marital difficulties with the film actress Arlene Judge, formerly Dan's wife, had put both Toppings into headlines. Cries of "Cut" and "Hold it" drowned out whatever else the Yankees' new manager had in mind for his opening sentence. Then, after everybody had rewound the equipment, Casey took another cue and made another start.

"This is a big job, fellows," he said, with no trace of his customary plunges into slapstick. "And I barely have had time to study it. In fact, I scarcely know where I am."

"There'll likely be some changes," he said, turning to the team's situation. "But it's a good club, and I think we'll do all right. We'll go slow, because you can tear down a club a lot quicker than you can build it up."

Baseball writers who had covered the Yankees in their glory days enjoyed Stengel but suspected that he was miscast. John Drebinger wrote in *The Times:* "There is much work to be done before the Yankees can ever hope to reclaim their baseball leadership." Ben Epstein wrote in the *New York Mirror:* "Casey Stengel will be the fifth candidate to have stabbed at this morning glory since 1946."

They were right: It was an ordeal. It was also a time of some tension between Stengel and DiMaggio, who seemed wary of each other and who never settled into an easy relationship. Stengel praised Joe as "the best I've ever had." But he sensed that DiMaggio symbolized a Yankee tradition that Stengel had never shared. And DiMaggio sensed that Stengel needed him but suspected that Stengel also wondered about him and the aching heel.

"He was a very worried man," Arthur Daley wrote in *The Times,* reporting on DiMaggio's changed moods in spring training. "Strangely abrupt, and almost surly."

The mood thickened when the Yankees announced on April 12 that he would miss yet another opening game. Then he was flown directly to Johns Hopkins in Baltimore, and the mood grew worse. Or, as Jerry Coleman described the feeling: "It took the heart out of the ball club, and made everybody grouchy."

DiMaggio was certainly grouchy, and with good reason. He stayed in the hospital only overnight, but he was constantly pestered and badgered by reporters asking the same questions. When a photographer tried to take his picture while he was being wheeled into an operating room for treatment on his foot, he screamed at the man. When he walked on crutches through the lobby to leave the hospital, he called to the crowd of writers and cameramen: "Don't you think you've gone far enough?" And *Time* magazine reported that he added: "You guys are driving me nutty. Leave me alone."

Here was a man who couldn't even walk without pain, and everybody kept asking when he expected to play ball. He was making $90,000 now, and for once in his career he didn't have to wage wars of strategy over his contract. But he was crippled, and he was missing. He went back to New York, shut himself into his hotel room, listened to the games on the radio or caught some on television, and lived the life of a recluse.

"For the first time," Mel Allen remembered, "he began to think he was through, finished, washed up as a ballplayer. Always a loner, Joe really shut himself off from the world. George Solotaire and Toots Shor, his two closest friends, were the only two people who saw him at all when he returned to New York alone after taking more treatments in Baltimore. He just stayed locked up in his room at the Hotel Madison on Fifty-eighth Street, killing time and brooding."

When the Yankees announced that he would miss the opening game, they were understating the problem. He missed the first sixty-five games, in fact. And then it became an epidemic. The backup power hitters became hobbled, too: Tommy Henrich (wrenched knee, three broken vertebrae), Charlie Keller (chronic back ailment), Yogi Berra (broken finger). Seven different men played first base at one time or another: Henrich, Johnny Mize, Dick Kryhoski, Jack Phillips, Billy Johnson, Fenton Mole, and Joe Collins. Third base was shared by Johnson, a part-time first baseman, and Bobby Brown, a part-time medical student, who probably could have helped the team more as a doctor than as a player. Two small but accomplished acrobats played shortstop and second base, Phil Rizzuto and George Stirnweiss, with support from Jerry Coleman, a Marine Corps Reserve pilot who shuttled between the Yankees and the Marines for years. Berra, an outfielder, was made a catcher; Johnny Lindell, a pitcher, was made an outfielder.

Every day when he arrived at the stadium, Stengel would check with the trainer, August R. Mauch, to learn how many able-bodied men were available so that he could write nine names onto his lineup card. He wrote the names of the three middle batters — Henrich, DiMaggio, and Berra — as a unit only seventeen times in 154 games.

Mauch, a trim man who wore white slacks and tennis

sneakers, held degrees as a Doctor of Naturopathy and as a Doctor of Chiropractics. He had treated professional baseball players, college swimmers, and football players at every level, George M. Cohan, Jimmy Durante, and even George Bernard Shaw, and he played a calculated hand of bridge, besides.

He was the trainer for the football Giants in New York for seventeen seasons, the football Yankees for four, the baseball Yankees for sixteen, New York University for six, and Manhattan College for twelve. He eventually trained eleven baseball pennant winners, eight World Series winners, two National Football League champions, six American League All-Star teams, one National League All-Star team, and one All-Star team each in the NFL and the All-America Football Conference.

He once helped keep Cohan dancing onstage for weeks while the entertainer was suffering with a sprained ankle, a pulled hamstring muscle, and a case of influenza. Bernard Shaw visited him at the McAlpin Hotel's roof club in 1926 for massages. Durante called on him for help during his Copacabana appearances in 1940. And Admiral Richard E. Byrd was a fairly regular patient starting in 1927.

"He looked a little pale," Gus Mauch reported, "when he came back from the North Pole."

But he added that the busiest year in his career was 1949.

"Every day, I'd walk into Stengel's office," he recalled, "and I'd say, 'Your star outfielder is hurt and can't play.' And he'd say, 'Thank you, doctor.' He never blinked an eye. He grew tougher later, but that year he was gentle. If the team was on a winning streak, he might howl and shout, but he was mild when we were losing or when we were hurting."

The Yankees grew so accident-prone that even Mauch became a casualty. They were in Boston near the end of the season, and Charlie Silvera, a second-string catcher, was in a doughnut shop when he noticed Mauch walking by. So Silvera picked up two doughnuts, put them over his eyes like spectacles, peered through the holes, and rapped on the window. Gus was so amused that he started to laugh — and walked into a parking meter, breaking two ribs.

"But the biggest pain was the one in Joe DiMaggio's heel," he told me later. "It was like the pain of a hundred carpet tacks. He had a flock of tiny calcium deposits that had to solidify into one before the pain would stop. We could have filled a closet with all the contraptions the shoe companies sent us to correct the problem. They sent shoes with half-soles in the front and iron bars in the rear to act as a cradle for Joe's foot. People who had bone spurs sent advice and even medicine."

DiMaggio's personal life was causing pain, too. He still seemed to be brooding over the breakup of his marriage. His father died in May of 1949, just one month after passing his written examination to become a naturalized citizen.

By late June, the Yankees were struggling to stay in sight of the Red Sox, who were fielding an even more powerful offense than in the past, led by Ted Williams, Bobby Doerr, and Dominic DiMaggio. And they had a pair of professional pitchers: Ellis Kinder and Mel Parnell, all under the command of Joe McCarthy, the longtime manager of the Yankees.

But the ordeal of 1949 was about to be transformed somehow into the fantasy of 1949. And it began to unfold one day late in June when DiMaggio stepped out of bed in his hotel and discovered that the pain in his right heel was gone.

The Yankees were scheduled to play an exhibition game a few nights later, on June 27, against the Giants. And DiMaggio walked into Stengel's office while Casey was fiddling with his lineup card, as usual, and said without warning: "I think I'll give it a whirl tonight, Case."

"Great," Casey croaked. "You can play as long as you want. Just let me know when you're ready to quit."

But instead of giving it a whirl for a time, he played the whole game. And the next night, against the Red Sox in Fenway Park, he got back into the regular lineup for the first time that season.

He hit a single the first time up and a home run the second time. Then he hit two home runs the next day, and another the day after that.

Before the last one, he hit a long foul ball that just missed being a home run, and McCarthy shot out of the dugout waving his arm and scowling toward his pitcher on the mound. He was getting weary of DiMaggio's theatrics. He retreated back into the dugout, and just had time to sit down before Joe rocked the next pitch even farther, and this time there was no doubt that it was a fair ball — or that the Yankees had started to revive mightily.

They revived, all right. His first home run helped them win the opener, 5-4. The next day, his second home run started them back into a game they were losing, 7-1, and his third home run won the game, 9-7. And the day after that, his fourth home run helped them sweep the series from the Red Sox, who had won ten of their last eleven games before the Yankees arrived.

Joe got five hits in eleven times up during the three games, and knocked in nine runs. A small airplane flew over the ballpark before the final game carrying a streamer that read: "The Great DiMaggio."

One month later, handsome and toothy, he made the cover of *Life* magazine with a widening smile and the title: "It's great to be back." Inside, the byline "By Joe DiMaggio" was set in fifty-four-point black type alongside a subhead that read: "Baseball's biggest hero, his bad heel cured, tells how it feels to sit on the sidelines, worry that your $100,000-a-year career is over — and then start hitting homers again."

The foreword to the article reflected the national response in these words:

"During the week of June 26, a $100,000-a-year baseball player named Joe DiMaggio — a shy and retiring young man who up to then had been noted chiefly for his easy grace in the outfield and his mechanical proficiency at punching out base hits — suddenly became a national hero. After being out for nearly half the season with a bad heel that threatened at times to end his career, he got back into uniform and — in perfect fairy-tale fashion — began breaking up game after game by hitting the ball out of the park.

"It was one of the most heart-warming comebacks in all sports history, and from one end of the country to the other it became the summer's prime topic of conversation, even among people who never saw a game in their lives. DiMaggio had always been a great player, and now he took his place in that select circle of athletes, like Babe Ruth and Jack Dempsey, who are not only admired but also beloved."

He was certainly treasured, almost like a national resource, and his moodiness and his privacy now became accepted as elements in that resource. After all, it *was* a mighty performance and a melodramatic comeback, and it carried him from one level of public praise to another dimension. He despaired, he survived, he conquered the odds.

"Every athlete has to face it," he wrote. "Sooner or later, as you get up in the 30's, your legs are going to go back on you — and then you're through and there's nothing anybody can do about it. But when it's just a heel, something that you never thought about in your life, then it's hard to take."

During the depths of the time when he was hurting, he said, "I really was almost a mental case. The only two people I could stand to see regularly were my closest friends, Toots Shor and George Solotaire. I tried to avoid everybody else. Most of the time, I was alone in my hotel room."

But once the heel stopped aching, he related, he plotted his return methodically. The Yankees were traveling in the Midwest when the pain suddenly left, so he had a few days to prepare. When they returned to New York, he startled them by showing up for light batting practice; the heel felt fine, but his hands became blistered from the new irritation of gripping the bat. But he stayed on course, worked his transition to the point where he was able to take the full fifteen minutes of batting practice, worked out in the infield, shagged flies in the outfield, and even stayed late after the game one day to chase fly balls hit to him by Gus Niarhos, the third-string catcher.

Even then, his appearance in the exhibition game against the Giants was more of an audition than anything else. And when he passed it, he still was wary about testing the heel on the great stage of Fenway Park.

"On the day the team left for Boston, on a morning train," he said, "I still wasn't quite sure. In a way, I suppose I was almost afraid to make the decision. I stayed behind and had lunch with Toots Shor, thinking it over. At 3:15, I caught a plane; at 5:15, I was at the clubhouse in Boston and at 6 o'clock I told Casey Stengel I was ready if he wanted me."

Stengel wanted him, all right. But it still seems strange, decades after the fateful decision was made, that he made it only after consulting Toots Shor, who was outranked by very few people as a partisan of Joe DiMaggio. It was doubtful then, and it remains doubtful now, that he could have received guidance or informed opinion from Shor. More likely, he got what he wanted from Shor: stroking.

But DiMaggio's impact on the fortunes of the Yankees in 1949, when his impact was delivered with the greatest force, was so stark that much of the public and the media got caught by surprise. After all, when the season opened, he was crippled and the Yankees were devastated. Or so people thought.

Three months before he came back from the dead and rocked the Red Sox, the common wisdom suggested that both DiMaggio and his team were declining. He made the cover of *Look* magazine on April 24, too, an endearing picture showing Joe Jr. gripping a baseball bat rather tentatively (wearing a Yankee uniform, of course), while Joe Sr. stood behind him holding the bat for greater control. But there was nothing endearing about the title of the article: "Is the Yankee Empire Crumbling?"

"Today's Yankee roster," the article said with a doomsday tone, "indicates that major rebuilding will be necessary before the team will win again. Joe DiMaggio's physical condition is dubious. So is Charley Keller's. The only postwar farm product measuring up to traditional Yankee specifications is pitcher Vic Raschi, 19-game winner in '48."

Then, indulgently and incorrectly, the report looked into the future, and missed the mark colossally.

"Eventually, the Yankees will win again," it predicted. "They have money, front office direction and a manager, in Casey Stengel, who should do well. *But they will never again dominate baseball as they did for a quarter of a century.* No team will. There is too wide a distribution of money, brains, talent — and, presumably, luck."

Considering that they won ten American League pennants and seven World Series in the next twelve years, history would have to agree that was a prediction worth even less than the newsstand price of the magazine in those days: fifteen cents.

With DiMaggio back in the lineup, physically and emotionally, the Yankees hammered the Red Sox into second place and at one point eight games behind in second place.

"It was hard to believe," Gus Mauch remembered, "but Casey would take a guy out of the lineup and the substitute would do better than the original. He moved players around, he switched positions, he did everything, and everything seemed to work."

Yogi Berra, a twenty-three-year-old junior member of the lineup who was paid ninety dollars a month when he signed with the Norfolk farm club six years earlier, hit twenty home runs and knocked in ninety-one runs. Allie Reynolds, the part-Cherokee "chief" from Oklahoma who later struck oil, literally, won seventeen games and lost six. Joe Page, the straying but sizzling left hander, pitched in sixty games in the late innings and won thirteen of them.

"If Casey pulls this one out," said Bill Dickey, the graduate catcher who by then was one of Casey's coaches, "he's a Houdini."

Somehow, with clutch performances up and down the batting order and with heavy reliance on intuition and Gus Mauch's wizardry in the trainer's room, Houdini led the Yankees home on September 26 in a tie for first place with the Red Sox and with one week to go in the season.

When they arrived in Grand Central Terminal that Sunday night, they were astonished to find a crowd of seven thousand jamming the station waiting for them, including Mrs. Johnny Mize, the wife of the veteran first baseman the club had bought from the Giants (who was injured, naturally), and Mrs. Babe Ruth. A detail of policemen escorted the players out through side exits through the cheering mob and, as they did, Stengel said above the noise: "We're still up. Tomorrow, we'll have them on our home ground, and tomorrow's a big one."

It was a big one, all right. Before 66,156 in Yankee Stadium, the Red Sox showed up for the showdown and muscled their way into first place by scoring four runs in the eighth inning and beating the Yankees, 7-6.

The game ended in a tumultuous argument when Johnny Pesky slid across home plate on Bobby Doerr's squeeze bunt as Ralph Houk lunged to tag him out and the home-plate umpire, Bill Grieve, called him safe.

The Yankees not only lost the game and the league lead but also $500 in fines — $150 each for Houk and Stengel and $200 for Cliff Mapes, an outfielder who wasn't even in the game but who was tactless enough to ask Grieve, as the players and umpires headed for the dressing rooms: "How much did you bet on the game?"

Four days later, after the Yankees had played three games against the Philadelphia Athletics, the Red Sox were still clinging to a one-game lead with two to go — against the Yankees in New York. And as the teams grappled toward the close of their war, *The New York Times* paused in its coverage of world affairs and, in an editorial titled "Days of Anguish," set the stage:

"In times like these, we customarily repair to the classics for what calm we can discover. We like the soothing cadence, marching though it does to doom, of the Ernest Thayer lines:

Oh, somewhere in this favored land
The sun is shining bright.
The band is playing somewhere, and
Somewhere hearts are light.
And somewhere men are laughing, and
Somewhere children shout. . . .

"Charity and the fear of laying a hex on Casey Stengel lead us to draw a veil, temporarily, over the last line of this masterpiece. We will not believe that our Casey has struck out until the baseball mathematicians say the Yankees are impossible."

They certainly looked impossible: one game behind with two to play. They had to win two, Boston had only to win one. And the odds were grimmer than that: DiMaggio had at length exhausted his strength, come down with a viral infection, dropped fifteen pounds in weight, and for the last several weeks presented a ghostly image of himself. The heel was cured, but now the whole body was weary.

As if the world knew and shared his suffering, an immense crowd of 69,551 filled the stadium to watch the weekend's wonders and to watch the final salutes to the player who had helped make the weekend so meaningful with his heroic comeback three months earlier. It was "Joe DiMaggio Day," and close to $50,000 worth of gifts were showered on the pale and drawn man in the blue windbreaker as he took the salutes from family, friends, and foes alike.

Dominic DiMaggio came out of the Red Sox dugout and stood next to Joe and their mother at home plate. They all knew that one of the brothers would make it to the World Series.

Joe McCarthy came up to home plate, too, and congratulated Joe, who had helped him win six pennants. Mayor William O'Dwyer said over the public-address microphone: "You came here from San Francisco. After today, you will never leave New

York." And Ethel Merman made it official, *fortissimo,* by singing "Take Me Out to the Ball Game."

The gifts included a Cadillac for Joe, a Dodge for his mother, a Chris-Craft speedboat, two television sets, mounds of personal jewelry, two rifles, a carpet, a baseball and bat made of Christmas candy, a set of electric trains for his son, a four-year college scholarship for anybody else's son he selected, a cocker spaniel, and, as the commercial centerpiece, a case of frozen lima beans. He also received numerous cash gifts, which he turned over to the Damon Runyon Cancer Fund and the Heart Fund.

Mel Allen, the radio and TV voice of Yankee history, served as master of ceremonies and said later:

"He stood on the infield for a full hour before the game, standing there at home plate trying to keep the emotion out of his eyes and out of his voice."

Then DiMaggio got his moment at the microphone, and made the most of it.

"I'd like to apologize," he said, opening with a beau geste, "to the people in the bleachers for having my back turned to them."

Then, hitting oratorical line drives to all fields, he said:

"This is one of the few times I've choked up. Many years ago, Lefty O'Doul told me: 'Joe, don't let the big town scare you. New York is the most generous town in the world.' "

He paused for emphasis, and added: "This day proves it."

"I've played for three managers," he went on, "and they all taught me something. If we don't win, I will say to Joe McCarthy: 'If we couldn't win, I'm glad you did.' The Red Sox are a great bunch of guys. But that doesn't include the guy in center field who spends so much time annoying me."

It wasn't the greatest line in the world, but it covered the brother connection. And then he concluded with the winner: "I'd like to thank the good Lord for making me a Yankee."

In the home dugout, old Casey Stengel trained his mind on the nine innings that would make or break his team in his first season as manager, and said: "I think we've got 'em. I feel it in my bones."

But the Yankees, who felt fatigue and pain in their bones, fell into deep weeds at the start when Allie Reynolds lost his control and gave up four runs in the first three innings. But somehow, six innings from losing it all, they scraped together some hits here and some hits there and survived, as though having been through hell almost every day for six months, they had asked, why panic now? And when Johnny Lindell unfurled a home run in the bottom of the eighth inning, they finally wrested the lead from the Red Sox, 5–4, with Page pitching in long relief to preserve it. And later he said that he kept looking out to center field to his dog-tired idol, DiMaggio, and thinking: "If he can play the way he feels, I can pitch forever."

"And so, it develops," John Drebinger wrote after the game, "that those battered Bombers with their countless aches and bruises weren't ready to be rolled into a boneyard, after all. At least, on this final day of the American League championship season, they are still standing as well as their formidable rivals, the hale and hearty Bosox."

And, on the final day, they fought the final battle before 68,055 fans, winner take all.

It was 1–0, Yankees, until the last half of the eighth inning with Vic Raschi pitching for New York. Then the Yankees fired their last salvo of the season for four more runs, only to see the Red Sox roar back with three in the top of the ninth. The most dangerous shot was a triple that Doerr hit over DiMaggio's head in deep center field, putting the season on the line. But Joe made a decision on the spot, and it was as noble as it was memorable: He signaled to call time-out, then limped off the field to a standing ovation. He had nothing left to give. And the Yankees held on to win, 5–3.

"We had seventy-two injuries that season," Gus Mauch said. "I mean seventy-two injuries that kept a man out of the lineup. And when Henrich caught the foul ball that ended that last game and gave us the pennant, Bill Dickey jumped up in the dugout and cracked his head on the roof. That made seventy-three."

"It was," Henrich said, reaching for the favorite cliché in sports, "a team of destiny."

The "team of destiny" still had to survive more adventures in the World Series, and the National League meanwhile was providing an opponent with almost as much style and destiny. The St. Louis Cardinals had already begun selling tickets and distributing them for the Series, then lost four straight games to the sixth-place Pittsburgh Pirates and the eighth-place Chicago Cubs. That gave the Brooklyn Dodgers a last-minute chance, and while the Yankees were slicing past the Red Sox on the last day of the season, the Dodgers were slicing past the Phillies, 9–7, in ten innings on the last day in Philadelphia.

What would they all do for an encore? Well, they thought of something suitable. On October 5, the first day of the Series, 66,224 persons packed Yankee Stadium and watched Don Newcombe allow the Yankees only five hits while striking out eleven. But Allie Reynolds allowed the Dodgers only two hits and struck out nine. They were still scoreless when Henrich led off the bottom of the ninth, with Newcombe keeping an eye on Joe DiMaggio in the batter's circle and letting the count on Henrich slip away to two balls and no strikes. By then, Newcombe was entering the danger zone, and he did not survive. He got the next pitch over the plate, and Henrich hit it into the right-field seats.

The next day, Preacher Roe, a left-handed country boy, stopped the Yankees on six hits while the Dodgers made seven off Raschi and Page. And Brooklyn won that one, also 1–0, this time before a bulging crowd of 70,053.

In the third game, they were all tied at 1–1 after eight innings in Ebbets Field. Then the Yankees scored three times in the visitors' half of the ninth, the Dodgers scored twice in the home half on two home runs, and lost by a score of 4–3.

In the fourth game, the Yankees scored six runs inside five

innings, then gave back four runs and Stengel had to call in Reynolds to protect what was left of his lead. Reynolds did, striking out four of the seven batters he faced.

Finally, in the fifth game, the Yankees treated Stengel to the luxury of a nine-run lead. But Gil Hodges, who once received the prayers of an entire congregation in Brooklyn during a batting slump, hit a three-run home run in the seventh. And Stengel, his season of suspense not yet done, signaled Page into the game. Page did his thing, and the Yankees won their twelfth World Series.

"It was part of the greatest rebuilding job in baseball," said Arthur E. (Red) Patterson, who worked as the public relations impresario for the Yankees in New York and later for the Dodgers in Los Angeles. "Between 1948 and 1953, Dan Topping and Del Webb gave George Weiss the authority and the money, and Weiss rebuilt an organization. Stengel had been hired with the complete respect of all three. They didn't think he was a clown or a buffoon. They knew he had a record in the minor leagues that maybe nobody else could match, making out with old players, new players, finished players, professional players. And they brought him to the Yankees with their eyes wide open. It was no diversion to keep the public amused enough to forget the club's collapse.

"He took a few veteran ballplayers who required special treatment, like Joe DiMaggio, Charlie Keller, and Tommy Henrich, and he blended them with kids who needed encouragement and experience. And when things got rough, Weiss bought several established stars like Johnny Mize, Johnny Hopp and Enos Slaughter to keep the mix from coming apart.

"I think he was the father of the two-platoon system. He was criticized for overdoing it. But he'd say: 'If I had DiMaggio, Keller and Henrich in their prime, I wouldn't platoon. But I don't.'

"And the seventy-three famous injuries. It would be like this: During one doubleheader in July of 1949, just after Weiss bought

Mize from the Giants for $40,000, Mize played first base, and Henrich was bumped into right field. In the first game, Henrich crashed into the wall and broke three vertebrae. He was carried out on a stretcher. In the second game, Mize dived to make a tag, threw his shoulder out, and for the rest of the year all he could do was pinch-hit. So now both first basemen were out.

"Not only did Stengel make changes that paid off in situations like that, but he made the Yankees more popular, more likeable than they ever had been. They always won everything but love. But when they started getting hurt, they won that, too."

Joe DiMaggio, who coveted love and approval more than most, ended the season in some tatters. He got only one hit, a single, in the first four games of the Series, then curled a home run down the left-field line in the final game and closed the performance with two hits in eighteen times at bat for a batting average of .111. He also closed it with a case of complete exhaustion, and with growing awareness that he couldn't keep it up forever.

But if the season of 1949 was the first of his curtain calls, it was a rave. To the public, he was not growing old; he was growing older, and doing it gracefully. He was nearly thirty-five years old, and he still hit .346 after missing the first half of the season. He was still the center fielder and cleanup hitter on the "new" Yankees and the living link to the "old" Yankees going back nearly to the days of the first dynasty established by Ruth.

Most of all, he was the fallen hero who spent months brooding over the pain in his right heel — the Achilles heel of the Yankees until the day he stepped out of bed and felt no pain. Then he was the revived and aroused hero who gathered his teammates, led them against the enemy, and touched the national imagination the way he had done during the great streak, eight years before.

Self-centered, aloof, vain, remote. Yes, all of that. He could sulk in his tent with the best of them. But when he rose up in splendor and played the game, he *was* the best of them. He was a landmark. As *Life* magazine said, panting a bit, he was at last like Babe Ruth and Jack Dempsey, "not only admired but also beloved."

"If you saw him play," Jimmy Cannon wrote, "you'll never forget him."

9

EXIT, STAGE LEFT

IN JANUARY of 1950, the front office of the New York Yankees mailed questionnaires to the players, asking them, among other things, to name their "baseball model" and "the player you most admire." In a landslide, they named Joe DiMaggio.

Whitey Ford, the city slicker who joined the Yankees in 1950, not only admired DiMaggio but also feared him.

"When I came up to the club," he said, "Pete Sheehy gave me a locker near DiMaggio. I couldn't believe it. I just stared at the man for about a week. He'd say things like hello, things like that, but I think I would've fainted if he'd said more than that to me."

It wasn't easy to intimidate Whitey Ford in those days. He was born on East Sixty-sixth Street in Manhattan, between First and Second Avenues, and he was street-smart and as brazen as they come. After he signed with the Yankees in 1946 for a minor-league salary of $250 a month, he was invited to spring training with the big club the following spring, failed to make even their Class-A farm team, and was assigned instead to their Class-C team at Edenton, North Carolina. The manager was Lefty

Gomez, who had been DiMaggio's roommate, running mate, and teammate.

"I guess we deserved each other," Ford conceded, "because we were always pulling stunts on each other the way he used to pull stunts when he was pitching back in the Thirties and was nicknamed Goofy.

"Gomez had a rule that we all had to be in our rooms by ten o'clock every night, and you don't have to be a genius to see trouble right there. We tried, though. But one night about nine-thirty, one of my room-mates and I decided to go to a carnival in town, we wanted to take a ride on the Ferris wheel. You know, we figured about five minutes of that and we'd be back in our room on time. So, we got on and rode for about ten minutes, but then we couldn't get off.

"Every time it came our turn to get off, the guy running the ride would pass us, and he kept doing this till 10 o'clock. I didn't know why, then.

"We finally got off and ran back to our hotel, which was only about two blocks away. We got there about five minutes after ten, and there was Gomez in the lobby. I said, 'Skip, you'll never guess what happened. We got on the Ferris wheel, and the guy wouldn't let us off.' And Gomez said, 'You're fined five dollars each.'

"Years later, Dizzy Dean had Gomez as a guest on his after-the-game television show from Yankee Stadium. And Lefty tells this story — how he'd given this guy a couple of bucks to keep us on the Ferris wheel. Now, I'm in the clubhouse watching the show and, when it's over, Lefty comes into the clubhouse and I say, 'You son of a bitch. All those years, you never told us.' And he says, 'I just never told *you*.'

"So, I say, 'Give me my ten dollars back.' Now, he's laughing his head off, but he gives me ten dollars. Then I say, scoring big, 'Good, you son of a bitch, you only fined me five.'

"Maybe that's why they call me Slick."

But slick or not, Ford admitted that he was terrorized by the proximity to DiMaggio after he made it to the varsity team four years later. "Joe and everybody else in there," he said, "looked twelve feet tall."

When Mickey Mantle joined the team the next year, he came apart at the emotional seams whenever he passed DiMaggio en route to his locker. He remembered that Casey Stengel, like Lefty Gomez, kept order and decorum in numerous little conspiratorial ways. But he admitted that ultimately, the level of decorum was maintained by the presence of the legends who dressed silently at the nearby lockers.

"You couldn't fool Casey," he said, "because he'd pulled every stunt that was ever thought up. He didn't mind it too much, either, so long as you didn't start to lose it on the ball field. That's where it all came out, on the field. You could run around like some of the guys, or you could travel with the club looking like DiMaggio in those beautiful blue suits and Countess Mara ties."

"Either way you did it," Mantle concluded, "if you played like DiMaggio, you'd keep Casey off your back."

Billy Martin, the bad boy from Berkeley, California, preceded both Ford and Mantle to the Yankees early in 1950 and shared the same sense that they were new members of the cast of the longest-running show in baseball. They were the next generation; DiMaggio was the senior star of the last generation. And probably because of that stark fact, Casey Stengel gave everybody — especially Joe DiMaggio — the idea that he indulged his rookies and slighted his veterans.

"My first day with the club," Martin said, "we were losing 9 to 0 in Boston, and the Old Man put me in. The first time up, I doubled off the left-field fence in Fenway Park for one run, and later in the same inning I got a single with the bases loaded for two more. Two hits in the same inning, my first two times up. We won the game, 15 to 10. The Old Man liked me, I guess, because I was a lot like him when he was young. I suppose I had a lot of balls for a rookie.

"But," Martin said, "there wasn't anything I wouldn't do for

the Clipper. I was just thrilled to be around him. He was everything I dreamed he would be. When he walked into that clubhouse, it was like a President or Senator walking in there.

"For the two years Joe was there with me," Martin remembered, "I always rooted for him to have a big game, not only for
himself and the club but for me. If Joe had a good day and we
won, we would go out. If we lost and he had a bad day, he would
eat in his room. I would have to join him because he didn't like
to eat alone."

When Martin made his resounding debut, it was opening day,
April 18, 1950. They not only trailed the Red Sox, the team they
had swept in Yankee Stadium for the pennant seven months before, but Mel Parnell was pitching to protect Boston's lead.
That's when the Yankees came back with fifteen runs. No
wonder the Old Man liked him.

It wasn't so clear why DiMaggio liked him, or even tolerated
him. With almost all of the people who worked or lived around
him, DiMaggio was either proper or removed, even remote. But
with the chosen few, the rather crude few like Toots Shor,
George Solotaire, and Billy Martin, he was tight, confiding, even
isolated from the world outside. They had one trait in common,
besides any other traits he regarded as virtues: They didn't challenge him, they fawned over him.

"Joe DiMaggio was my hero," Mantle recalled, "but Billy used
to play jokes on him and hang around with him. Billy wasn't
afraid of Joe, maybe because they both came from San Francisco.
Besides, Billy was a fresh kid, and he even pulled some stunts on
Joe. There was one in particular I'll never forget.

"Billy had one of those pens with disappearing ink. Well, Joe
would always come to the ballpark in a shirt and tie — I was
wearing brown crepe-soled shoes and one of those ties with
feathers. Anyway, I just couldn't believe that Billy would squirt
ink all over Joe's nice-looking suit. I can still see it. Billy would go
up there and ask Joe for an autograph and shoot the ink all over

him. Joe would just say, 'Damn it, how could you do that?' And Billy got away with it, and always went out to eat with him.

"I used to watch and ask Billy what Joe was like. And he'd say, 'Shit, he's just like anyone else. All you have to do is open up when you're around him.' And I'd say, 'Shit, I couldn't do that.' "

Whitey Ford analyzed the poles of behavior this way: "I acted like a rookie; Billy didn't. I probably would have fainted if Di-Maggio came up to me that spring. I was a kid from New York and knew all about DiMaggio. I knew his *personality,* and you just didn't parade up to Joe. Not Billy. He got away with it."

Some people believed that the Olympian view of DiMaggio prevailed because it made more dramatic written history, and the New York press tended to protect him, anyway. Lots of sports stars are considered aloof and selfish; he was usually portrayed as aloof but noble. And the memory of the noble DiMaggio was chiseled into the public's consciousness when Ernest Hemingway published *The Old Man and The Sea* in 1952, and old man Santiago thought to himself along these lines as he dealt with his sea:

"I must have confidence and I must be worthy of the great DiMaggio who does all things perfectly even with the pain of the bone spur in his heel. . . . Do you believe the great DiMaggio would stay with a fish as long as I will stay with this one? . . . I am sure he would and more since he is young and strong. Also, his father was a fisherman. But would the bone spur hurt him too much?

" 'I do not know,' he said aloud. 'I never had a bone spur.' "

Or, as Eddie Lopat put it, in terms that Santiago might have better understood sailing on his silent sea: "Joe was the loneliest man I ever knew."

Lopat also remembered that the rookie Billy Martin not only ingratiated himself to the great DiMaggio but even endeared himself, and he did it so slavishly that the rest of the Yankees called him "Joe's Little Bobo." The outfielder Cliff Mapes nagged

Martin: "What in hell does the big guy see in you?" And bold Billy replied: "He can recognize class."

But class couldn't have had much to do with it; Billy Martin wasn't famous for being a class act. He was belligerent and brazen, and DiMaggio could handle both strains, especially since Billy teased him but never threatened him, intellectually or professionally.

Besides, time seemed to be running out, or at least running short, and Joe more and more distrusted his critics and cherished his loyalists. Meanwhile, he was still riding into town on a white horse and burying the Boston Red Sox with the old firepower in a new moment of urgency, his bone spur and his image pain-free.

But his transition from his role as the show-stopper to something less, or at least to something less constant in stopping the show, was not pain-free. The symptoms of withdrawal began to surface in 1950, which would have been a difficult year under the best of circumstances for anyone to stage an encore after the melodrama of his comeback in 1949.

With retirement in the back of his mind, he agreed to appear on two radio series, both aimed at an audience of children asking questions on baseball. He admitted that he was "no crackerjack yet," but he clearly was exploring the frontier beyond baseball for the first time.

He also spent some time trying to rekindle the old torch with Dorothy Arnold, but he fretted that her *third* marriage was probably confusing to their son Joe Jr., who was then eight years old and living with his third father. Nothing came of the close encounter, but it confounded him for a while in one more lingering lost cause.

Then he opened the season back at the old stand, but struggled. He went to bat thirteen times with getting any hit, went through ten games without getting an extra-base hit, and closed the first two months with a .243 batting average and a strained muscle in his back.

But he also was suffering from strained relations with Stengel. They seemed respectful of each other at a distance, but they now had divergent priorities.

DiMaggio wasn't the only member of the Old Guard who felt uncomfortable, even unappreciated, by Stengel. They were all more or less amused at the old manager's style of talking and acting, and they didn't exactly begrudge him the spotlight, which Casey had a way of hogging just by being himself. He spoke in colorful, convoluted, and never-ending clauses that were spiced with antique usages and words like "commence" and that usually ended with a question or a wildly unrelated observation like: "And the shortstop could go back and ketch the ball."

John Lardner once said: "He can talk all day and all night, on any kind of track, wet or dry."

Quentin Reynolds, marveling at Stengel's life as a baseball nomad, once said: "Every time two owners got together with a fountain pen, Casey Stengel was being sold or bought."

Stengel, always willing to trump somebody else's verbal ace, replied: "I never played with the Cubs, Cards or Reds. I guess that was because the owners of those clubs didn't own no fountain pens."

One of his most celebrated capers came after he was installed as a one-man triumvirate running the Boston Braves' farm club at Worcester, Massachusetts, in the Eastern League in 1925 as his own playing career was winding down.

He was made the president of the club, the manager of the team, and the right fielder, as well. It was his first experience with the disciplines of command, and he felt surrounded by responsibility after years of being surrounded in the big leagues by jolly teammates and drinking cronies. But he wore all three hats for one maddening season, and even played in 100 of the team's 125 games (and the team finished third).

Then, as soon as the season ended, he executed a monumental front-office triple play to escape. As the manager, he released

Stengel the player. As the president, he fired Stengel the manager. And as Stengel, he resigned as president.

He once slid into a potted palm in the Sheraton-Cadillac Hotel
in Detroit to demonstrate Ty Cobb's famous fallaway slide. But
when he was cricized for not sliding home during a close game
when he was, according to his own judgment, a grossly underpaid member of the Pittsburgh Pirates, he replied: "With the
salary I get here, I'm so hollow and starving that I'm liable to
explode like a light bulb if I hit the ground too hard."

When umpires pulled rank to thwart his tricks, he sometimes
counterattacked with passive resistance. He might swoon in a
mock faint and just lie down on the ground while they raged.

He pulled this bit of toomfoolery once when Beans Reardon
was umpiring behind home plate, but Reardon, one of the National League's senior disciplinarians, went even farther by lying
down alongside him near the plate. Stengel admitted later:
"When I peeked outta one eye and saw Reardon on the ground,
too, I knew I was licked."

When another umpire once rejected his suggestion that it
was growing too dark to continue playing, Stengel goaded him
by signaling his pitches with a flashlight.

When John McGraw, his idol as a manager, attempted to stifle
him and his wayward behavior, Stengel rebelled somewhat more
gently. McGraw hired a private detective to shadow Stengel and
Irish Meusel, the two most renowned hell-raisers on the New
York Giants. So the two players simply split up, forcing
McGraw's man to track one but neglect the other. Stengel then
went to McGraw and said, with pretended resentment: "If you
want me followed, you'll have to get me a detective of my own."

Later, when he was a manager himself, Stengel looked back
on his running years and said: "Now that I am a manager, I see
the error of my youthful ways. If any player pulled that stuff on
me now, I would probably fine his ears off."

Indeed, he was frequently accused of intolerance in the face
of other people's antics. When he was the manager at Toledo in

the American Association before making his assault on dugouts in the big leagues, his players, like most other working adults in the country in the 1920s, became Wall Street buffs who played the stock market and showed more frenzy over the stock averages than their batting averages. The team slipped from first place and plunged to eighth in 1929 just before the market plunged even deeper.

Casey called his team of investors together one day at the peak of the boom and said with a tone of formality: "You fellows better start buying Pennsylvania Rail Road and Baltimore & Ohio stock, because when we start shipping you out to the bushes next week those roads are going to get rich."

A quarter of a century later, after he took charge of the Yankees, he watched his players easing into a game of Twenty Questions aboard a train en route from a catastrophic series against the meek Philadelphia Athletics. When he could stand the frivolity no longer, he poked his head around from the manager's front seat in the special car and growled: "I'll ask *you* a question: How many of you fellas think you're earning your salary?"

By the time the Yankees were deep into the 1950 season, scrambling to defend the improbable championship they had won the year before, Stengel wasn't browbeating on a massive scale. But neither DiMaggio nor Phil Rizzuto felt amused anymore. They believed that he overmanaged, overplatooned, and overreacted, and they resented it.

He especially riled DiMaggio on July 4 when he suggested that Joe try playing first base. He sensed that the suggestion would outrage DiMaggio after more than eleven seasons as the premier center fielder in the game, so he nudged Dan Topping into the role of messenger. DiMaggio was infuriated by the implied notion that he might be losing some range in the open reaches of center field, but he acquiesced and actually played first base that day.

He didn't argue, at least not publicly, and the next day he was returned to center field because new injuries on the team forced

Stengel to juggle his lineup one more time. And that was the point of irritation: Stengel may have had good tactical reasons for wanting to make room in his outfield for some young hitters like Hank Bauer, Gene Woodling, Cliff Mapes, and Jackie Jensen. But *no* tactical reasons were compelling enough to switch DiMaggio from his position of distinction.

Stengel probably had good tactical reasons for trying another switch, but DiMaggio was just as insulted. The Old Man dropped him for a time from the cleanup spot in the batting order to the number five spot below, and awarded the cleanup role to Johnny Mize, who was a year older than DiMaggio but who nonetheless hit twenty-five home runs in only ninety games. DiMaggio bristled at that demotion, and he bristled even more in August when Stengel sat him on the bench for a few days for a rest that Joe didn't think he needed.

When he got back into the lineup in the middle of August, he went on a rampage, hitting .400 for the next two weeks and .373 for the month of September. He then finished the season with a fairly low batting average of .301, but he hit 32 home runs, knocked in 122, and again led the Yankees to the pennant. It would have taken a brave or reckless man to intimate to DiMaggio that maybe Casey had handled it smartly and rested him at exactly the right time.

One year later, Stengel dropped him down to fifth in the lineup again, replacing him as the cleanup hitter with Yogi Berra, and the reaction was identical: DiMaggio resented the move mightily, but vented his resentment on pitchers and not on his own teammates or his own meddling manager.

In his first game batting in the fifth spot, he knelt in the on-deck circle in the first inning and watched Berra nail Bob Feller for a triple and a 1–0 lead. DiMaggio followed with a grounder back to Feller and swallowed his pride.

The next time he went to the plate, he did even worse, grounding into a double play. But in the fifth inning, Feller tempted fate when he walked Berra intentionally with a runner on second base and two down. Joe knelt in the circle and watched that time, too, taking it as the ultimate insult at a time in his career when insults seemed to be coming in waves.

He walked to the plate, Mel Allen remembered, "with solemn interest." Then he got behind in the count, one ball and two strikes. But when Feller went for the kill, he rocketed the hard slider 450 feet to the fence in deep left-center for three bases and two runs.

When anybody dared to broach the subject, Stengel reacted with just as much sensitivity as DiMaggio. The manager may not have marched through the generations of baseball time wearing the toga of Yankee tradition, but when he was inducted into the Hall of Fame twenty years later, he reminded people that he had been in touch with greatness, too. He carried the crowd at Cooperstown back through the decades and the eras of baseball, and said: "I chased the balls that Babe Ruth hit."

So, when he was questioned about his tactical moves with Joe DiMaggio, he said with heat: "DiMaggio? They said I didn't like him, but I *played* him. What more could I do than that? There were a lot of great ones, and Ruth could pitch, too. But this man is the best I had."

But Stengel had other problems besides his uneasy relationship with his best player. Joe Page suddenly lost his effectiveness as the "stopper" who came out of the bullpen with the game on the line and fired left-handed hardballs. So George Weiss had to go shopping for an experienced relief pitcher, and got one: Tom Ferrick of the St. Louis Browns, one of Connie Mack's pitchers of 1941 on the Philadelphia A's when Mr. Mack instructed them to give Ted Williams a fair chance at the .400 mark, and they did. And when Tommy Henrich added a battered knee to the club's medical log, Weiss went shopping again in September and bought Johnny Hopp from Pittsburgh to take his place.

But the move that paid off the most, and for the longest time, was the elevation of a twenty-one-year-old left-handed pitcher from the farm team at Kansas City. He was Edward Charles Ford, the fresh-faced city slicker from Manhattan Aviation High School, but more prominently a graduate of the city's sandlots. He opened his professional career in 1947 by winning thirteen games and losing four at Butler in the boondocks leagues. By the time the Yankees brought him up to the big leagues two and a half years later, he was about to enter military service for two years. But before he did, he pitched in twenty games for them, started twelve, won nine, lost one, completed seven, and finished with an earned-run average of 2.81.

When the trading, promoting, and wheeling and dealing were completed, the Yankees somehow were leading the league again on the final day, with Detroit, Boston, and Cleveland chasing in that order.

In the National League, the Philadelphia Phillies — who had won only one pennant in eighty-one years — held a seven-game lead on September 23 and seemed in no danger of not winning their second in eighty-two years. But they won it the hard way. They lost nine of their final thirteen games, let their lead dissolve to one game, then had to play ten innings on the final afternoon of the season at Ebbets Field before subduing the Dodgers on a home run by Dick Sisler, with a young right-handed pitcher named Robin Roberts outlasting Don Newcombe.

If there ever seemed to be a chance for Cinderella to become the star of the ball, this was it. In the thirty years before 1950, the Phillies had finished in last place more than half the time. They also had lost two bright young pitchers, Bubba Church and Bob Miller, to injuries. Curt Simmons, the twenty-one-year-old left-handed ace of the staff, was inducted into the Army during the pennant race in September, and got back to watch the World Series only by dispensation. And what he watched was a massacre of sorts, David against Goliath, except that this time David didn't make it.

But the Phillies opened with surprise, and nearly got away with it. Their manager, Eddie Sawyer, started Jim Konstanty against Vic Raschi in the opening game, and that was after Konstanty had set a major-league record by pitching in seventy-four games, winning 16, losing 7, and starting none.

In fact, he had never started a game for the Phillies. But he started this one, and nearly finished it, allowing only four hits until he left for a pinch hitter in the eighth inning after coming close to one of the great coups of World Series history: the career pitcher *de luxe* who muzzles the mighty defending champion Yankees.

But Stengel had horses, too, starting with Raschi, who meanwhile was stopping the Phillies on two hits and winning the game, 1-0.

The next day, Robin Roberts tangled with Allie Reynolds for ten innings until he made a mistake on Joe DiMaggio, who had popped up the last six times he batted in the Series. But this time he popped one into the upper grandstand in left-center field in Philadelphia, and the Yankees won it by a score of 2-1 and went two games in front of the "Whiz Kids" of Philadelphia, who were aging quickly but gracefully.

The Phillies were still tenacious in the third game when the Series shifted to New York. They even went into the bottom of the eighth inning with a 2-1 lead. But they lost the lead when shortstop Granny Hamner made an error with the bases loaded. And they lost the game in the bottom of the ninth when Jerry Coleman singled home Gene Woodling, and the Yankees moved three games in front.

In two World Series thirty-five years apart, the Phillies now had lost seven games in a row by the margin of one run. They did it in the final four games of the 1915 Series against the Red Sox, and they did it in the first three games in 1950 against the Yankees. They finally managed to break that particular streak the next day against Whitey Ford when they lost by three runs and also lost the Series in four straight. And suddenly, old Casey Stengel and his mixed team of senior stars and junior prodigies were winners again.

To the senior of the senior stars, Joe DiMaggio, the Series was something of a milestone, even though it was his ninth in twelve years. He was being analyzed and inspected by the hour for signs of erosion. Actually, despite his slumps and switches, it had been a resounding season by any measure. But the "DiMaggio watch" had begun, and the critics were circling.

Because of that, he allowed himself extra pleasure over the home run off Robin Roberts in the second game. Roberts, a relentless right-hander headed for the Hall of Fame, came within one pitch of achieving a baseball rarity: He got DiMaggio to pop up four times in a row (after two pop flies the day before), and he went for one more but made the pitch too good and DiMaggio pounced. Afterward, Joe said it was the most important home run in his career. He was probably reaching, but these days he seemed to be reaching more than usual.

One month after the Series, in an article title that seemed typical of the type of press he was receiving, *Sports* magazine asked: "What About DiMaggio Now?" But it didn't seem able to supply the final answer, saying instead: "Harassed by physical difficulties and batting slumps, the Yankee Clipper was having a tough season. The experts started to write him off. But they buried him too soon."

Joe, who felt the slings and arrows even before they stung, promptly raised the question with Dan Topping. He was absolutely secure in the knowledge that nobody would ever shove him, but he also was absolutely sure that nobody had to. When the time came, he would be the first to know, and the first to go.

DiMaggio conceded that he felt as though he were "just about stepping off the hill and going down the incline." But Topping reassured him that he would not be taking the money under "false pretenses," persuaded him to accept one more year at $100,000 again, and sent him home with handclasps, backslaps, and huzzahs.

But "home" was precisely the heart of the problem for DiMaggio. He had been raised in a bustling, crowded, and endearing home, but for the last fifteen years, though successful and

even renowned beyond expectations, he had been living the life
of a well-paid hermit. He had fans, friends, and legions of
women, but they didn't add up to a home.

To steepen his sense of loneliness, Rosalie DiMaggio had died
on June 18 when he was struggling to establish some level of
performance for the 1950 season. She was seventy-two years old
and she had been suffering from cancer for several years. So in
little more than a year's time Joe had lost his father and mother
at a time when he also seemed inevitably in danger of losing his
command on the ball field, where he had become the power
and the pride of the family.

DiMaggio was still wrapped in a heavy mood when he reported to spring training in February 1951, and even that bit of
routine represented a change: The Yankees and Giants had
agreed to switch training camps, so the Yankees pitched their
tents in Phoenix while the Giants opened in St. Petersburg. It
was the Yankees' first penetration of the West, and their training
base was embroiled with speculation about DiMaggio and the
rookie Mickey Mantle. The timing was dramatic: DiMaggio
hinted at times, and announced at times, that this would be his
final year in uniform. And there came Mantle, the man most
likely to succeed as his replacement in center field and as the
heir to the empire.

"Mickey Mantle, rookie from Commerce, Oklahoma," wrote
James P. Dawson in *The New York Times,* "will be the subject of
an extensive experiment in the Yankees' training campaign. No
less an authority than Manager Casey Stengel revealed this infor-
mation today, one of those rare days when rain dampened activities in the Valley of the Sun.

"Stengel said he would work the 20-year-old Mantle in center
field, and immediately speculation arose over whether the Yanks
regarded the rookie as the eventual successor to the great Joe
DiMaggio."

The great Joe DiMaggio added some urgency to the speculation by declaring again that he intended to retire after the

season. If so, then Stengel had little choice but to groom a replacement. And if the replacement was to be Mantle, who had played at Independence, Kansas, in 1949 and at Joplin, Missouri, in 1950, then the grooming process suddenly had become a quandary.

"The husky blond," one report intoned, "has the speed of a deer, the swinging power of a seasoned hitter and the throwing arm that compares with anything in camp right now. But he is both a delight and a problem. Should Casey play him or let him ride the bench after a jump from Class C at Joplin, Missouri?"

Well, it was no problem as long as Joe DiMaggio was playing center field. But that foreshadowed a problem in itself, of course, because DiMaggio opened the season in center field, Mantle opened alongside him in right field, and people on the sidelines waited for one changing of the guard, one more time.

As it turned out, neither one of them got off to a rousing start. Mantle exuded power and force, but he was overmatched by big-league pitching and kept striking out. Stengel even sent him back to the minor leagues for six weeks. And DiMaggio labored against insult and injury both, played in only 116 of the 154 games, batted only .263 with 12 home runs and 71 runs batted in. It was his worst, and predictably his last, season.

Also his most contentious season. The strain with Stengel crossed the line into some public bickering, notably in early July when the Yankees and Red Sox, who were both a game back chasing the Indians, opened a series. The Red Sox promptly mauled Yankee pitching and delivered a knockout in the first inning. So Stengel made one of his sweeping moves on the spot: Billy Martin replaced the veteran Phil Rizzuto at shortstop, Gil McDougald took over for Coleman at second, and, *mirabile dictu,* Jackie Jensen trotted out to center field and replaced Joe DiMaggio.

When DiMaggio was questioned later about the move, he replied with anger. When Stengel was questioned, he replied with vagueness. He insisted that he had sent Jensen to the outfield only to ask if DiMaggio wanted to take a rest, not to tell him to take a hike. But who, let alone Joe DiMaggio, could accept that explanation?

In *The Times* that day, John Drebinger wrote: "This has been DiMaggio's mood for a long time. In fact, he rarely talks to his teammates or manager, let alone anyone remotely associated with the press. On a recent train ride following a night game in Philadelphia, DiMaggio, in the Yanks' special diner, sat by himself at a table set for four. It's a queer set-up, but almost everyone traveling with the Bombers is leaving the Clipper severely alone."

Severely alone. Even he could see the irony in it. "When I get a hit now," he said, receiving congratulations after a game-winning hit in September, "they send me a telegram."

At the end of the season, his batting average was the lowest among all the team's outfielders, even four points lower than Mantle's .267. But the Yankees had so many professionals on their roster that they won the pennant by five full games over Cleveland and by eleven over Boston. Then they settled back to watch the National League play out its melodrama: The New York Giants, who had lost eleven games in a row at the start of the season, were still thirteen and a half games behind the Brooklyn Dodgers in the middle of August. But under the goading of Leo Durocher, they caught and tied the Dodgers on the final day of the season, then defeated them in the third and final game of the playoff when Bobby Thomson hit his famous three-run home run off Ralph Branca in the last half of the ninth inning.

The World Series started the next day and became something of an anti-climax, although the Giants won the opening game and appeared on the way to certifying themselves as the ultimate storybook team in baseball. But the Yankees, old hands at surviving the perils of any short series, won four of the next five games and swept to their third championship in a row.

In the first three games, DiMaggio got no hits. But in the

fourth game, he singled and hit a home run off Sal Maglie, and he ended the Series with six hits in six games and five runs batted in. It was his tenth World Series in thirteen years.

But it was also his most bitter World Series. Twelve days after it closed, the Dodgers' scouting report on the Yankees was published in *Life* magazine, and it was humiliating to him. It was the last straw.

Worse, the only reason the report surfaced was because it had become the object of intrigue. The intrigue was hatched by Clay Felker, a statistician on the Giants' broadcasting team, who wanted to land a job on *Life*. He reportedly was told the price of admission was the National League scouting report on the Yankees.

Once the Dodgers were blasted out of the playoff by Bobby Thomson, the scouting report should have stayed in a drawer in the desk of Buzzy Bavasi, the general manager. But Felker persuaded him to unzip the report and promptly leaked it to *Life*. It was written by Andy High, a onetime third baseman who was now a superscout for the Dodgers, and in it he reported that Joe DiMaggio was no longer the star of the cast.

"His reflexes are very slow," he said, "and he can't pull a good fastball at all. He cannot stop quickly and throw hard, and you can take the extra base on him. He can't run, and he won't bunt."

Angry? Beyond belief. Embarrassed? Beyond reason. The Yankees won the Series, true, and he played a role of some strength. But either his skin was too thin or his pride too deep. And, approaching his thirty-seventh birthday, he decided that the final game of the World Series on October 10 was the final game of his career. As his friend Jimmy Cannon remembered later, this was the time when "despair seized him about his vanishing gifts."

He carried his "despair," if that's what it was, across the Pacific to Japan as part of a lengthy tour the Yankees took after the Series. He even hit a home run in Tokyo on November 16. But when Dan Topping offered him one more year at $100,000, no strings attached, he refused. The die was cast.

It was two o'clock in the afternoon on December 11, and the Yankees gathered the clans for the announcement in their offices in the Squibb Tower at 745 Fifth Avenue in midtown Manhattan.

Dan Topping came out, stood in front of the massed microphones and cameras, and said:

"Del Webb and I worked until ten o'clock on Joe last night, but he wouldn't change his mind."

DiMaggio, serious but not somber, stood alongside while Red Patterson went to the microphones and read the farewell speech for him:

"I told you fellows last spring I thought this would be my last year. I only wish I could have had a better year. But even if I hit .350, this would have been the last year for me. You all know I've had more than my share of physical injuries and setbacks during my career. In recent years, these have been too frequent to laugh off. When baseball is no longer fun, it's no longer a game. And so, I've played my last game.

"Since coming to New York, I've made a lot of friends and picked up a lot of advisors, but I would like to make one point clear: No one has influenced me in making this decision. It has been my problem, and my decision to make. I feel that I have reached a stage where I can no longer produce for my ball club, my manager, my teammates and my fans the sort of baseball their loyalty to me deserves.

"In closing, I would like to say I feel I have been unusually privileged to play all my major league baseball for the New York Yankees. But it has been an even greater privilege to be able to play baseball at all. It has added much to my life. What I will remember most in days to come will be the great loyalty of the fans. They have been very good to me."

He was asked if he had any ambitions to become a manager, and he said: "The fact is, I don't want to put on a baseball uniform again at all, and I certainly don't want to have to worry about twenty-five other men."

He was standing now in front of a mural that looked as vast as center field in Yankee Stadium. It pictured him as a young man swinging a bat. His back was turned to the wall while he repeated: "I've played my last game of ball."

One more time, he was asked why. And this time he cut through the words and the memories, and said:

"I just don't have it anymore."

In San Francisco, a continent away, his older brother Tom was asked the same question, and he said:

"He quit because he wasn't Joe DiMaggio anymore."

10

MARILYN

SHE WAS THE IRRESISTIBLE FORCE; he was the immovable object. She was the love of his life, and the torment of his life. She was goddess, she was demon. They had a courtship that lasted two years, and a marriage that lasted 274 days. It happened so fast that his best man, Reno Barsocchini, was still on the scene nine months later to help him move out of the apartment.

Tolstoy had it right when he wrote, in the opening words of *Anna Karenina:* "Happy families are all alike; every unhappy family is unhappy in its own way." But this one was happy *and* unhappy because he was Joe DiMaggio and she was Marilyn Monroe. The rub was that, happy or unhappy, they were never quite a family.

But they were a fantasy, starting with the way they met: in the All-American tradition, on a blind date. Also, the way they were introduced: through a baseball player named Gus Zernial, who was a bit of a fantasy himself with home-run power, Li'l Abner muscles, and the nickname Ozark Ike. And yet, the fantasy that Gus Zernial helped to shape came to a tragic ending, and it deepened the solitude and the secrets surrounding Joe DiMaggio.

It might not have happened at all if he hadn't retired from baseball near the end of 1951, because he was finally free from the itineraries and schedules that dictated his time and travels from February until October every year and even beyond, if the Yankees were in another World Series, which they usually were. But there was even irony in that: *With* DiMaggio playing the lead role, they won nine World Series and ten pennants in thirteen years. *Without* him, they won six World Series and ten pennants in the next twelve years.

But he quit while he was still on top, as it were; at least, still on top of the town. Not long after he retired, he went to Yankee Stadium one night to watch the fights. He loved the fights, and he went this time in distinguished company.

He was accompanied by Edward Bennett Williams, the renowned lawyer, who soon became his personal hero and perhaps his most cherished friend; Toots Shor, whose "joint" was facing the prospect of losing its marquee attraction; W. Averell Harriman, the diplomat and later the governor of New York; and Ernest Hemingway and his wife, Mary, who should have needed no introduction, except maybe to the fight mob surging into the stadium.

But even in this phalanx of world-class stars, the mob had eyes only for one, and they swarmed around DiMaggio clamoring for his autograph. Then they realized he was walking with some obviously major talent, and that piqued their interest, too. One kid in the crowd even looked at Hemingway and asked: "Hey, you're probably somebody, too, right?"

And Hemingway, who didn't need to be told that he was unknown and unranked in this particular pit, laughed and replied: "Yeah, I'm his doctor."

When he flew home to San Francisco later that winter, it was like stepping through the looking glass. His mother and father were both gone, his active days as a ballplayer were gone, his times at bat were gone. Even his brothers and sisters were pretty much gone. But Joe realigned the old household on Beach Street in the Marina district, within sight of Fisherman's Wharf on one side and within distant sight of the Golden Gate Bridge on the other side. He anointed his widowed older sister, Marie DiMaggio Kron, as the head of the house and the keeper of the keys. And he became the traveling head of household. But even in later years, he would instruct his friends, if they sent something to his home by mail, to separate it from the flood of mail that somehow reached the house by writing in the corner of the envelope: "Attention, Marie." That way, he knew it was personal, and so did Marie.

But life in retirement was also something like life in exile with new scenes, new routines, and new slumps. And even when he was drawn into new ventures, he wasn't as comfortable as when he had been straining to overcome the aches and pains of spring training and six months of ball games.

He agreed to take part in a pregame television show for the Yankees. But Jackie Farrell, the wispy and wee little man who pieced together shows like this for the club, remembered later that "Joe was very nervous about the show."

"He just didn't like to talk in front of people, on camera or off," Farrell said. "He had to have everything written out on cue cards. Once, he misplaced his cue card and wouldn't go on until we found it."

The crucial card read: "Hi, I'm Joe DiMaggio."

Not that he was in danger of being mistaken for anybody else. But even then, undefeated and unchallenged, as it were, also newly unemployed and certainly unencumbered, he was uptight and at times terrorized by the demands of public appearances. There was something about the scripted confines of television, something about the stopwatch timing, something about the whole contrived checklist that gave him instant malaise. He was always infinitely more at ease ad-libbing his way through a turn at bat against, say, Bob Feller than he was sticking to the instructions for a thirty-second commercial.

He also cringed at the thought that commercials or other performances on camera or microphone weren't usually done on his home turf or on his terms. You had twelve guys running around with clipboards and scripts telling everybody to stand by. Even when he agreed to appear in a spaghetti commercial for the Yankees' pregame show, things got out of hand: To make the point that pasta provides energy, he persuaded people to let his friend and disciple Billy Martin slide into second base instead of a professional actor. This was in St. Petersburg in the spring of 1952, and Martin slid with so much energy that he fractured a bone in his ankle.

But except for the perils of reading cue cards on spaghetti, he was finally trying the life of the idle rich. And one day in March that spring, Gus Zernial made it richer.

Zernial was a six-foot Texan with hard biceps, an easy personality, and fresh-faced good looks, and he had just made a name for himself by hitting thirty-three home runs for the Chicago White Sox and the Philadelphia Athletics in 1951. He did even better two years later when he hit forty-two. But he was already one of the rising stars of the game that spring on a baseball landscape that for the first time in a generation lacked Joe DiMaggio.

For all those reasons, Zernial was the right man in the right place when the Athletics got a phone call one day from a Hollywood agent named David Marsh. He was calling to ask the A's if their new star would pose for some publicity pictures with Marsh's new star client, a twenty-five-year-old actress named Marilyn Monroe.

She was, Zernial confessed after they met, "the most beautiful girl I had ever seen." On the spot, he also confessed, he was tempted to ask her out to dinner that same night; but on the spot, he remembered that his wife was watching from the grandstand, and so he missed his rendezvous with destiny.

Marilyn Monroe owned some exceptionally minor film credits at the time. But she owned some exceptionally major personal credits. She was five feet five inches tall, she weighed 118 enticing pounds, she stared into space through wide, oval eyes, and she topped it off with a spectacularly blond and at times platinum mane.

There were probably a thousand great-looking starlets in Hollywood in those days, all of them panting and jostling for the big break. But she was already beginning to rise in the standings, not because of her assets as an actress but because of her assets as a woman. She also posed for large, splashy calendars for five dollars an hour, wearing as little as possible. And she finally hit a grand slam, as it were, wearing nothing but an arched and haughty look on a calendar that sold six million copies and made $750,000 for the John Baumgarth Company. She made fifty dollars for posing.

But the eyes of the nation were trained on her now, and Joe DiMaggio didn't need any prompting after the photographs of Marilyn and Gus Zernial started to appear in newspapers from coast to coast in one of those typical shots of life in the baseball camps, and can spring be far behind? A few days after the pictures began to show up in the papers, the Athletics played a charity game against a bunch of retired players from California, and DiMaggio went straight for the target.

"How come I never get to pose with beautiful girls like that?" he asked, gibing at Zernial as though he had never posed with coveys of beautiful girls like that.

Zernial, whose marriage so far had survived the photo encounter, told him that it had been arranged by David Marsh in Hollywood. Joe took his best shot at that one, and didn't miss.

A few days later, Marsh did the only logical thing any press agent could do: He telephoned his client and invited her to dinner with his wife and Joe DiMaggio.

It wasn't exactly a marriage of true minds. While Marsh and his wife sat and waited at the Villa Nova in Hollywood, their celebrated guests preened. Joe was fifteen minutes late; Monroe nearly two hours late. They shook hands and settled back somewhat awkwardly. Nobody said: "Dr. Livingston, I presume?"

Nobody said much of anything until the conversation got around to the film Marilyn was making then, *Monkey Business.* She played the sexy secretary to Cary Grant, who played a prim research chemist and who presumably was no match for his bombshell secretary. Everybody knew what Cary Grant could do on the silver screen, but Paul Beckley brought you up to date in a hurry on the somewhat unknown Monroe when he wrote, in his review in The *New York Herald Tribune:*

"Not having seen Miss Monroe before, I now know what that's all about. She disproves the old stage rule about not turning one's back to the audience."

The evening took a turn when Mickey Rooney caught sight of DiMaggio from another table and instantly crashed the party. He began to babble about DiMaggio's baseball exploits, especially the clamor of his dramatic return in Boston in the middle of the 1949 season, and painted him in titanic terms.

Nobody who attended the dinner that night has said much about it, but several second-guessers and Monroe-watchers have suggested that Rooney's prattling somehow made an impression on her, elevating DiMaggio in her realization to his full status as a public hero. But it couldn't have made too much of an impression because she announced at eleven o'clock that she had an early call the next morning, and she stood to leave.

DiMaggio, who still didn't like to drive cars, had come to the restaurant by taxicab. He also stood and said good night. She offered to drop him at his hotel in her car, and they left together.

What happened after that? The speculation and gossip that enveloped them from that night forward now runs the range of theatrical possibilities. One version says they parked in front of his hotel for a time. Another version says he requested they take a drive, and they did. David Marsh reportedly telephoned her

the next day and asked: "How did you like him?" And she supposedly laughed and replied: "He struck out."

If he did, he kept striking out for a while. During the next
few days, he called her at home and asked for another date, but
she was "busy." He called again the night after that, and she was
still "busy." He called the day after that, and she probably was
really busy then because she struggled through her films trying
to learn her lines, remember her cues, and primp for her scenes.
He didn't know it at the time, but his beautiful blind date was a
bundle of anxiety and dread, spectacular to look at, impossible
to tame.

But after striking out for a week on the telephone, he suddenly connected. *She* called *him* one day, and asked if he would
take her to dinner. Would he take her to dinner? At that point, he
would have crawled over the polar ice cap to take her to dinner.
He may have been unflappable about most things, but this
wasn't one of them.

Jimmy Cannon, who liked to hang out with Joe back in New
York and who wrote columns fixing his place in the history of
our times, sensed that this was the start of some pure fantasy.
They were storybook stars trying to find private joy in their public world, for better, for worse.

"They are folk idols, Marilyn and Joe," he observed later, "a
whole country's pets. They are the fulfillment of the uncompli-
cated desires of the obscure and those troubled by poverty and
insecurity. What is simpler than being the greatest ballplayer of
your generation? What is easier to be than the most sensational
actress of this age?

"We are people," he said, getting to the essence of the public's rapture, "who pine to be what Marilyn and Joe DiMaggio
are."

Or, he might have added, what they seemed to be.

She was born Norma Jean Baker on June 1, 1926, in the Los
Angeles General Hospital. Her mother was Gladys Monroe, and

her father was Jack Baker, although some people have doubted that he was actually her father.

But something else could not be doubted: There was a dark side to her family's history, and it would stalk her for the rest of her life. Her mother spent long stretches of time in a mental hospital. Her grandfather Monroe spent his final years in an asylum. Her grandmother, Della Monroe Grainger, underwent treatment in psychiatric wards. And her mother's brother committed suicide.

She was raised in a foster home by Ida and Albert Bolender, who cared for as many as half a dozen children at a time. But in 1935, when she was nine years old, she went to the Los Angeles Orphans' Society Home and stayed for nearly two years. Then she was released and placed with Grace McKee Goddard and her husband, Ervin "Doc" Goddard, an aircraft factory worker, and they became her legal guardians.

But the Goddards farmed her out frequently, and for the next five years she did a lot of drifting. But she still had at least the framework of a home with the Goddards. She went to Van Nuys High School with their daughter, who took the well-trodden path to the film studios and became the starlet Jody Lawrence at Paramount. For that matter, Grace Goddard, the mother, had long since traveled the same path to a different destination: She worked as a film librarian at Columbia.

Norma Jean didn't have to look far for attention. The boy next door was James Daugherty, who had been a popular student at Van Nuys High before she got there. He was good-looking and well employed in one of the aircraft factories that boomed in southern California during the war years. And on June 19, 1942, just like that, they got married. He was twenty-one, she was sixteen. He joined the Merchant Marine in 1943, and they were divorced in 1946.

Meanwhile, in 1942, the year she married the boy next door, the year after Joe DiMaggio was hitting in fifty-six straight games, she joined the tide and went to work as a paint sprayer in a defense plant. And that was where a photographer at the factory started taking pictures of her. Not only that, he also brought the pictures to the attention of Miss Emmeline Snively, who was running the Blue Book School of Charm and Modeling, and Miss Snively knew a good thing when she saw one, too. She tutored Marilyn on things like walking and posing and making up that fair face and bleaching that bleached hair.

She also took new photos of Marilyn and circulated them around town, and a model was born, a busy one. It was a new world for Marilyn, but she embraced it and even wallowed in it, and later remembered: "I mostly answered calls for a girl in a bathing suit. One month, I was on five magazine covers."

She also was on a bunch of calendar covers, and it was only a nudge or two to the movie studios, where she soon was steered by Harry Lipton, an agent for Helen Ainsworth of the National Concert and Artist Corporation. It took some persistence, but he eventually wangled an appointment for her with Ben Lyon, the casting director at Twentieth Century Fox. He said she reminded him of Jean Harlow. But he didn't exactly put his money where his mouth was: He signed her to the standard don't-call-me-I'll-call-you contract for the standard seventy-five dollars a week. She wasn't exactly in the big leagues, but a big-league team was signing her to a minor-league contract. She was in the Fox farm system, and it had a cast of thousands.

Lyon even arranged for her to get a part in a movie. It wasn't much of a part, and it wasn't much of a movie. In fact, it had the unthinkable title of *Scudda Hoo! Scudda Hay!* And her part called for her to recite one word: "Hello." And the line was cut.

Within a year, though, she was cut, too. Fox dropped her from the payroll for no known reason, except the obvious one that she had no training and nobody knew if she had any talent. She did not shoot down speculation that she was fired for having turned down Darryl F. Zanuck, the impresario of the studio, who just happened to keep a pied-à-terre for exceptional privacy behind his office.

She repeated the same cycle at Columbia, and was turned loose there possibly for the same reason: Harry Cohn, who was known and detested for coming on too strong, may have come on too strong.

She finally landed a walk-on part with the Marx Brothers in one of their romps, *Love Happy,* and Groucho not only leered at her for years after but also announced for years after: "She's got the greatest ass in Hollywood."

If there was a turn of fortune, it probably came in 1950 when she played the baby-doll house pet to Louis Calhern in *The Asphalt Jungle.* It was her customary decorative role, but this time she made an impact. She made such an impact that Fox promptly signed her back for five hundred a week, nearly seven times her old retaining salary. She was twenty-four years old, and arriving.

But she was arriving because of her stunning looks, not because of her stunning talent. Nobody knew if she had any talent, and they weren't likely to know as long as she was playing baby-doll roles. She was smart enough to realize that doors were opening, and she also realized they were opening because of the way she could light up the screen. And she was beginning to appear in casts headed by established stars. The only problem was that she also was beginning to cherish the idea of making it as an actress, not just a knockout. It was an ambition that kept growing until it became an obsession, and by then it was consuming her.

But for now, she accepted the Hollywood equation: Sexy face, sexy body, and sexy voice equals sexy roles, and they paid the bills.

After *The Fireball,* also in 1950, a roller-derby saga with Mickey Rooney, came *The Asphalt Jungle* and *All About Eve,* followed by *Love Nest* in 1951, in which she played one of the points of a triangle that also involved William Lundigan and June Haver. The same year, she played a secretary in *As Young As You Feel,* and she moved into stronger company in *Let's Make It Legal,* with Claudette Colbert and Zachary Scott.

She hit the jackpot in 1952 when she was cast in five pictures, starting with *Clash by Night,* in which she played a cannery worker opposite Barbara Stanwyck and Robert Ryan. Next came *We're Not Married,* a farce with a manic story line about six couples who discover that their marriage licenses aren't actually valid. The story may have been trivial, but the cast also included Ginger Rogers, Fred Allen, and David Wayne. And she once more caught the approving eye of a reviewer for the *New York Herald Tribune,* this time Otis Guernsey, who wrote that she "looks as though she had been carved out of cake by Michelangelo."

In her next film, she got the chance to perform in a broader role. She played a disturbed young woman in *Don't Bother to Knock,* with Richard Widmark. But if this was her debut in something more demanding than the customary roles as a sexpot, she received a rude greeting from Bosley Crowther, who wrote in *The New York Times:* "Unfortunately, all the equipment that Miss Monroe has to handle this job are a childishly blank expression and a provokingly feeble, hollow voice."

Regardless, she took the blank expression and feeble voice straight into *Gentlemen Prefer Blondes* and *How to Marry a Millionaire,* and then *Monkey Business,* the film she was shooting with Cary Grant when DiMaggio entered her life. And before the year was out, she would play a streetwalker in *O. Henry's Full House,* starring the giant Charles Laughton.

So her career was bustling when DiMaggio began to court her. By the time she had finished her five films that year, he had thought enough was happening in their relationship to take her home to San Francisco to meet his sisters and brothers. And by the following summer, *she* thought enough was happening in their relationship to send him an SOS from Banff, Canada, and he came running.

She sent the distress call because she was starting to suffer from the pangs of anxiety and fear over the demands of her work. It was a cycle of pressures that haunted her as the film opportunities grew bigger and the demands grew bigger and her fear grew bigger. She was being overpowered this time by the pressures of acting opposite Robert Mitchum under the renowned director Otto Preminger in *River of No Return.* She didn't like the script, she didn't like Preminger's strict instructions, and she didn't like straining a ligament in her leg during warmups for a scene on a river raft.

It was the first time since they had met that she appealed to DiMaggio to rescue her, but not the last. He was already sensing some anxiety himself: anxiety that her career might put too many demands on both of them. He even wanted her to be his wife, but he didn't want to share her with ogling film audiences or with ogling film executives. Somehow in the far reaches of his mind, he wanted her to come home and stay home. He was in love with the idea of loving and having her, but he was in dread of the idea of other men loving and having her, even in the lustful thoughts that her movies were designed to create.

But when she called, he came running. He flew to Banff and shepherded her back home to San Francisco, where he could comfort her and protect her far from the film studios in Los Angeles or their location sets in places like Banff. And they were already getting into the geography that reflected their separate worlds: She represented Los Angeles and its schmaltz; he typified San Francisco and its ethnic hominess. She wanted a career; he wanted a ménage, and he wanted to run it.

They were still in San Francisco mending her mind when DiMaggio suffered a loss that overpowered *him.* His older brother Mike drowned in a fishing accident. In just three years, he had lost his father, mother, and brother, and he was shattered.

Now it was Marilyn's turn to console him, and she did. Somehow, out of the depths of her own misery over her career, she reached out and comforted him over the loss of his brother. In some ways, they may have been closer at that time of mutual sorrow than ever again. They were emotionally torn, and they needed each other. And carrying their closeness one long step farther, they agreed that the time had come when they should do something about it.

It was three o'clock in the afternoon on January 14, 1954, when they walked into the chambers of Municipal Court Judge Charles S. Perry in the San Francisco City Hall. He was dressed with all due solemnity in a blue suit with a blue polka-dot tie. She wore a chocolate-brown suit. They were flanked by Lefty O'Doul and his wife and by Reno Barsocchini, his friend from the old neighborhood, who had set the stage by making the arrangements quickly and simply. It took five minutes.

It took about five minutes more for them to find out that they were not exactly alone. When they walked out of the judge's chambers arm in arm, they were engulfed by the one hundred or more reporters and photographers who had been tipped off and who were massed in the corridors waiting.

It also didn't take five minutes for them to cast shadows into the immediate future. Joe was asked, "Where are you going to live?" And he replied: "Here, in San Francisco." Marilyn was asked: "Are you going to continue acting or settle down?" And she replied: "I'm going to continue my career, but I'm looking forward to being a housewife, too."

The implausibility of handling both roles — Marilyn Monroe and Mrs. Joe DiMaggio — didn't strike people then. Everybody was swept up in the implausibility of the baseball hero marrying the Hollywood queen, a pair of people from humble backgrounds who had made it big and who now were taking the ultimate step. It was a royal coming-together, maybe even a royal wedding, and the cheers drowned out any questioning thoughts such as: Can it work?

For the time being, at least, this was Joe DiMaggio's hometown and Joe DiMaggio's wedding day, and that was good enough. Well, actually his second wedding day, fifteen years after the wedding day he shared with Dorothy Arnold. And it looked as though the whole town had been tipped off. More people were massed outside, and they surged around DiMaggio's blue Cadillac with the "JOE D" plates, and this time he did the driving.

Three hours later, after cruising south along the Pacific Ocean, they pulled into the Clifton Motel in the beach town of Pasa Robles, and Joe asked for a room — with a television set in it.

Asking for a television set on the first night of your honeymoon with Marilyn Monroe may seem like one of the all-time outrages in history. But he may have wanted to pick up newscasts on the voting for baseball's Hall of Fame. And the voting for the Hall of Fame became one of the mysteries of the ages.

It was bad enough the year before, when he had appeared on the ballot for the first time since retiring and got only 117 votes out of 198 cast. He finished *eighth* on the list. How was that possible? The evidence suggests that the ballots were still carrying the names of many of the old-time stars of baseball who were not selected for the Hall of Fame by acclamation, the way the first group was selected in 1936: Ty Cobb, Honus Wagner, Babe Ruth, Walter Johnson, and Christy Mathewson. Further evidence suggests that DiMaggio may have lost some votes because of resentment against the Yankees and against the sportswriters in New York who were suspected of glamorizing the hometown heroes. The ballots were cast by senior baseball writers around the country, and they were not immune from provincialism, even though DiMaggio's career seemed to have carried him far beyond the confines of provincial thinking.

If that was the case, DiMaggio wasn't alone. Bill Terry, the longtime first baseman and manager of the New York Giants, also labored under the burden of geography. He had closed his career with a batting average of .341, and he joined DiMaggio on the list of rejected candidates.

In his second year of eligibility, DiMaggio figured to break clear of the strictures of petty minds and to power his way into

Cooperstown. So with all due respect for the charms of his bride, he knew the results of the voting were being released and he had every right to be curious. But while he and Marilyn were passing their first day or so at the Clifton Motel, the results of the voting were announced — and, this time, he missed by fourteen. He got 175 votes, 189 were needed for election, and the man who later was named "the greatest living ballplayer" failed to make the Hall of Fame for the second straight time.

Ironically, his old teammate Bill Dickey did make it along with Bill Terry and Rabbit Maranville, but that did nothing to soothe his feelings, which were easily bruised, anyway.

Even when he finally made it the following year, in 1955, the distinction was diluted. He won the most votes that time, but he wasn't alone: Ted Lyons, Dazzy Vance, and Gabby Hartnett also made it, and they were inducted en masse.

"He was leaning toward Cooperstown the first day he chased a baseball," Jimmy Cannon wrote when the deed was finally done, "because this was a boy formed early to be what he became. It appeared to be a talent untouched by emotion but it wasn't, and he was made despondent by temporary failure and was elated by success. He took it out on himself and was cruel about it.

"The loneliness was always in him and the shyness and the circus of his fame depressed him. But no one ever had more dignity on a ball field and remember this is a place where a lot of them use the sneaky little tricks they call showmanship. There was none of it in DiMaggio and he came to the big leagues that way and that's the way he left."

Well, if he was truly despondent when he missed the Hall of Fame in 1954, he had a major consolation at his side. And he and Marilyn drove on down to the mountains above Palm Springs for a couple of weeks more and then took their honeymoon all the way back to San Francisco and the house he had given to his mother and father years earlier. His sister Marie did the cooking and the housekeeping, and they spent time sitting with Tom at the family restaurant on Fisherman's Wharf, and for the time being they were "at home" in San Francisco while Marilyn's career marked time in Los Angeles.

One of the reasons her career was marking time was an increasingly familiar one: She had been suspended by Fox for not accepting scripts. But she was still riding the wave of public acclaim, and even hysteria, as the storybook bride of the storybook baseball star. As hype, at least, it could not have been a better match. So her troubles with the studio weren't disabling.

Jimmy Cannon compared them to Mary Pickford and Douglas Fairbanks as America's sweethearts, and although it wasn't a very good comparison, he said:

"They were bigger than Mary and Doug while it lasted because their range of identity was wider. They are Marilyn and Joe, like symbols created for kids to cherish. You don't need any prolonged education or prestige of birth to be Marilyn or Joe. Wealth doesn't help you, either. It happened fast for them and they got it while they were still young enough to enjoy it.

"It might have been an idea Zanuck had. Nunnally Johnson could have turned out the screenplay. Billy Wilder may have directed it. And why shouldn't it star Marilyn Monroe?"

It *did* star Marilyn Monroe, and that was becoming the problem. Even when DiMaggio was the center of attraction, all she had to do to upstage him was walk into view. And it happened soon after they rang down the curtain on the honeymoon when they flew to Japan on a baseball mission.

The mission involved a favor for DiMaggio's old friend and mentor Lefty O'Doul, who was leading a tour of Japan and enlivening it with exhibition ball games and seminars on baseball, and Joe had agreed to appear as a coach and even as a player a few times. It was late in January when he and Marilyn flew from San Francisco to Honolulu and then Tokyo, and he was cheered wherever they went. He probably wasn't expecting her to steal the show, but she did, receiving thunderous welcomes at every stop. The Korean War had ended six months earlier, but there were still a million American soldiers in the Far East, and no beautiful blond actress could ask for more.

For a possessive man like Joe, the sight of his wife being mobbed by cheering, leering young men violated the very essence of his possessiveness, and did it on a gigantic scale. He was proud of her but tortured by the show-business values that made her alluring in a rather brazen way. Worse, every mob scene nudged her career one step farther along the road to the super-celebrity status that seemed to be the point of it all — for the people who cast her and paid her, for the publicity flacks who flaunted her, for the fans who bought the movie magazines and movie tickets. And she seemed to treasure the adulation and even to crave it.

Consequently, when she was asked by some high Army officers at a cocktail party if she would take a sidetrip to Korea to entertain the troops, she accepted — and Joe fretted.

She not only made the trip but made a blockbuster scene or two, arriving by helicopter and then sliding onto the outdoor stage in a sequined gown and singing "Diamonds Are a Girl's Best Friend" while thousands of howling G.I.'s from the First Marine Division hooted and hollered. And when she sang "Do It Again" as an encore loaded with suggestive lines and wiggles, they tore the place apart. Even the Army was impressed and a little intimidated by that performance, and discreetly suggested that she drop that particular number from a repertoire that needed no extra tease.

As she left Seoul to fly back to Tokyo, where her anxious husband was waiting and pacing, she said: "This is the best thing that ever happened to me." She may have said it out of zeal or even patriotism, but she gave the impression that she mostly said it out of sheer exuberance over the waves of rapture that cascaded down on her otherwise fearful mood and mind.

Back in the Imperial Hotel in Tokyo, she was both exhilarated and exhausted and went to bed for four days with a touch of pneumonia while DiMaggio treated her and gave her antibiotics and sheltered her from the world.

It was during this time that she supposedly told him that he couldn't imagine how it felt to be cheered by fifty thousand people. And he supposedly replied: "Yes, I do." Neither of them ever confirmed that this exchange took place, but it has been told and retold as the perfect example of their diverging personalities and views: the wide-eyed aspiring actress basking in the applause; the solemn and enshrined folk hero stating simply and sadly that he had been there before, many times. They may never have said it, but the story served its purpose whenever people later began to search for clues to the downfall of their marriage.

They went back to San Francisco, spent some time idling with his family, took rides on his boat, *The Yankee Clipper.* But they missed the chance of spending time with Joe Jr., who was twelve years old then and away at boarding school. (His mother, Dorothy Arnold, referred publicly to Marilyn as "that woman.") But "that woman" had a bigger problem than that: She was growing bored.

They both knew it was time for her to get back to work, so they made the inevitable move to Los Angeles, rented a house in Beverly Hills, and centered their life on her long days at the studio filming *There's No Business Like Show Business,* with Donald O'Connor and Ethel Merman. It was her first film in eight months, and it was important because she was hoping to use it as a stepping-stone to a major role in *The Seven Year Itch.* But she paid the price for the long hours: She came home weary most nights after he had tried to keep busy playing some golf or joining her on the set or watching TV. And now it was Joe who was getting bored.

He was also getting angry. Part of her job included Hollywood parties, which he hated. And most of her job included concentrated efforts to create and sustain an image of smashing sexiness, which he hated even more.

"My life is dull," he confided to Jimmy Cannon. "I never inter-fere in Marilyn's work. She goes to the studio and I don't go with her anymore. It's the same stuff all the time. They do a scene and then they hang around a long time waiting to look at it.

"I don't resent her fame. She was working long before she met me. And for what? What has she got after all these years? She works like a dog. When she's working, she's up at five or six in the morning and doesn't get through until seven at night. We eat dinner, watch a little television, and go to bed."

He complained to another friend, Arthur Richman, the New York writer and baseball executive, that their house in Beverly Hills was "like Grand Central Station — there was no privacy, and the phones never stopped ringing."

But DiMaggio kept missing the signs. When he had begun to court her two years before, he had seemed certain that the real-ity of her career would never interfere with the fantasy of their being together. And even when her career was clearly interfer-ing with their closeness, he still seemed certain that she could make the right choice when the choice had to be made.

"She's a plain kid," he told Jimmy Cannon. "She'd give up the business if I asked her. She'd quit the movies in a minute. It means nothing to her."

He meant that love would conquer all. But he still refused to admit that love would have a terrible time conquering anything in her frantic and even tragic life after she had made the long climb from foster homes to movie studios and lighted marquees. He wanted to hide; she wanted to grab the brass ring.

Her dresser and longtime companion Lena Pepitone quoted her as putting it this way: "I had always been nothing, a nobody. I couldn't give it up, just when things were looking good for me. Not just to be a housewife, not even Joe's housewife."

By contrast, Jimmy Cannon remembered, "fame irritated Di-Maggio.

"He ducked attention before and after he married Marilyn," he said. "He told me that his golf-playing, television-watching life in Hollywood was dull. He is one of the loneliest men I've ever met, and usually he moved through crowds. The flattery most men enjoy embarrasses him."

The gist of this got back to Marilyn, who pouted to Joe: "You told Jimmy Cannon it was dull living with me."

"No," he replied. "I said my life in Hollywood was dull."

The skirmishing grew more serious when Marilyn flew to New York late in the summer of 1954 to begin work on the "big" film on her agenda, *The Seven Year Itch.* The story was set in the city, and the outside scenes were shot in midtown Manhattan, for all the world to see. But even before she left Los Angeles, they headed for trouble. She announced that she was going to be accompanied by her drama coach, Natasha Lytess, who was a member of her inner circle of support, emotional and professional. DiMaggio resented the coach's influence over his wife, as he resented almost everybody else's influence over her, and he said that he wouldn't go if Lytess did. Marilyn insisted, Joe insisted, and he drove her to the airport but declined to fly with them.

A couple of weeks later, he did join them in New York, but by then Jimmy Cannon was writing what other people were thinking: "All over town, people they didn't know were concerned about Marilyn Monroe and Joe DiMaggio. It's a shame it didn't work. Maybe it can. Maybe it can be patched up. I hope so, anyway."

But any hope that "it" could be patched up faded after DiMaggio arrived in New York and stood watching on the corner of Lexington Avenue and Fifty-first Street while Marilyn played what might have been her most famous and most provocative scene. She had made sixteen films, and in almost all of them played a dumb but devastating blonde, including Miss Caswell opposite George Sanders in *All About Eve* (1950), one of the Bette Davis classics. And here she was starring in George Axelrod's comedy about a summer bachelor, played by Tom Ewell, and his sensational upstairs neighbor.

It was midnight late in September when they shot the celebrated scene: Marilyn playfully standing over a subway grating in
a billowing white skirt that was blown over her bare thighs by
electric fans that had been planted beneath the grating. The
scene was shot at midnight to avoid snarling traffic. But a huge
crowd of onlookers still thronged the sidewalks behind police
barricades, whistling and cheering as the gusts inflated her skirt.

DiMaggio stood off to the side watching with Walter Winchell.
The wind blew and the skirt flew and the crowd screamed, and
DiMaggio bristled.

He was still bristling when he arrived at Toots Shor's a few
blocks away, and he was steaming when he left. And after he
reached the St. Regis Hotel, where they were staying, he got into
a pitched shouting match with Monroe that other guests in the
hotel said they could hear, loud and clear. The next morning, he
flew back to their home in Beverly Hills. Two weeks later, she
announced that she was filing for divorce.

By then, to put it bluntly, Joe had cleared out. He and his
trusty best man, Reno Barsocchini, packed his suitcases and golf
clubs into the car and headed north back to San Francisco.
Whatever it was, a test of willpower, a conflict of careers, a clash
of personalities, it came unraveled with electrifying speed. She
testified, sounding something like Dorothy Arnold thirteen years
before, that he was cold, indifferent, moody, and silent. The pre-
liminary decree was granted on October 27, nine months and
two weeks after they were married.

But the end of the marriage by no means marked the end of
the relationship. He yearned for her, she called for him, especially when she needed strength and protection from her mis-
eries, her pressures, her demons. They finally were admitting
that they couldn't live with each other, certainly not as long as
she pursued her career with passion and he detested it with
passion. But they also sensed that they couldn't live without
each other.

Her lawyer, Jerry Giesler, reported that DiMaggio had caused her "grievous mental suffering and anguish." On the other hand, he acknowledged that there was no community property, and she did not ask for alimony.

The mood swings were extreme. On the dark side, DiMaggio and Frank Sinatra were implicated in a clumsy caper that may have started as a stakeout on Marilyn a few weeks after the divorce. She apparently had parked her car outside an apartment building to visit a woman friend, and was followed by a pair of private investigators on the trail of "divorce evidence." At least, that's what Sinatra called it later when he testified before a legislative committee in California that was looking into the operations of private eyes. But the stakeout reached comic proportions when several men kicked in the door of the wrong apartment. The men weren't identified, but the woman whose door was kicked in later sued Sinatra and DiMaggio for $200,000 in a "wrong-door" action that was settled out of court for $7,500.

On the friendlier side, within months after the divorce, DiMaggio escorted Marilyn to the premiere showing of *The Seven Year Itch* and even escorted her another time to Cedars of Lebanon Hospital, where she underwent minor surgery for a gynecological problem.

But even the good times had bad times. After the premiere of *The Seven Year Itch* at Loew's State Theatre in New York, they went to Toots Shor's for the cast party and got into an argument. It was just like old times, and it ended like old times when Marilyn left by herself.

The peculiar pattern of splits and reunions was interrupted when she began to see the playwright Arthur Miller regularly. They had apparently gotten to know each other even before the divorce, but they grew serious during 1955 and married in June of 1956. It took no stretch of the imagination to follow her feelings: Miller offered her the same sense of security that DiMaggio had, the same shelter against her own storm-tossed fears. And he was an intellectual, which DiMaggio wasn't, and she was now trying to escalate her career into more of an art form than a physical form.

DiMaggio was predictably wounded, and he was even more wounded whenever Marilyn did anything that seemed to puncture the lingering notion that they were a pair of star-crossed but long-term lovers. Edward Bennett Williams, who became his counselor and confidant as the years passed, told Maury Allen later how vulnerable Joe remained.

"I was with Joe when Arthur Miller was called to testify before the House Un-American Activities Committee," he said. "Joe and Marilyn had been divorced, but Joe was still carrying the torch. Marilyn had married Miller, and Joe was upset. Marilyn volunteered to testify for Miller at the hearings. She got up before the committee, defended Miller vigorously, and said: 'Arthur Miller is the only man I ever loved.'

"I knew that would hit Joe like a brick wall. I figured he would cancel our dinner date that evening. He didn't. He never said a word about Marilyn all night. Joe has a way of blocking unpleasant things out of his mind like that."

But Marilyn Monroe's marriage to Arthur Miller was soon beset by the same emotional devils that had haunted her marriage to DiMaggio. In 1957, they flew to England for the filming of *The Prince and the Showgirl*, putting her on the same stage with the king of British acting, Laurence Olivier. But there was pressure in that, too, and it started to build when she turned off the press in London by pretending to be a devotee of great music. She was coaxed to name names and came up with Louis Armstrong and Beethoven, but couldn't name anything by Beethoven that she liked.

Then she turned off Olivier by arriving late for work repeatedly, and the malaise next spread to Miller, who was getting embarrassed and irritated himself. To treat her galloping nerves, she reportedly was taking sleeping pills now. And to stroke her runaway anxieties, she sent a distress call to New York for Paula Strasberg, her friend and patron, and for her analyst.

She made *Some Like It Hot* with Tony Curtis, Jack Lemmon, and Joe E. Brown; and she made *Let's Make Love* with Yves Montand, and it was no secret that they did make love until he retreated home to his wife Simone Signoret. Then in the summer of 1960 she made *The Misfits* with Clark Gable and Montgomery Clift. The film was written by Arthur Miller and directed by John Huston.

But her alliance with Miller was unraveling after four years, and her career was unraveling, too, just when she was working with major scripts, directors, and actors. Actually, her career was probably unraveling precisely because she was working now in the highest levels of Hollywood's big leagues, and she could not handle the demands of being there. She was often sick, regularly late for work, always wracked by a morbid fear of memorizing, analyzing, and delivering her lines. She loved Gable as a kind of kingly father figure, and she loved Clift as a friend. But she still dreaded each day's call. Miller arrived to comfort her; DiMaggio arrived to comfort her. But within one year's time, all the strands of her world came undone: Gable and Clift both died, and she divorced Miller in Mexico on January 20, 1961.

She now was cut adrift from most of the anchors in her life, and she also seemed to be sabotaging her career just when it was offering its best opportunities. So, she committed herself to the Payne Whitney Psychiatric Clinic in New York, and promptly plunged into panic. As in the past, the SOS went out to Joe Di-Maggio.

It was March and he was in Florida then, appearing in the spring training camp of the Yankees for the first time since he had retired ten years earlier. He was there at the invitation of the club to serve as an unpaid deputy to Ralph Houk, the manager, mostly because he and the owners of the Yankees had been sparring since then over his proper role in the family. He had always said that he had no interest in becoming a manager, but he always had the conviction that the Yankees should develop an

interest in hiring him back as something grander than a broadcaster who shilled for spaghetti on the pregame show. When he
was asked why he had returned after ten years, he replied: "Because I was asked for the first time."

The Yankees were still training in St. Petersburg then, and he
was savoring his return as the senior eminence of the empire
when the distress call came: She was desperate to leave Payne
Whitney and needed him to make it happen. He promptly flew
to New York, quickly and firmly arranged for her to be trans-
ferred to Columbia-Presbyterian Medical Center. He was *this* re-
sponsive, or this gallant, to her cries for help: She telephoned
him during the daytime, he flew to New York the same evening,
he personally led her out of the hospital the next morning.

Three weeks later, she returned the favor and flew south to
join him at the Yankees' camp, where they relaxed and walked
the beach and he shielded her from the tortures of her mind.
"The whole ball club," Mel Allen remembered, "was crazy about
her."

But her emotional spiral steepened into a tailspin.

She was devastated when she read in a newspaper column
that Kay Gable suspected that Marilyn had "brought on Gable's
fatal heart attack from tension and exhaustion." Then she underwent surgery to remove her gallbladder. And then she began
commuting from New York, where she was living most of the
time, to Los Angeles, where her analyst was living. Then in June
she was fired by Twentieth Century Fox and sued for $750,000
for repeatedly missing work.

The work was a film titled *Something's Got To Give,* a comedy that might have suited her. But she was absent from the set
exactly half of the time in the first month of shooting. Nunnally
Johnson, the writer and director, even telephoned DiMaggio in
London and asked him to fly to Los Angeles to rescue her, one
more time. DiMaggio said he was in no position to solve the
problem that way, but promised to telephone her.

She was hiding out in her home in Los Angeles then, taking

Nembutol by prescription and struggling to clutch some wisp of reason in her life. Early in the morning on August 5, 1962, her house companion found her dead in the bedroom of her stylish house in Brentwood. She died of an overdose of barbiturates. She was thirty-six years old.

Joe DiMaggio had arrived in San Francisco to make an appearance in a charity baseball game when he got the call. He immediately flew to Los Angeles, where he had planned to go the following day to see her.

He was shocked and sorrowful, but driven to save her in death from the people and the values that he felt had stalked her and violated her in life. He went straight to her home and took charge.

He took charge with a series of decisions that he enforced like an avenging angel: The memorial service would be held in the Village Church of Westwood, burial in the Westwood Memorial Park; only twenty-three close friends would be admitted. This was his chance to purge the Hollywood flocks, and he did it relentlessly. He barred the Rat Pack, specifically Frank Sinatra, Dean Martin, and Peter Lawford. He barred Lawford's wife, Patricia, the sister of President John F. Kennedy and Attorney General Robert Kennedy. For a time, he even excluded Marilyn's attorney, Milton Rudin, but relented and let him in. The rumors linking both Kennedy brothers to Monroe had not surfaced yet, at least not publicly, and years later nobody could demonstrate that they were true. But Joe grouped them in his judgments with the celebrity hordes who had used and abused her, and this was the chance to wage his crusade against them.

He kept the service short and simple, and even stood at the door of the chapel afterward shaking hands and thanking the visitors for coming.

"He had always come through for her," Lena Pepitone said, "and he came through again in the end, when for all her fame, she had no one else who would take care of her burial."

Three times a week after that, six red roses in a small vase were delivered to the Westwood Memorial Park and were placed next to her crypt. They were sent by DiMaggio, who also appeared there twice a year or so unannounced, stayed quietly for a few minutes, and then left.

Sid Luckman, the onetime quarterback for the Chicago Bears who became a business associate and friend of DiMaggio, selling supplies to military post exchanges around the world, said later that DiMaggio believed that she had been ready at last to give up her career, marry him again, and settle down in San Francisco. It was hard to believe that DiMaggio truly expected this to happen. But then he always expected her to make it happen.

"When she died," Luckman said, "he was devastated. He didn't come out of his house for six weeks."

Jerry Coleman, the smart second baseman for the Yankees and later a manager and broadcaster in San Diego, said: "Nobody ever brought up anything personal with him. I have never mentioned Marilyn's name to him, and he has never mentioned it to me. But I'm sure Joe deeply loved that woman. Even after they split, he was still carrying the torch."

"Joe carries a bigger torch than the Statue of Liberty," Edward Bennett Williams said years later. "It has not lessened through the years. He was crazy about her, and still is."

11

A WITNESS TO HISTORY

THEY RAN INTO EACH OTHER by chance in the airport in Los Angeles, and Joe DiMaggio rushed over to Arthur Daley, the columnist for *The New York Times,* and clutched his arm and steered him through the crowds of newspaper and radio reporters and the packs of passersby he was drawing like the Pied Piper.

"Why can't they leave me alone?" he asked Daley. "They're driving me nuts. Why can't they forget me?"

He didn't pause to test the logic or likelihood of his own question, and he didn't seem to notice that he had spent a generation becoming unforgettable and now he wanted most to be forgettable. Or maybe unapproachable.

"I want to be forgotten," he said, sounding like a man spelling it out, once and for all. "I want to be able to walk down the street without being recognized and stopped."

"Maybe you won't like it when it happens," Daley said. "One day I was talking to Jack Sharkey, the old heavyweight champion. He told me that he knew he was washed up when the crowds stopped booing him whenever he was introduced from the ring. It was something he'd always wanted. Yet, when it happened, he discovered he didn't like it."

"I'll take my chances," DiMaggio replied. Then, spelling it out with finality, he said: "I want to be alone, ignored, forgotten."

Alone, maybe. Ignored, hardly. Forgotten, far-fetched. But for thirty years and more after he had set the tone and the rules and selected the audience for Marilyn Monroe's memorial service, he charted a course through his own life that was aimed at keeping him alone most of the time, ignored much of the time, and forgotten hardly at all. Like Monroe, he had come too far and endured too much to simply let go. Like Monroe, he wanted to decide *who* should leave him alone — without forgetting the legend that he had created by not being alone.

At the funeral, he heard the minister read the Twenty-third Psalm and excerpts from Psalms 46 and 139, and heard him recite The Lord's Prayer. Then he heard Lee Strasberg, the artistic force of the Actor's Studio, as he isolated the same theme in his eulogy:

> Marilyn Monroe was a legend. In her own lifetime, she created a myth of what a poor girl from a deprived background could attain. For the entire world, she became a symbol of the eternal feminine.
>
> But I have no words to describe the myth and the legend . . . a warm human being, impulsive and shy and lonely, sensitive and in fear of rejection, yet ever avid for life and reaching out for fulfillment.

Joe DiMaggio, distrustful and even scornful of the Hollywood crowds surrounding and badgering Monroe, nonetheless accepted Lee Strasberg and his family as exceptions. The Actor's Studio over the years had cultivated artists: Marlon Brando,

Paul Newman, Steve McQueen, Geraldine Page. It taught acting, not swaggering. It didn't strike DiMaggio as hostile Hollywood; it was benign. And the Strasbergs offered Marilyn the same thing DiMaggio was almost desperately trying to offer her: a home.

"Marilyn was special," Susan Strasberg remembered in *Marilyn and Me,* her book about the closeness between them. "She was welcomed in our home even at 5 in the morning, and there was a bed for her and arms to hold her. She permitted us to see her angels and her demons without fear of rejection. . . . For eight years, Mother, Marilyn and I tap-danced for the love of one remarkable man, 'Pop.' "

She told how she had visited the Fox lot when she was fifteen and met Monroe for the first time. She also met DiMaggio, who was watching from the wings while Marilyn cavorted in front of the cameras.

"I'd read all about how DiMaggio wanted to change her," Susan Strasberg wrote. "He wanted her to wear high-necked dresses, be more demure. Marilyn wanted to please him and do anything to make him happy."

At the time, Marilyn was dancing and lip-synching the "Heat Wave" number from the film *There's No Business Like Show Business,* and was screwing it up. Once she gyrated and fell down. Then she ran "to the man in the shadows."

"As she neared him," Strasberg recalled, "he seemed to withdraw behind some invisible shield."

Joe apparently was also upset because she had been cast as a prostitute for the film. But Marilyn in turn had some uneasy moments of her own trying to play the role of Mrs. Joe DiMaggio. "When she went with Joe," Strasberg said, "she was afraid of his friends."

After they were divorced, Marilyn reportedly told a friend she had another misgiving: "Bored, he bores me."

But at the court hearing on the divorce, she was dressed in

black, as though mourning her lost marriage, and tears were flowing. And she later said in an interview: "I'm just a pretty girl who's soon forgotten, but Joe's an all-time great."

In another interview, supplying another ray of insight, she said: "When I married him, I wasn't sure why."

She knew why she was drawn to him; she just didn't know why they took the ultimate step and encased their attraction within the confines of marriage. She clearly had no intention of surrendering her career to settle down and thereby settle his nerves; or, at least, she made no move to surrender it or even to narrow it. But to the end, he cherished the notion that it would all come to a happy ending and that she would come home, place an apron around her waist, and keep their nest. The world always jolted him back to reality. The press agents always staged her arrivals and appearances in a way that jolted him back to reality. And she kept landing bigger roles and kept building bigger anxieties that softened his resistance and prolonged the alliance.

But even his most touching gesture could not survive the crudeness of the mob surrounding them: the roses that he sent to her crypt in Westwood three times a week. After fifteen years or so, he canceled the standing order because souvenir-hunters kept coming to her grave to marvel at the marriage of the century and to shed a tear at its short, sad course — and kept stealing the flowers.

Life after Marilyn was probably best portrayed by Paul Simon in his 1968 song "Mrs. Robinson" from the film *The Graduate*. In the second verse, he asked the question that became part of the language:

> *Where have you gone, Joe DiMaggio?*
> *A nation turns its lonely eyes to you.*
> *(Woo, woo, woo)*

Joe appreciated the sentiment, but he once confided to a friend: "I've never been able to figure out what that song means."

But it seemed true: He had gone away. He now was no longer a star player, no longer a star husband, in some ways no longer a star ex-husband. He just slipped from sight. He signed for a few commercial missions, which mostly involved his name and prestige, but he was no longer onstage. Then the telephone rang one day, and Charles O. Finley was on the line offering him a role back in baseball. Not a starring role, but a role in the show.

Finley was the baseball rebel of his time, and the natural opposite of Joe DiMaggio. He was a onetime semi-pro first baseman who nearly did not survive a siege of tuberculosis after World War II but recovered and started building an empire in life insurance. He bought the Kansas City Athletics, who had existed for years as a kind of talent pool for the New York Yankees, sending selected stars to the big team in exchange for several players of far less magnitude. One of the first things he did after taking control was to order his people to cut off the traffic to New York.

He employed one of the best spy systems in America, and he used it to sign young players named Reggie Jackson, Catfish Hunter, and Vida Blue. Then he trundled them off to the West Coast, where they became renowned as the Oakland Athletics and won five consecutive divisional championships and three World Series in a row in the early 1970s. But the A's merely won; they didn't draw. And Finley later said that moving them to Oakland was his big mistake. He apparently didn't count things like firing the manager almost every year, suspending Mike Andrews for making two errors at second base in one inning during the 1973 World Series, and threatening to send Jackson to the minor leagues after he hit forty-seven home runs.

He also released his home-run hitter Ken Harrelson for calling Finley "a menace to baseball," whereupon Harrelson promptly signed with the Boston Red Sox and helped to power them to the American League pennant while knocking in more runs than any other hitter in the league. And, of course, he also was the only owner in baseball history who took a Missouri mule on the road as a kind of team mascot.

But Charley Finley did some things that were shrewd. He attracted attention by lobbying for orange-colored baseballs and for night games in the World Series; and, while the former brainstorm was abandoned, the latter wasn't. He also hired pretty, young ball girls to sit in the open down the foul lines and chase stray baseballs. And he installed mechanical rabbits and elves who popped out of the ground and handed new baseballs to the umpire.

With the same sense of stoking public interest, he telephoned DiMaggio one day after the 1967 season and offered him a job as coach, consultant, and community hero. DiMaggio normally shunned commitments that might anchor him too firmly, but this commitment came with certain plus signs: The A's were moving to Oakland, across the Bay from his home in San Francisco, and he didn't have to travel with the team or do anything else that didn't appeal to his laid-back, lazy lifestyle. He looked overdressed in his yellow, green, and gold uniform, but for two years, he was back in baseball.

But being a coach with the Oakland A's just *before* they became spectacularly successful in the seventies did not thrust DiMaggio back into the public spotlight, or even the public mainstream. He seemed content, but he also seemed tactful to a fault: He did not especially want to upstage or distract the team, so he did not encourage interviews from the waves of newspaper writers who passed through Oakland during the summer's travels. He also did nothing to encourage speculation that he might be waiting in the wings for Finley to swoop down and execute another manager.

Jimmy Cannon remembered that he once had been asked to

sound out DiMaggio for a vacancy in the manager's job somewhere else, and Joe replied: "No, I'm not interested. See if you
can send in Lefty O'Doul."

Even when speculation turned to the Yankees, he did nothing
to spice the intrigue. He seemed to feel that the Yankees owed
him respect and permanent status, and he was quick to resent it
when they did not, whether he felt slighted on World Series
tickets or on the pecking order for Old-timers' Day. But managing
the team was one reward he did not particularly covet.

"There were some things he simply didn't want to be pinned
down on," Edward Bennett Williams said, "and I think a permanent job with the Yankees was one of them. He got some feelers
about managing clubs, but he wouldn't have enjoyed the responsibility."

He was past fifty now, and maybe he was mellowing, or simply aging. But he was growing into a more reflective state of
mind, and it was adding to the general image he projected: civil-
ity, dignity, grace. When he visited the Yankees' training camp
one day, he managed to look and sound avuncular, the elder
statesman at peace with himself and his world.

"Kid ballplayers are about the same as they used to be," he
observed. "But where are the .300 hitters? Maybe the pitchers
are better now. But I wouldn't be too sure of that. If some of
these kids concentrated on batting .300, some of them would
become more important ballplayers."

You couldn't argue with that, whether you were a pitcher or
hitter. And after he had spent seventeen days and nights touring
American positions in Vietnam in November of 1967, he reached
new heights of feeling in public and new levels of expressing it.
He made the trip with Jerry Coleman, his former teammate on
the Yankees; Pete Rose of the Cincinnati Reds; Tony Conigliaro
of the Boston Red Sox; and Bob Fishel, longtime public relations
director of the Yankees.

When they landed back in San Francisco, there was no doubt
DiMaggio was exhausted and no doubt that he also was touched.

"Let me assure you," he said, "those kids out there have guts. We visited hospitals and forward areas and talked to the men in bunkers and aboard the aircraft carrier *Intrepid* and, well, what wonderful kids they are. Wherever we went, we could feel how welcome we were, how glad they were to see new faces from home among them. Wherever we went, there was a hand to shake."

There was a kind of poetry in this, and it came from a man who had been considered a bit of a stiff when he was the player's player a few years earlier. In those days, he was lionized as the star of stars on the field, but he also was recognized as either lazy or uncommitted off the field. Now, he was history on the field, and he was becoming grace and goodness off the field. His timing could not have been better.

But his attention span was still likely to be brief, at least in terms of staying absorbed in something like a job. He was still gratified to be back in baseball as a coach with the Oakland A's, but he was also still wary of carrying on the commitment. As Ed Williams put it: "Joe stayed with Finley for two years, and then he got tired of being tied down again."

The best of both worlds for DiMaggio was to be cheered but not committed, to keep his rank alive without working at it. And he achieved both goals in a historic way in the summer of 1969 when the All-Star Game was played in Washington, D.C., just two days after men had landed and walked on the moon, men of the space mission Apollo 11, men who received baseball scores across the remote reaches of space en route to their epic destination. The setting was properly momentous in Washington, with astronauts landing on the moon and planting the flag on a barren plain a quarter of a million miles from Earth, where baseball heroes were arriving in the capital in the surge of national pride. They were there to stage their annual All-Star fantasy and to celebrate the one hundredth year of professional baseball, and they were there at precisely the right time.

Richard M. Nixon, on the eve of flying to the Pacific to

welcome the astronauts home from their cosmic journey, invited the baseball clans to the White House and greeted them in a massive reception. Later that night, baseball entwined itself even more deeply into the public mood when it bestowed awards for achievement that cut across generations.

The award for "greatest manager" went to John McGraw. For "greatest living manager," to his disciple, Casey Stengel. For "greatest player," Babe Ruth. And the "greatest living player" was Joe DiMaggio. It was half a century after McGraw, Stengel, and Ruth had played the dramatic leads in the Battle of Broadway, the series of confrontations that showcased the sport, and the heritage they created with bats and balls and crystal radio broadcasts was now enshrined.

He was in his middle sixties now and openly cherishing the revival of acclaim triggered by the television and radio role The Bowery had cast him in, the role that resurrected him from the recesses of retirement, even from the benign obscurity that had surrounded him since the death of Marilyn Monroe. Even out of sight and mind, he had been esteemed as one of the demigods of *the game.* But now he was back onstage, and people finally had the answer to the question that had become part of the folklore of the time: Where have you gone, Joe DiMaggio?

He was more than a cult hero; he was more of a culture hero, and the aura kept growing as he kept retreating into the folds of his obsession with privacy. Every now and then, he would unbend. But he always refused to tolerate any discussion of Marilyn, or even any reference to her. No one was allowed to pry at the memory.

The mystique proved irresistible, and almost impenetrable, for the waves of people stalking the "real" Joe DiMaggio for an endless series of literary, psychological, or historical purposes. In 1979, when he was sixty-four years old and secure in his revival role as a TV "spokesman," he was stalked by one of the country's cerebral giants, Christopher Lehmann-Haupt, the book reviewer of *The New York Times,* who had committed himself to a mission of discovery: "to spend the entire 1979 baseball season exploring the world of baseball."

He wound up exploring the world of DiMaggio, as he later recounted in a book of fervent memoirs titled *Me and DiMaggio: A Baseball Fan Goes in Search of His Gods,* published by Simon & Schuster in 1986. The emotional high arrived when he traveled to Seattle for the All-Star Game, then to Portland for an Old-Timers' Day gala that regularly drew major-league superstars to a minor-league park that housed the hometown Beavers. And in the trainer's room there, he found himself in the company of the most divine of his "gods."

"I was now alone in a tiny room with Joe DiMaggio," he wrote. "I opened my mouth to apologize, but, luckily, no sound came out. DiMaggio finished signing the baseball he was holding, put it down, and picked up another from an open box beside him on the table.

"Now I began to recall all the lore of DiMaggio's legendary reticence. The man simply didn't talk to strangers. When Gay Talese had tried to interview him for an *Esquire* magazine profile, DiMaggio was supposed to have told him, 'You're invading my rights.' Talese had to write his piece without talking to his subject."

But after Lehmann-Haupt explained who he was and why he was there, DiMaggio responded. Lehmann-Haupt asked: "What brings you to Portland?" And he replied: "Well, I was at the game up in Seattle, and I have some friends in this town. So, it was convenient to drop by. Also, the Beavers made it worth my while."

They continued the dialogue in person and on the telephone over a period of months while Lehmann-Haupt tried to elicit the facts surrounding one of the lost episodes in the mystique: a Sunday game in Cleveland in May 1948 when DiMaggio hit three home runs, two of them against Bob Feller, the third against Bob Muncrief. But the mystique in this case was embellished by a rumor that DiMaggio had spent his Saturday night with a noto-rious mob figure at a gambling joint and that the companion had poured Joe into bed at the Hotel Cleveland at five-thirty in the morning. Then the mob's man supposedly telephoned his bookie and bet big on the Indians "because there is no way Di-Maggio is going to be able to play."

DiMaggio played, all right. He not only reached Feller for two home runs and Muncrief for another, but he knocked in all six runs while the Yankees were beating the Indians, 6–5. He al-ways seemed to rise to the occasion, so there was nothing ex-traordinary in his performance, as such. The only question was whether he also managed to rise to the occasion after spending all night drinking with the big boys. And even that wasn't a burning question thirty years later unless you were so fascinated by the DiMaggio mystique that you pursued pieces of intrigue within it, and Chris Lehmann-Haupt was in full pursuit.

He had a friend in Cleveland who had told him that DiMaggio was taken on the town by John Angersola, known informally as Johnny King, who supposedly outranked even Moe Dalitz, the don of Cleveland's Jewish mafia. Even Elvis-watchers might have had trouble matching *that.*

Months later, Lehmann-Haupt arranged to meet DiMaggio at the Sheraton Heights Hotel in Hasbrouck Heights, New Jersey, where DiMaggio frequently stayed during visits to New York. But as Lehmann-Haupt tracked the issue into lengthy detail, Joe seemed to grow bored or, as Chris surmised, afflicted with "in-jured wariness."

"You never hear about the ones that stay up all night and they go for a horse-collar and maybe make an error or two," DiMaggio said. "I wasn't a drinking man, I can tell you that. I didn't do a hell of a lot. I wasn't *that* kind of heavy hitter."

Lehmann-Haupt persisted, and DiMaggio persisted: "I never raised a hell of a lot of hell. I mean, we had rules on our ball club."

He conceded that Toots Shor had introduced him to the Cleveland "team," and that he had met Morris Kleinman at the Desert Inn in Las Vegas, but noted in mitigation that Kleinman was "a very dear friend of Bob Hope's." Zeroing in, they eventually concluded that it was Lou Rhoda (aka Rothkopf) who had been Joe's host and that Johnny King might have been boasting, as he did when he sometimes compared himself to Don Corleone in *The Godfather.*

But Chris Lehmann-Haupt, relentless in his search for the quintessential DiMaggio, stayed on the trail. He next questioned Bowie Kuhn, the commissioner of baseball, and then got a call from Edward Bennett Williams, the friend and confidant of DiMaggio and also his counselor. Williams had recently bought the Baltimore Orioles, but he was calling about the Yankees and Indians thirty years earlier.

"He tells me the story is not true," Williams told Lehmann-Haupt. "He conceded to me that he did go to the Mounds Club; he apparently went there with people whose reputations were not of the best. But he denies vigorously that he got drunk, passed out.

"I've known Joe, I think, for thirty-three years now, and I've spent many, many hours with him. I've never seen him drunk. In fact, he's a very light drinker."

"I'm sure," Williams said, delivering a kind of summation, "half the mythology around Babe Ruth is of the same character."

As unlikely conversations go, this one was pretty unlikely: a renowned criminal lawyer talking to a renowned book reviewer about a night that Joe DiMaggio spent in Cleveland in 1948 before hitting three home runs the next day. Lehmann-Haupt still sensed that the history of the twentieth century demanded more, so he telephoned DiMaggio in San Francisco to see if his memory had improved.

Joe was clearly growing weary of the whole thing and reminded Chris that he had agreed to meet "the book man from

The Times" at the behest of the author. And he finally deflected the inquiry into the mythology of Joe DiMaggio by saying, with some heat: "I was just trying to do Joe Durso a favor."

Lehmann-Haupt, reasoning, came to this philosophical conclusion: "If you were going to be a hero in America, you had to live like a hero." And he added, with some regret showing: "Joe seemed to have a kind of divided awareness of himself."

But then, the public also seemed to have a divided awareness of him, seeing and hearing and speaking no evil and excusing any suggestion of it. Heroes were getting harder to come by as the century spiraled into its final violent decades, and there weren't many heroes with the enduring grace of this one.

When the New York Board of Trade saluted him in 1980 at a luncheon on the Starlight Roof of the Waldorf-Astoria, he was extolled as "Mr. Bowery and Mr. Coffee and Mr. New York." Senator Jacob K. Javits sent a message that said, perhaps a little vaguely: "Joe DiMaggio is synonymous with what's great about New York." And Mayor Edward I. Koch, reaching for a bon mot, said: "He is probably the only athlete who could attend fifty-six consecutive luncheons and score a hit at all of them."

Slightly stooped, but still stately and handsome, DiMaggio rose to *that* occasion, too, and replied to all the toasts and salutes by saying: "I should be thanking New York. Everything I have, I owe to New York. I had a great friend when I was playing, George Solotaire. Whenever he had to leave town, he would tell me: 'I've got to go camping for a few days.' And when he returned, he would say: 'It's so good to be back in America.' "

Some extra elegance was bestowed on the occasion by Lillian Gish, the actress, who was seated near DiMaggio on the dais. She was there as a friend: For years, she and her sister Dorothy lived in the Elysée Hotel in midtown, where DiMaggio sometimes lived during his many summers as a hotel-dweller. She liked to tell how she had asked for an autographed baseball, took it on a trip to Spain, and placed it in a window in Madrid. Crowds gathered in the street just to view it. She did the same thing in Barcelona, and the crowds gathered there, too. The mystique crossed international frontiers.

But another old friend, Til Ferdenzi, the sportswriter, preferred to remind DiMaggio how far in time and importance the mystique had traveled. Before he started covering the Yankees for the *New York Journal-American,* he played quarterback for Boston College. About ten years later, after he had left school, someone from back home mailed him a copy of an Italian newspaper from Boston dating to the middle thirties. The eight-column banner line read: "Ferdenzi to Start for B.C." At the bottom of column eight, a one-line head reported: "Yankees Buy Coast Star." And the brief said: "The New York Yankees today purchased Joe DeMagio [sic], outfielder, from the San Francisco Seals."

Ferdenzi said he saved it to show Joe, "just so you know who was the big *paisan* in Boston in 1935."

It was December in 1987 and he was seventy-three years old now, and he was reaching out to the world for more of the symbols of honor and reassurance that he might have avoided in the past. It was as though the image fit, and he finally was appreciating the fact that it fit, and even cherishing the way that it fit. He still ducked crowds, but not distinguished crowds.

The crowd that seemed to please him most was as distinguished as they come, and he was so proud of it that he took a long hot drive up Florida's turnpike one day early in 1989 to tell me about it.

Joe Camilleri, one of his trusted allies from Miami, did the driving; Joe did the squirming as the sun rose and the traffic thickened. They didn't have to be caught in that particular trap, but DiMaggio decided to spare me the drive down the coast, so he and Joe Camilleri made the trip themselves to join me in Port St. Lucie, where the New York Mets were playing a spring training game against the Boston Red Sox.

They even parked the car in the far reaches of the public lot and walked several hundred yards in the heat to the trim little stadium, where they never did get to watch any part of the game. Instead, we got them some turkey sandwiches and cold drinks and settled down in Arthur Richman's office, and DiMaggio finally cooled off and started to tell the story of his favorite crowd.

"Early last December," he said, "I got a call at home in San Francisco on a Friday, inviting me to the White House for dinner. I said I didn't know if I could make it. I had to be in Florida. I said I'll let you know Tuesday.

"Early Monday, I got a call from my sister Marie at home in San Francisco saying to call the White House. I did, and the lady there said: 'Can you make the state dinner? It's the hottest ticket around, just 126 guests.' I said, 'I'll be there.' "

It was the hottest ticket in town because it was a formal bash at the summit: President Ronald Reagan was introducing the Soviet leader, Mikhail S. Gorbachev, to a cross section of stars from American life. Nancy Reagan was there with Raisa Gorbachev and Secretary of State George P. Shultz, Senator Bob Dole, Secretary of Defense Caspar Weinberger, the writer Joyce Carol Oates, the columnist George Will, Maureen Reagan, and Joe DiMaggio, who got there the hard way but with a high purpose.

After accepting the invitation on the telephone, DiMaggio realized that he had let himself into a quagmire of logistics. He was in Florida by then, and he had a tuxedo stashed for such emergencies at Camilleri's home. But he had no formal shirt, no airline reservation, no transportation, no place to stay in Washington.

But with one swing, so to speak, he solved all problems. He placed a call to Edward Bennett Williams, and waited to be rescued. Not everybody would telephone Edward Bennett Williams just to come up with a dress shirt, airline reservations, and a hotel room in Washington. But even his best friends agreed that, over the years, DiMaggio had been spoiled by doting friends and had come to expect them to continue to spoil him. Even the high and the mighty like Ed Williams gave advice, logistical support, and personal favors, and that was fine with Joe. Whether it was Williams in Washington or Joe Camilleri in Miami or Eddie Liberatore in Philadelphia or half a dozen other friends in half a dozen other cities, he accepted the caring attention as something earned by high rank.

"He called me back on his car phone," he remembered, sounding as though Williams had his priorities straight. "And I asked him, 'Ed, did you get an invitation to the White House dinner?' He said no. I said, 'Well, I did, and I need some help.'

"He arranged my flight to Washington. He sent his driver, Leroy, to meet me at the airport in his limo. He put me up at the Jefferson Hotel, which he owned. He even gave me one of his six overcoats he kept in his office. And Leroy went out hunting for a formal shirt my size, and found one in Georgetown on the third try."

By now, DiMaggio had a purpose to go with his finery. But he needed a baseball in a hurry to carry out his purpose, so he asked Leroy to drive to one of the Baltimore Orioles souvenir shops (also owned by Williams), came out with a box of a dozen baseballs, and headed for the White House.

"I took one of the balls and put it in the pocket of Ed's overcoat," he said. "But how do you get a baseball signed at the White House? It was a million-to-one shot.

"But when I checked my coat, I asked the checkroom lady to keep the coat nearby because I might want to come back and get something out of the pocket. And all during dinner, I kept thinking about it.

"On the receiving line, the greeter asks how you'd like to be introduced. I said, 'Just Joe DiMaggio.' When I got to the head of the line, the President introduced me to Mr. Gorbachev and added, 'This is one of our greatest players in the United States.' Mr. Gorbachev looked as though he knew me.

"I said, 'Mr. President, I'd like to get your autograph on a baseball.' He smiled. Then the interpreter told Gorbachev, and he smiled, too. But remember, the ball was in the coat pocket in the checkroom.

"The dinner was relaxed, really beautiful. I was seated with Maureen Reagan to my left, Mrs. Shultz to my right. She said she was a Red Sox fan. Around the table, Bob Dole and Caspar Weinberger, and across from me, George Will. He likes baseball, but the flowers were blocking us out."

The evening grew longer, and DiMaggio grew warier: The baseball was still stashed in the coatroom, still unsigned. None of this was exactly in character for him, but he decided on the spot to make his move.

"I'd met Maureen Reagan in Saigon years before," he said, "and I turned to her and said, 'You know, Maureen, there's something on my mind. I'd like to have Mr. Gorbachev's signature on a baseball.'

"She told me to get the ball and take it to the office of the chief Marine usher and leave it there for her. She said, 'I've got good contacts, Joe.'

"I went to the coatroom downstairs without wasting any more time and got the ball, and went back up to the dining room and gave it to the chief usher. The ushers are all Marines, and they've got this office just off the dining room.

"The next thing, we all went in to hear Van Cliburn play the piano."

The next morning, DiMaggio was back in his hotel watching the two leaders on television. They were giving a report on the summit, wrapping it up for the world, and suddenly he did a double-take.

"There they were," he said, "sitting six feet apart at a table, and the President was rubbing a baseball in his hands. Unbelievable.

"Some time later, Maureen sent it to my home in San Francisco. Reagan's signature is very precise and readable. Gorbachev signed it the way a doctor writes a prescription. But the mission was complete."

So, what do you do with a baseball signed at the summit? Hide it, he decided; probably in a bank vault. Or give it to someone: His son, Joe Jr., who had carried the family into a new dimension by studying at Yale and had two daughters who were the pride of their grandfather's life. Or add to its value by adding the one other signature that would enhance it: Joe DiMaggio's.

"That's a good thought," he said, meaning the general thought of what to do with the ball. "I haven't made the decision yet. I have two granddaughters, and I think of them all the time. I've already had requests to buy it. But there's no way in the world I'll sell it."

He no longer looked or sounded like the imperturbable old Joe DiMaggio. In his senior years, maybe in his old age, he was cultivating or experiencing a sense of belonging, a yearning to be part of the scene that he had always skipped and even scorned. Could anyone on the old Yankees imagine that he would sneak a baseball into the White House?

"In my life," he said, giving the caper its full value, "that's the only time I ever asked anybody to sign a baseball."

I asked him whose autograph on a baseball he would have wanted the most. He peered back across the years, and replied with respect: "I would have liked Babe Ruth's."

Then, marching down from the mountain where he had chosen to live his life and waving a large flag with none of the old flinching, he said:

"I have done a lot of things in my time. But that day became one of the nicest days of my life, and one of the most meaningful. I was a witness to history."

12

THE LAST KNIGHT

WHEN THE EARTH BEGAN TO TREMBLE, the teams were on the field warming up for the third game of the 1989 World Series, the first in Candlestick Park in San Francisco, and Joe DiMaggio was sitting in a lower box with Dr. Bobby Brown, his onetime teammate and now the president of the American League. It was eighty-three years after DiMaggio's father had felt the ground shake when the shattering earthquake struck the Bay Area and destroyed entire stretches of the city with force and fire.

There was no doubt in anybody's mind on that October afternoon that San Francisco was taking the fury of another major quake, especially since it rocked the region on national television: The pregame show was setting the stage for the big battle of the Bay, the Oakland A's in command after winning the first two games at home and now shooting for a sweep in the rugged and angular old ballpark of the San Francisco Giants. And throughout the long and black night that followed, Al Michaels of ABC played the strange and historic role of anchorman to an earthquake from inside the television trailer parked outside the stadium on the roadway behind the life-sized statue of St. Francis.

They have a statue of Stan Musial outside Busch Memorial Stadium in St. Louis. They have a statue of Henry Aaron manning the entrance to Fulton County Stadium in Atlanta. They have monuments to Babe Ruth and Lou Gehrig in center field at Yankee Stadium in New York. They even have a heroic statue of the great racehorse Swaps outside Hollywood Park racetrack. Only in San Francisco do they have a statue of St. Francis standing on a bluff looking out over the city that took his name, and standing in all majesty and benevolence outside the ballpark.

In the press box behind third base, we got the first clue that this was a major earthquake when somebody's portable radio carried a bulletin reporting that it had been felt as far south as Los Angeles. The next bulletin reported that the Bay Bridge had been severed.

The public-address announcer said in a calm way that spectators sitting in the upper deck should walk down the ramps in an orderly fashion to the lower deck and that spectators in the lower deck should walk out onto the field.

But the people of San Francisco, who knew all about life on the San Andreas Fault, in their own calm way stayed in their seats.

After telephoning details to *The New York Times* until the phone line went dead, I left the press box and trotted down the ramps to see what was happening on the playing field. I went past Bill Walsh, the longtime coach of the San Francisco 49ers, who stopped to say he had lived through enough tremblers there to know that this one was memorable; past Jim Palmer, the longtime pitching star of the Baltimore Orioles, who was broadcasting the World Series with Al Michaels; past Orlando Cepeda, the longtime star of the Giants, who was making a swift exit from the celebrity tent outside the lower level. Yes, past St. Francis.

By the time I arrived on the grass field, players from both

teams were escorting their wives and children from the box seats and heading them toward the long corridor in right field that led to the locker rooms and eventually to the players' parking lot beyond. They were methodical but impressed by the power of the earthquake and those that were sure to follow.

DiMaggio and Bobby Brown had already joined the cavalcade streaming slowly in the general direction of downtown. And when they got there, they already knew from radio reports that massive fires were burning through the Marina district, where DiMaggio lived.

His home on Beach Street was showing cracks in the masonry, the natural-gas lines were ruptured or turned off, the telephones were silent. Worse, his sister Marie was missing from the house.

He started searching for her around the neighborhood and in the shelters, which were already crammed with people dispossessed from their homes, and he kept searching until he found her in the home of family friends. The police still wouldn't allow them and many other people in the Marina district to go back into their homes, so Joe and Marie camped out with friends for several days.

Like many other sportswriters, I was covering the earthquake by then on both sides of the Bay. But whenever I ran into Bobby Brown in the St. Francis Hotel, where we both were staying, we would ask each other about Joe. We were telephoning his home every day but getting no answer. Then, five days after the quake struck, we both got through to him about five minutes apart. He had just walked in the front door when the phone rang for the first time in five days.

There was something stoic about the way people all over San Francisco and Oakland endured the earthquake and the hundreds of aftershocks, and DiMaggio reflected the public response. He was troubled but not panicked, and I encountered the same kind of sturdiness one afternoon when I walked through the streets of the Marina district with Billy

Graham, who had flown into town to raise money and raise spirits.

He looked big and husky and weather-beaten, and he was asked the same question by dozens of people who went up to him, many with babies in their arms: *Why?* And Graham, standing for hours on the sidewalk half a block from DiMaggio's house, replied to all of them: "There is no explanation for this in the Bible. But God isn't punishing you. God loves you."

He was seventy-five years old now, and standing on the pavement outside the Low Memorial Library on the Morningside Heights campus of Columbia University in uptown Manhattan, and *The New York Times* put it this way:

"More than 7,000 students received degrees from Columbia University yesterday and gave Joe DiMaggio the kind of ovation he used to hear regularly at Yankee Stadium.

"Mr. DiMaggio received one of seven honorary degrees awarded at the 236-year-old university's commencement. When the lithe and silvery-haired Mr. DiMaggio was spotted in the procession, applause swelled and was followed by the chant, 'Joe D., Joe D., Joe D.' Mr. DiMaggio smiled and waved."

One of the students broke ranks and rushed up the steps of the library, threw his arm around the hooded hero, and posed for his picture in fond embrace. DiMaggio didn't flinch, as he once might have flinched. He looked strange, wrapped in cap and gown. But he also looked properly impressed by the thought that he was stepping into a new dimension in his life, and it suited him fine at this time in his life.

The pièce de résistance came when Michael I. Sovern, the president of Columbia, bestowed an honorary Doctor of Laws on the man who had once dropped out of high school in San Francisco, and said: "You are unabashedly our hero."

He was also unabashedly Morris Engelberg's hero.

Morris Engelberg is a lawyer, a tall expatriate from New York who cheers for the Miami Heat basketball team at all its home games and who cheers for Joe DiMaggio at all times and all places, at home and away.

But he has grown into a far greater presence than just the cheerleader. He has become counselor, confidant, majordomo, money manager, agent, and strategist for the man and his mountain. And he directs the marketing of Joe DiMaggio from a compound of law offices at 3230 Stirling Road in Hollywood, Florida.

When you turn your car past the green hedges into the compound, you don't have to wait long to get the full message. In big, bold letters across a horizontal sign, you are advised that this is the "Yankee Clipper Center." Then when you look for a parking space, you notice that the parking lot in front of the neat, low building is lined precisely to acknowledge the rank of the law firm's executives and clients. But the number one space isn't reserved for the boss; it's reserved for the boss' passion in life, Joe DiMaggio.

At the head of the first parking slot outside the solid wooden door to the office, the standing sign proclaims: "Reserved for the Yankee Clipper, No. 5." On the ground, someone has painted the number 5. At the head of the *next* space, one slot farther away in rank, the sign reads with all due deference: "Reserved for Morris Engelberg." And if you have any doubt who *he* is, the plaque on the wall says: "Engelberg, Cantor & Kushner."

Beyond the wooden door, the law office stretches into a suite of rooms that are dedicated to the proposition that Joe DiMaggio is the world's greatest citizen. There are DiMaggio bats and DiMaggio dolls and DiMaggio pictures from one side to another, most of them samples or relics of ventures past and present and of business deals yet to come.

Every now and then, DiMaggio arrives at the office, presumably parks in the spot reserved for the Yankee Clipper, and strides inside to be greeted and lionized by the Yankee Clipper's disciple. They will sit at a large conference table and review the stack of propositions on the agenda. Engelberg insists that most are rejected: not enough class or not enough money. But there are plenty of others with both the class and the cash, and those are tested against Engelberg's sense of business and DiMaggio's sense of outrage. The bottom line comes down to this, in most cases: Which deal will make the most money for the least work?

Imitations aren't tolerated, and counterfeits are pursued relentlessly. When baseballs supposedly signed by DiMaggio began to flood the market, Engelberg summoned the Federal Bureau of Investigation. He was the swift sword of justice, and he also reckoned that phony signatures could only dilute the value of the real McCoys. On the other side of the coin, he demands that DiMaggio be paid by certified check for attending card or memorabilia shows, the idea being to foreclose any dirty little suspicion by the federal tax people that a baseball player might be crass enough to take something on the sly and not report it to his nearest IRS office.

Their business activities are grouped inside a corporate structure known as Yankee Clipper Enterprises, which promotes and protects DiMaggio and screens the constant flow of offers that all seemed based on one thing: his name and his fame. He also became a legal resident of Florida, which had no income tax, even though his family home was still in California, which had a hammering income tax. And so, the revival in his public image and popularity led to a revival in his personal fortune. Forty years after he retired as the center fielder of the Yankees, twenty years after he signed on as the trusted voice of the Bowery Savings Bank, a longtime official of Yankee Clipper Enterprises reported that "Joe did five or six million last year, his best year ever."

"Morris has an almost adolescent excitement over Joe," the official said. "It's consumed his life. But he's also pushed Joe's income to peak levels that he never could have reached without Morris."

Sometimes, things fall through the cracks of the empire. Late in 1993, the Home Shopping Club launched something it called a

"celebration" of Joe DiMaggio. And if you wanted to help celebrate, you could purchase an autographed baseball for $300 and
an autographed bat for $4,000, just by shopping on TV.

In the background, two uniformed guards took their posts to
"protect" the bats from predators while salesmen in tuxedos
hawked them on the screen. And Whitey Ford, known affectionately as "Slick" to the Yankees forty years earlier, gave the product a push by remembering that Joe had been telling him that he
hadn't signed a bat "in five or six years." One of the TV hucksters
then told the home audience that Joe hadn't signed a bat in *fifteen* years. Either way, you were supposed to get the idea that
signed bats were rare, indeed.

"He won't even sign a bat for his own grandchildren," Whitey
Ford said, lending even more weight. To which Phil Mushnick
commented in the *New York Post:* "Well, if that's true, DiMaggio's a sick man. If it's untrue, consider the people to whom
DiMaggio has sold his name."

The heading on the column read: "Home Shopping Club: A
Yankee Clip Joint." And beneath an unflattering picture of Di-
Maggio, the caption read: "Peddling autographs."

There were 1,941 bats in this particular offering, and even
the number had a meaning: to capitalize on the memory of
1941, the year of The Streak. To sign that many bats, he sat in a
room in the Louisville Slugger factory in Jeffersonville, Indiana,
and started signing. About 1,600 of the bats went on sale; Di-
Maggio kept 191 for his estate. He also stipulated that he would
not take part in another commercial bat signing for five years.
He was seventy-nine years old at the time, which reminded
some people of the time old August A. Busch offered Whitey
Herzog a "lifetime contract" to stay as manager or general manager of his St. Louis Cardinals and Herzog replied: "Whose
lifetime — yours or mine?"

For the heat he took, and for his arduous day of sitting and
signing, DiMaggio went home with close to two million dollars.

He also went home with no lasting damage to the image of

grace that he projected to the public, an image that the public preferred and protected. If the baseballs were overpriced and the bats oversold, somebody else was the shill and the source of the slur on the shield of the old hero.

It wasn't that Joe DiMaggio was unaccountable; he was just unassailable. He didn't rule; he reigned.

Putting it bluntly, he might be described as arrogant, pampered, selfish, vain, and slow to spend. But nobody seemed interested in putting it bluntly. Instead, the same traits were likely to be given a benign spin that pictured him as classy, revered, self-assured, proud, and thrifty.

Eddie Arcaro, who was a master jockey when DiMaggio was a master baseball player, lives near him in the Miami area and sees him regularly at the LaGorce Country Club. I asked Eddie to size up his friend and contemporary, and he touched all the ambivalent bases.

"Joe has an inferiority complex," he said. "He strikes people as aloof and distant. But he's relaxed and one of the boys when he's with the guys.

"He comes over to LaGorce, where I play golf, nearly every day. He doesn't play much golf anymore. He likes the baths and the club for lunch. And he doesn't pick up many tabs. Once, I signed about eight straight times, and I yelled at him: 'Hey, asshole, when are you going to get one?' He laughed, but he didn't sign.

"People ask him for autographs, and he tells them: 'I'll sign for you, but not here. Too many people would see us and cause a commotion.'

"He was always shy socially. He's a good guy. He's kind to people. But he stays to himself. He's not good to people he doesn't know."

But many ballplayers go through life walking a red carpet; it is a royal way of life, and they grow accustomed to it. In his earlier years, DiMaggio was criticized for not getting involved in causes or even charities. But in his later years, he became involved in some major activities, plunging into them as though making up for lost time.

If you drive south along I-95 from Fort Lauderdale to Hollywood, his face and his public virtue welcome you from a broad billboard on the side of the interstate. It shows him with a child who is clearly a hospital patient, and the message in large letters reads: "DiMaggio and the Babe."

It's a bit of a reach, but it lets you know that he is now involved with kids in the hospital, and you can find out why if you take the exit at Hollywood Beach Boulevard and continue on to the Hollywood Hospital, where the name jumps out again: Joe DiMaggio Children's Hospital.

Paul Schneider, for years the chief accountant in Morris Engelberg's office and in Yankee Clipper Enterprises, remembered that it happened this way:

"Morris also got him involved in the Hollywood Hospital. He put some of Joe's memorabilia up for auction to finance the Joe DiMaggio Children's Hospital within the Hollywood Hospital. He visits the hospital. On Many Fridays, he and Morris have lunch there. It's become important in Joe's life to be attached to something with this kind of dignity and this enduring quality."

It became important because by then he was a grandfather and a great-grandfather, and a lifetime spent mostly living by himself could now be shared with his son and his son's two daughters and their children. The hermit as paterfamilias. He relished it, and he also relished the sense of goodness that the hospital gave him at a time in his life when he seemed to be reaching for fulfillment.

"You walk through there and see those children," he said during a visit to the hospital in 1993, "and you don't care how much money it takes. You've got to do it. And no kid is ever turned away."

But nothing in his life cloaked him in more nobility than his steadfast fixation on Marilyn Monroe. He not only idolized her; he idealized her. If her bounce and beauty tormented him when they were together, the memory of her comforted him when they were finally apart. She riled him in life; she calmed him in death. If her name came up in conversation, he cut it off. He possessed her now, and he tolerated no intrusion. You might wonder about it, but you couldn't argue against it. As the Bard said: Love is "an ever-fixed mark that looks on tempests and is never shaken."

Whatever it was, he would not allow it to be shaken.

He also would not allow his sense of general security to be shaken as he grew older, the hair spare and white, a pacemaker implanted in his chest, the shoulders sloping. In 1994, he was asked how it felt to be approaching his eightieth birthday, and he smiled and said: "Well, it's reachable."

More important, his own sense of destiny also was reachable. He had overtaken the public image of Joe DiMaggio, and now he embodied it. However he was cast, he played the part and eventually mastered it. He even *lived* the part.

It was like the time in 1948 when a famous American died, and the *St. Louis Post-Dispatch* portrayed him in an editorial in terms of the image he had created:

"There he stood, a great tall inverted pyramid at the plate. At the top were two of the broadest, most powerful shoulders the bleachers had ever seen. His slender legs hugged each other and his feet came together like the dot of an exclamation point. He was not fussy. No nervous swinging of the bat. No uneasy kicking of his shoes. No bending over. No straightening up. Just a deliberate getting set. Maybe a little motion at the wrists — that and a death watch on the man on the mound.

"Then the first pitch. Low and outside. Everybody tense except the inverted pyramid. Another pitch — low and away. Were they going to walk him? With two on and the winning run at bat, a walk was the play. Then a third pitch. The pyramid gathers himself, steps into the ball and swings — all in one motion.

"Before the crack of the blow reaches ears in the stands, the ball is lofting away on wings. It rises right of second, arches higher and higher over right field and drops into a sea of up-raised hands for another home run. He is jogging around the bags, two runs scoring ahead of him.

"Another game won for the New York Yankees, another game nearer the American League pennant and still another World Series. Jogging on, around second, up to third as the din rises, now spikes down on the plate and home again — *home for all time.*"

Now, *that* is image. So much image that they didn't even mention his name in the editorial they wrote to memorialize his life. They didn't *have* to mention his name. All they had to do was recreate the image that he projected to the public, to summon the symbol that told it all — the symbol of Babe Ruth in the years before "the replacement for Babe Ruth" arrived and began to project an image of his own.

As he neared eighty, Joe DiMaggio considered the durability of that image and said he had never been able to figure it out.

"I don't know where it comes from," he said. "I've often wondered. I'm still the same kid who played on the San Francisco Seals years ago. I feel like the same person. I don't think I've changed. I don't hurt anyone."

He didn't even hurt anyone's perception of himself, either. Babe Ruth, roistering and rumbling, was the symbol and spirit of the Roaring Twenties. Joe DiMaggio, poised and proper, was the symbol of the sobering and more solemn thirties. And the public, searching for heroes in the decades of Depression and war, not only found DiMaggio but also endowed him with the dimension of heroism. He wasn't a selfish hermit; he was a proud, private person. He wasn't the superjock who had no intellectual friends and who surrounded himself with cruder types and cheerleaders like Toots Shor and George Solotaire; he was the toast of the town. He wasn't the eager lover who misjudged and mishandled his marriage to Marilyn Monroe; he was the noble but starcrossed lover who bestowed on the public the fantasy of his marriage to Marilyn Monroe.

Which was the "real" DiMaggio? The one that people perceived, or the one that played the part that people perceived?

In the long run, what difference did it make? People projected an image, and he grew into it. And in six words, his old teammate and ally Lefty Gomez caught the secret of it all: "He knew he was Joe DiMaggio."

INDEX